CEN 08/12

FINDING MY VOICE
The Elkie Brooks Story

ELKIE BROOKS

The Robson Press

First published in Great Britain in 2012 by
The Robson Press (an imprint of Biteback Publishing Ltd)
Westminster Tower
3 Albert Embankment
London SE1 7SP

ISBN 978-1-84954-299-9

10 9 8 7 6 5 4 3 2 1

A CIP catalogue record for this book is available from the British Library.

Set in Adobe Garamond Pro and Bodoni

Printed and bound in Great Britain by
CPI Group (UK) Ltd, Croydon CRO 4YY

CONTENTS

*'That Bookbinder kid has got such a tip about herself,
she thinks she's better than everybody else.'*
Overheard at The Manchester Ice Palace
one Saturday afternoon, aged eleven.

FOREWORD

I was never keen on doing this book. If it hadn't been for my loving husband Trevor Jordan and my great friend Wilf Pine, it would never have happened. They said, 'Elk, if you don't do it, someone else will do an unauthorised version and get it all wrong.'

But before you go any further, let me be very clear: if you are after sensational celebrity stories from my fifty-two years in the music business, stop reading now; this book is not for you. This is the story of my very emotional journey through the highs and lows of my life in music.

My apologies now to all the musicians and associates I've met along the way if I haven't mentioned you; you either pissed me off or I've genuinely forgotten you.

My sincere thanks for all his patience in helping me with this book goes to my fellow aikido student Simon Williams 3rd Dan who I met through our late master Soke Eddie Stratton 9th Dan when he was a journalist in North Devon. For all their hard work editing, I thank Nicky Williams and Ljiljana Baird and my publisher Jeremy Robson and finally my daughter-in-law Joanna Jordan for initially starting this book with me many years ago.

I dedicate this book to the family – my husband Trevor, my son Jay, my daughter-in-law Joanna and my son Joey. I love you all, thank you for keeping strong.

CHAPTER 1

MUM AND DAD

Knowing the hardship and suffering that some of the world's best singers have endured in order to succeed in the music business – singers like Ella Fitzgerald and Billie Holiday who very much influenced me – I would love to be able to start by saying that my upbringing was tough and made me the artist I am today; fortunately for me, that couldn't be further from the truth. My childhood, to all intents and purposes, was very comfortable and, as it turned out, my struggle and suffering were to come much later in life.

I was born on 25 February 1945 at 1 Castleton Road, Broughton Park, in Manchester; the third and last child of Vi and Charlie Bookbinder – two fine members of the Jewish community in Prestwich ... well, at least on the surface.

Having two sons, Ray and Tony, my mum always wanted a girl, but I nearly didn't come along at all. After my brother Tony was born on 28 May 1943, my mother was advised not to have any more children because of her poor health, but a year later she became pregnant again. On previous advice she agreed to sign abortion papers, but she became increasingly confused and upset about the decision, especially as she felt pretty well in herself. She decided to seek advice from her GP, Dr Cupman, who was a German refugee and a good friend. He convinced her that she could have the baby safely. More importantly perhaps, he told her she was going to have a baby girl. Without Dr Cupman's counsel,

I'm pretty sure that I – Elaine Bookbinder – would not have been born.

The story, of course, goes back much further, but sadly my mum was always vague about her past, so I really have very little knowledge of her life before meeting my dad. Luckily, I'm much more familiar with Dad's past. His parents, Franklyn Bookbinder and Minnie Wientroube, were both brought to Britain by their parents from Gdańsk in Poland around the turn of the twentieth century. Together with hundreds of other Jewish families they fled the pogroms – organised massacres – and sought refuge elsewhere. Despite an improvement in attitudes towards the Jews in Poland in the late 1890s, my grandparents believed it was only a matter of time before things would change for the worse and therefore it was better to leave while they were still able to.

I recall my grandmother telling me that when her parents first arrived here, they thought they'd arrived in New York; it must have been quite a surprise when they realised their boat had actually docked in Hull and not 'The Big Apple'. The unfamiliar accents and architectural surroundings were far removed from what they had left behind. From the moment they boarded the boat they sacrificed their future to an unknown destination – all in the hope that they would find a better life than the one they'd left behind.

In 1911, my grandfather Franklyn met and married Minnie; shortly after, he opened his first kosher bakery 'Bookbinder & Goldstone' in Cheetham Hill, Manchester. He was a bit of a rebel and was refused kosher certification by the 'beth din' – the Jewish religious authorities. He had no doubt been spotted in a pub enjoying a few beers, which of course, wasn't the done thing for an Orthodox Jew as you had no way of knowing whether the beer was kosher or not. By today's standards this may seem a bit harsh, but while Franklyn practised Orthodox Judaism when he was at work, it is clear that he occasionally slipped when he wasn't.

This, however, didn't hinder him or his professional reputation and he made a great success out of his business. Franklyn and Minnie's second child, my dad – Kalmon Charles 'Charlie' Bookbinder – was born on 14 May 1915, shortly after grandfather moved the business to new premises in Bury Old Road, Prestwich, and dropped the 'Goldstone' from the shop front and replaced it with 'Son'.

My mother Marjorie Violet 'Vi' Newton was born on 29 August 1914. Despite being called Newton she told everybody her maiden name was Newman, which I think was because it sounded more Jewish. She was trying to hide the fact that she came from a very Catholic background, which, of course, I only found out after she died. While Mum had never been that forthcoming about her early life I remember her telling me that her mother, Maud Newton, was born blind in one eye. It was her parents' belief that this would limit her chances of ever finding a husband. And, although I never met my grandmother, I often wonder whether I got my musical talent from her because she was so passionate about music. Believing she wouldn't be able to rely on getting married her parents encouraged her to nurture her talents so she would be able to support herself independently. That must have been very unusual for the time. But they clearly knew a thing or two because Grandma won a scholarship to study music in Vienna. There she was classically trained and went on to become a concert pianist and violinist. Apparently, she used to give concerts at all the halls in Salford. In fact a few years ago I was asked to be patron of one hall where my grandmother used to play concerts.

Mum lost her father in the First World War and her mother remarried. Mum never took to the new man; in fact, she took an immediate dislike to him. Mum lived with her grandmother in Fleetwood, near Blackpool. When she left school in the 1930s she moved to Bury New Road, Strangeways, Cheetham Hill, and found work with a local Jewish family. This is where she met my dad, Charlie.

Despite Dad's strong Jewish faith, they got married at the local registry office in 1937. Unsurprisingly, considering the circumstances, it was a modest affair and they managed to keep things fairly quiet for a year until they got married again 'properly' in a religious ceremony at the United Synagogue, Leamington Road, Blackpool, on 4 January 1938. My brother Ray was born seven months later – illegitimately by Jewish standards – on 18 August 1938.

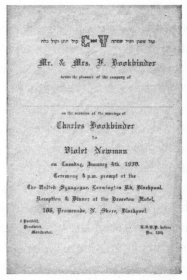

Mum and Dad's wedding invitation

Raised a Catholic and then marrying a Jew had major implications for Mum as she had to deal with converting to Judaism. I think this might partly be the reason why she was reluctant to speak of her life pre-Dad. There's a Jewish concept called Magae which, at that time anyway, required anyone converting to Judaism in Orthodox circles to distance themselves from things of their past that were not of the Jewish faith. Maybe Mum was obeying the custom, but then again, I'm sure she wanted to fit in with Dad's family, the business and the community. This must have been difficult for all concerned, but especially for Mum. The funny thing was that everybody else knew she wasn't Jewish apart from us: it must have been a bit of a scandal at the time.

I think another consequence of the Magae might have been her relationship with her brother and sister. It may also explain why I never met either of them. My brothers Ray and Tony, however, met Uncle Eddie once when they were mourning my mother years later in 1989, practising what is known in Judaism as 'sitting shiva', the tradition of seven days of mourning. I think Eddie was a Dominican monk who led a solitary life in a monastery – whether that was true I don't know; it could of course just have been an excuse to avoid his name coming up in conversation at home.

My mum's sister is quite another story and, to this day, a source of great intrigue to me. As a young girl, I remember a picture on Mum's bedroom mantelpiece of a wonderfully glamorous woman with a large cross around her neck. She was beautiful in her black sequinned leotard and long Crystal Gayle hair. I imagined she was the envy of all women and the object of every man's desire. I was transfixed by this image, but somewhat perplexed; why did my mother have a picture of a woman wearing a crucifix? And then there was the skimpy attire and the big hair. When I first asked who she was, Mum said she was her sister and that she was a trapeze artist in a circus. You can imagine my awe: how adventurous and romantic it seemed.

Mum never elaborated beyond those words; she wouldn't be drawn, no matter how I tried. I later learned from my brother Ray that our mysterious aunt had visited on a couple of occasions, arriving in true star style in a huge American convertible. My mum apparently was very hush-hush about it, not wishing to attract unwanted attention from the neighbours. It seems our auntie was whisked into our house as quick as she was whisked out.

I have little doubt that my mother loved her sister but their lives were obviously worlds apart. Perhaps there's another explanation: maybe my auntie was a stripper or something like that – that certainly wouldn't have been good for the family's reputation! Whatever the truth, I was – and still am – fascinated by the mysterious woman in the picture on the mantelpiece.

That's really all I know of my mother's past. She played such an important part in my life and I would dearly love to know more about her.

CHAPTER 2

119 CAVENDISH ROAD

I sometimes wonder where my love of music and singing actually came from. All I know for certain is that it wasn't from my mum and dad. In fact, let's not beat about the bush, Mum had a dreadful singing voice. Grandma Maud was obviously very musically talented, so I could have got it from her, or perhaps it had something to do with our neighbour at Castleton Road, Mr Gonski, who was apparently playing a wonderful classical piece on his piano at the moment I came into the world.

Joking aside, music just became part of my life. I think I had a good singing voice from a very young age. One of my first memories was my mum being poorly when I was three years old. She suffered bad health all through her life but at this time she had to spend a number of weeks in hospital. Knowing she would be away for a while, Mum arranged for a German au pair to look after me who taught me the German love song 'Lili Marleen' which became popular on both sides in the Second World War. Marlene Dietrich made it famous by singing it in German and English. By the time the au pair left, I could sing it fluently in German, but I'm sure I didn't understand what it was about, and I would certainly struggle to remember it now.

That was one of my few memories from our time at Castleton Road because we only lived there when I was very young. The other vivid memory I have is of moving house. I was in the back of my Auntie Betty's old black Austin A40 with all my mum's little knick-knacks from her dressing table all around me. Betty Roland was my dad's eldest sister. She and her husband were very well-to-do and worked in the car business; perhaps that's why she drove a car, because not very many women did in those days. Anyway, these glass and china bits were all around me and I can remember trying very hard to keep them all steady and stop them falling on to the floor. You would never do that now: put a three-year-old kid in the back of a car without a seat belt with all those loose things around them. Mum never got on with Auntie Betty and I never really liked her either. Dad's younger sister, Sylvia, I got on extremely well with. I was terribly upset when she died in 2008.

My memories of our time at 119 Cavendish Road, however, are vivid as that's where I grew up as a child – I say grew but perhaps brought up would be a better phrase as I did my growing a lot later on. It was a very big house for the area: a four-bedroom, one-bathroom, semi-detached house with leaded windows. It was pretty large, but we weren't that posh, although we did have a toilet, though in the cellar, full of coal and stinking of cat's pee; it wasn't very glamorous.

Looking back, Mum's taste was shocking. One of her most hideous choices was a very expensive, bright purple carpet with a gold pattern and you were hard pressed to find furniture to go with it. It was obviously all the rage at the time because Mum was very proud of it. She was a bit of a snob really.

But it was our big upstairs bathroom that set us apart from the rest of the houses on Cavendish Road. It was quite something: the suite was a deep avocado shade and was complemented by some black and green stripy lino. What a picture; enough to make you feel sick. I don't think you'd even accept a green bathroom suite today as a gift, but then it was considered the thing to have. I remember it being my mum's pride and joy. We were also probably the only family to have a bidet. How posh? Not sure what Mum said when Dad came back from the bakery and used it as a footbath.

Mum, of course, made lots of changes to the house. She was always saying, 'Oh, I'm going to have a vestibule built.' It makes me laugh now because she sounded just like Cissie and Ada – the two Northern housewives played by Les Dawson and Roy Barraclough on TV in the 1970s and 1980s. Mum got her 'vestibule' – in those days it was similar to a mini-conservatory – but to me it was just a tiny porch.

Our kitchen was very old-fashioned. It had a scullery and a separate dining area, which eventually was knocked into one. We also had central heating put in and this wrecked our grand piano so we ended up having to replace it with an upright. I still have it to this day – it's been moved a total of five times and it's in storage at the moment, but hopefully its resting place will be somewhere really nice.

The one thing I'll always remember from 119 Cavendish Road is the mirror, which hung above the fireplace my mother had built. It was very kitsch, with lots of different coloured mirrored strips spiking out. In fact, we were in Manchester not so long ago and went to look at the house, and I swear I could see that mirror still hanging there above the mantelpiece sixty years on. When I was moving into my first flat in London I said to my then manager Jean Lincoln, who was helping me because she lived in the same building, 'We'll have to put a mirror above that mantelpiece.'

With a look of pure disdain on her face she said, 'Oh Elkie, you can't do that, that would be horrible.'

I had acquired my mother's taste. Jean's words put a stop to that right then and I began to work on my own sense of style.

When the family moved to Cavendish Road we had a black Vauxhall Cresta with white wall wheels but no garage so Dad decided to have a double garage built underneath the house. This was a first for the road and really very unusual for those days. With the garage under the house we had a massive slope which my brothers and I used to use as part of a game. I had a pram, which being such a tomboy I never liked, so I would throw all the dolls out and my brothers would put me in and whizz me down the drive towards the garage. Luckily, they put cushions and an old mattress at the end of the garage so I had a soft landing.

At the back of the house we had a beautiful, big garden. There was a rockery outside the kitchen window, some lilac trees on either side of the lawn and banks of flowers, which Mum would lovingly look after. My brothers would play cricket or football on the lawn, but being a girl I wasn't allowed to join in. Having a big house, however, had its down side because when Granddad Frank became unwell, he and Grandma Minnie came to live with us. This meant my parents had one room, Grandma and Granddad had another, my brothers shared a room and I had the little bedroom at the back.

When I was about four years old, I remember going into my grandparents' room one day and Granddad saying, 'Go and get your mother, I'm not well.'

Not long after that he died, but Grandma stayed and that was to cause no end of problems for everyone, not least my mum. It couldn't have been easy for my mum sharing her home with her mother-in-law. As much as I love my mother-in-law, she's brilliant, I don't think I'd like to live with her. So I can fully understand how my mum felt, especially as Grandma was a traditional Jewish lady, which meant things always had to be done in a particular way. It was no great surprise, I suppose, that she ended up running the house and pretty much ruling the roost.

I'm sure my father understood what was going on and tried to give his mum something to do by buying another bakery shop in Didsbury, Cheshire, an area where a lot of the wealthier Jews were moving. Grandma, however, took umbrage and thought my mum had cajoled him into buying the shop to get her out of the way. In the end, Mum took the shop over and would drive there and back every day, but the trouble was she was a nervous driver, and, I have to admit, a terrible one! Even backing out of the garage was a major challenge. Like me she would probably have felt more at ease driving a tank. A few years ago, I ordered a brand new Range Rover, which I had completely customised, but I was always far too scared to drive it.

My brothers didn't like Grandma at all. I could tolerate her, probably because she used to let me stay up very late on Saturday night so I could watch the television with her.

She'd say, 'Elaine, come on, we'll watch the singing and dancing on the television.'

I used to love all that. I can remember watching Dickie Valentine and learning to sing 'Mr Sandman'. But even then you could see Grandma was a pernickety sort because she would stop watching the telly and start studying the carpet to see if there were any crumbs. If there were, she'd say, 'Pick up the crumbs, Elaine.' This clearly impressed me because I still do it today.

But the worst thing about Grandma by a long way was her cooking. I didn't like it, but Tony and Ray absolutely hated it. Everything was cooked in *schmaltz* (chicken fat), which meant meals were heavy and greasy. It wasn't cooked badly, it was traditional Jewish food: the old-fashioned Yiddisher kind. Our only respite from Grandma's cooking was when Mrs Matthews came to help out with the housekeeping and she would cook. It was great because we knew that that evening we would be eating a decent meal of meat and potato pie for supper. The boys loved Mrs Matthews and used her to mediate between themselves and Grandma.

The only dish that we liked of Grandma's was her chopped liver or herring with vegetables, which she would do for Shabbat (the seventh day of the Jewish week and a day of rest in Judaism). We loved it and she couldn't have made it often enough as far as we were concerned. Unfortunately for us though, we only had it once a week. Apart from that one highlight, her cooking was pretty grim.

I remember once her trying to get Tony to eat by waving a fork at him and saying, 'You've got to bloody eat.'

All Tony did was laugh, which made it even worse. After that Tony and Ray told Dad that they wouldn't eat her food again. My brothers were terrible, but good fun.

As you will have gathered, none of us got on with Grandmother Minnie, in fact she drove us round the bend. She caused a lot of arguments between our parents, although they very rarely argued in front of us. You didn't in those days; everything was always kept under wraps; people rarely showed any emotion. In fact, I hardly ever saw my parents be affectionate towards one another.

In the end though my mum gave Dad an ultimatum about his mother, saying, 'Either she goes or I do.'

There were lots of tears and I didn't understand what was going on. Apparently, right after that Grandma put her hat and coat on, stormed out and went round the corner to her daughter Sylvia. Grandma told Sylvia how Mum had forced her out and she let her move in. Afterwards Mum and Mrs Matthews were overjoyed and celebrated by getting thoroughly drunk on a bottle of brandy on the doorstep! There was such a fantastic sense of relief in the house. My brothers and I were just thankful that we would never have to face another one of Grandma's schmaltzy meals again!

Despite all the fuss with our grandmother, my childhood blossomed at Cavendish Road. Mum soon got help running the house as she was working all hours in the shop. A lot of the time, like Dad, she was up and out before any of us were awake and we wouldn't see her again until we were ready for bed or tucked up. We had a live-in au pair who slept in Grandma's old room. There were several over the years and they were nearly always Spanish. The one I remember most clearly was Petuka, a very pleasant woman in her early twenties. She was always teaching me Spanish songs and the one I recall is 'Bésame Mucho'. Years later, because of her influence, I wrote my own version.

I started my education at Broughton Jewish Preparatory School at three years old. I thought it was great, mostly because we used to have a nap in the afternoon. I can remember tasting orange juice from a tin there for the first time and loving it. It was marvellous and I wondered why we didn't have it at home. From there I went to Sedgley Park County Primary, which was a mixed school right in the heart of Prestwich where 99 per cent of the children were Jewish. This was because we lived right on the borders of Prestwich, Salford and Manchester. Throughout my career this has always been something that's annoyed me as everyone describes me as being from Salford, but as far as I'm concerned I am from Prestwich. Back then Salford was quite a rough and tough working-class area compared to where I lived and I didn't go there very often.

At home, my best friend was my cousin Hilary Gochin. I say was, but Hilary still is my best friend today. We may not see or speak to each other as regularly as we would like to, but when we do we always carry on as if we'd seen each other yesterday. She's like a sister to me and the years just disappear when we get together.

Hilary was very, very fat when she was a kid, which was fine until the summer when we would have to wear those awful elasticated stretch swimsuits: a look neither of us could pull off as I was the painfully thin opposite of Hilary. We looked a right pair! I was so thin that I was nicknamed 'Olive Oyl' after Popeye's skinny girlfriend. In the winter my brothers would make fun of me by asking if I'd put bagels in my tights because they were always so wrinkly! Hilary and I were terrible together. One of our favourite games was 'laughing bangs' as we called it. This involved taking turns sitting on the toilet and doing poos and every time one of us farted, we would laugh uncontrollably.

I was bossy in those days: so much so that I used to tell my brother Tony, who is a year and nine months older than me, what to do. Even Mum would ask me to take charge when she was out, which meant taking care of Tony and making sure he crossed the road to school safely. At school I was the leader of our little gang: Hilary, Sammy Portnoy, Lawrence Weiner, Noreen Rackien, Brenda Cohen, Rhona Stolberg, Sandra Oilberg, Barry Brownleader and me. We thought Sammy was a bit slow but we made him our treasurer nevertheless: quite funny really because he went on to become a well-respected Manchester solicitor. He was very sweet on me and as a token of his great affection he asked me to marry him. I was six years old. Of course, I accepted. My mother would have been so proud of her little girl marrying a treasurer. To mark our engagement Sammy gave me a brass curtain ring. I only took it off because it went green.

The gang would get up to all sorts of things, but as leader I didn't always accept responsibility for my actions. On one brilliant sunny day we went over to Heaton Park where the ground was bone dry and we did one of the most stupid things kids do, played with matches. One thing, of course, led to another and we started a fire, which quickly got out of control. Being kids we decided there was nothing else for it, and legged it. I ran home as fast as I could and hid in the cellar. It was awful because I could hear the sound of fire engines in the distance. Thankfully, the fire brigade put it out. They said a burning cigarette butt had probably caused it. None of us were caught and apart from that incident we were, for the most part, nice Jewish girls and boys.

CHAPTER 3

THE BOOKBINDER KID

At that time Cavendish Road and the wider Broughton Park area were almost entirely Jewish. Strangely, the only two non-Jewish households on our road were either side of us. On one side, we had Mrs Dewhurst, a sweet old lady who lived in a dark Victorian house with old-fashioned ornaments cluttering every available space possible. Her house had that old person look, feel and smell to it. She used to play the piano and one day she gave Mum a songbook, which was signed by Gilbert and Sullivan. Mum eventually passed it on to me and I still have it today.

On the other side, there was Mr Proctor and his house-keeper Dot who lived at the corner of the road in a huge detached house with the most fantastic garden. I would deliberately kick my ball over his wall just so I could retrieve it and walk around the garden. I got on very well with Dot and when the blackberries were in season she would make blackberry pie with custard and offer me some. This, of course, wasn't the sort of thing I would ever get at home, especially when Grandma was in charge of the cooking. The first time I tasted it, I loved it, but I knew it didn't seem kosher. When Dot invited me in for some she would sit me down at this huge walnut table, which was all very 'olde worlde' and so English, and proper, it was just the complete opposite of my everyday Jewish surroundings. I absolutely loved it.

Grandma was very religious, and this naturally had an effect on us when she was living under our roof, but the next generation of the Bookbinder family wasn't. On Saturday, for example, when most Orthodox Jewish families would be at the synagogue we would go to the shops. Our synagogue visits were saved mostly for festivals like Passover or Yom Kippur. Mum liked to dress me up for these special days, and she used our Saturday afternoon trips to Kendal's (now House of Fraser) to buy clothes. She would choose all these pretty dresses and fancy shoes, but I never wanted to wear any of them because I was much happier in more boyish outfits like my dungarees. I had a pair of blue ones and a pair of red ones, with matching ribbons. I'm not unlike that today as I'm always happier in jeans. I wear frocks on stage – raunchy frocks that is – because I feel the people who come to see me pay quite a bit of money and deserve to see me wearing something nice.

I don't know why Mum bought me so many clothes because she could make almost anything herself. I think she just got pleasure from buying things like that for me. She was an accomplished dressmaker and even created her own patterns. To do that, you really have to be very talented. Her grandma must have taught her because she was a trained seamstress. Of course, I was never interested in learning, but somehow over the years I've become pretty good at mending clothes. I did try to emulate Mum and I bought a sewing machine but quickly found out, however, that I didn't have the temperament for it. In fact, I got so exasperated with it I ended up throwing it away. I suppose I should have known better, especially when I think back on what I did to a dress with a pair of mum's pinking shears. I don't know why I did it but I started chopping away at it with the scissors and completely ruined it by cutting a great big zigzag pattern into it. I got a big whack on the bottom for that.

People always say that when you're the youngest child you get spoilt and get all the attention but I never felt that was the case with me. I can't deny that my mother didn't spoil me in a material way but I craved attention. Reflecting on my childhood, as I've done a lot over the years, I think what I really wanted was to feel that I was the centre of attention. I always felt it was my brothers who were the focus, and that bothered me a lot growing up.

A good example of this was ice-skating. Mum, and occasionally Dad, used to take us skating on a Saturday. I think I must have been about three years old when I started and I only got to tag along because my brothers were going. My first time on the ice was spent with Tony and Ray on either side of me, helping me along. I got the hang of it pretty quickly and, without wishing to brag, was something of a natural. Despite this, my parents never seemed to take me seriously and didn't push me to improve. Ray got all the tuition and became an incredible skater, winning lots of medals in competitions along the way.

My thing at that age was dancing. I excelled at ballet and tap but again I ended being frustrated because, despite having a talent for it, Mrs Cooper the teacher never gave me the lead roles. They always went to the kids whose parents were on the committee and were actively involved with the production. My parents just didn't have the time because of the bakery, so I would generally be given a chorus girl role.

One year though, I had my chance to star: a girl called Valerie was given the lead, probably because her mother had made all the tutus. Valerie, however, was taken ill and, at short notice, I was asked to take her place. While Valerie's mother was pinning me into the tutu, I was dying to go to the toilet. There was no getting out of that tutu and there was no controlling my bladder. I was so embarrassed, but thankfully nobody noticed and after the show I remember taking my hanky to it feverishly before handing it back.

The following year, the lead was given to a young boy whose father was on the committee and controlled the stage curtain for the shows. He also fell ill and so, out of desperation, the role was given to me again. This meant abandoning the tutu and wearing britches to play the little boy's part: not much of a problem for a born tomboy. As well as dancing, I had to sing 'Dear Old Donegal' and another Irish song called 'Shake Hands With Your Uncle Mac, My Boy' which had about fifty Irish names in it, but I just practised it really hard and got it down. For once – in those days – my parents actually came along to see me perform. I stole the show. And that was without really trying. That was a buzz I'll never forget. Again, looking back, all I wanted was to be noticed.

I was good at improvising my own routines when we were told to make a dance of our own. In fact, I used to hate it when I was being choreographed. I remember years later a manager suggested getting me a choreographer.

I snapped at him, 'No, you're bloody well not. I do it all myself. I want to feel natural.'

I believe it had always been my dream to go on stage because I can remember thinking, 'Oh, I'm going to be a big star. I'm going to have a big American car and come back home and flash around.' That deep-seated feeling of not getting my parents' attention as a kid must have driven me on, although I'm sure I wasn't aware of it at the time. Now, looking back, I can only think that's what it must have been: the burning desire to be noticed by my family and other people.

Another thing I was good at was Hebrew. Actually, I think I was better at Hebrew class than I was at school. I did brilliantly and got a certificate from the rabbi for my efforts. I could read from the Siddur – the Jewish prayer book – really fast. I can't do that now; I can just about say a few *broches*, or blessings, over wine and bread. I finished school at 3.30 p.m. and then had fifteen minutes to get to Hebrew class which would last for about an hour. In the winter, it would be dark when I came to go home and I used to get quite scared. The proper name for the class was *cheder,* which was the traditional Jewish elementary school for teaching the basics of Judaism and the Hebrew language. We had a lady teacher. I can't remember her name, but she had glasses and wore a *sheitel*, a wig that very Orthodox Jewish women wear when they get married to conform to the religious law that requires that their heads be covered.

My Hebrew certificate

I was obviously a lot better at Hebrew than my mum because she had married into Judaism. When we did go to the synagogue I can remember how all the women would have to sit upstairs and Mum would be mumbling, pretending to be reading along in Hebrew. I knew she couldn't read Hebrew, but I can remember wondering at the time why all the other women were able to read Hebrew and my mum couldn't.

Although Mum clearly couldn't fake knowledge of Hebrew, physically she fitted in better because she had this little Jewish-looking nose. At just five feet, she was a petite woman with a slight figure and thick dark hair, beautiful deep brown eyes and pale skin. She was an extremely attractive lady, a real stunner in her thirties and forties before she got poorly. She used to attract a lot of male attention, but she never strayed, she was incredibly loyal to Dad. In later years, I used to take her on my tours with the bands and they thought she was a corker, especially as she always dressed so beautifully.

I've got my mum's eyes but my dad's olive skin, which is lucky because Mum's very fair complexion could never tolerate the sun. Her hair was wonderful though and I certainly have inherited that aspect of her. In her youth, she had incredible thick hair and was always having it thinned.

Fortunately, I have been blessed with reasonably good health. She struggled with ill health. She had terrible ulcers, I suppose from all the stress of working in the business. It was quite ironic because she was always the one who looked after everyone else in the family. Grandma never liked Mum, but whenever she or anyone else was ill, it was always Mum they went to see. She was wonderful like that. She should have been a nurse. She was just one of those great women who always seemed to know what to do whatever you had wrong with you.

Mum could sort things out. I suppose she had to, being married to my dad who was completely useless with anything domestic. I've definitely got his cack-handedness. He couldn't even change a light bulb or plug. Most of the time, if something straightforward went wrong it was my mum who fixed it. She was one of the most capable women I've ever met.

Dad was a hard-working man. He was the son his mother wanted him to be: an upstanding pillar of the Jewish community. So that he didn't turn out like his father, she must have instilled in him a sense of responsibility from a young age. Although a good man and a great businessman,

Granddad hadn't always been as Orthodox as perhaps my grandma wished him to be. He liked a drink and he liked being sociable, neither of which she was keen on.

While Dad had been conditioned into thinking, 'I have to work hard to bring home the bacon' – or should that be the 'bread' being a baker, a Jewish one at that – he was also a bit like his father in not always being as Orthodox as he should have been. I suppose you could say he was kosher on the surface because, despite his strict Jewish upbringing, in fact he absolutely adored bacon, as did my brothers, even the smell made them go all tingly. I, on the other hand, have never been that keen on it and would definitely never touch it today. Dad would go to great lengths to get bacon for himself and the boys, and that meant driving to an area where he wasn't known. When he got back we'd race around the house opening all the windows, doors and curtains before we cooked it so the smell didn't linger. Deep down, I think he actually disagreed with quite a lot of the Jewish beliefs.

Whatever he thought, like all Jewish men he worked very hard and earned a good living for his family. Dad would get up at 4.30 every morning and be out of the door an hour later. By the time he got home at about 8 p.m. he would be shattered and good for nothing except eating his evening meal, reading the paper and falling asleep in front of the telly.

The only day of the working week that Dad would be home in time to eat with us was Friday night. I loved the Friday night meal. Mum and Dad would have the old Palwin sweet red wine and we were allowed to have a bit. We ate chopped liver which I adored, then chicken soup with *kreplach* or sometimes *matzah* balls, or *kneidlach* as they're also known, which I still make now. The main course was chicken that had been so over-cooked to make stock for the soup that it would be horribly dry and tasteless. I nearly always got the breast and it was like eating cardboard. I hated it but I was always full with chopped liver and chicken soup. That was the tradition every Friday night. Shabbat also highlighted the fact that Dad really wasn't a religious man because he would always rush through the *broches* for the bread and the wine and say, 'Come on, Violet, bring the dinner on.'

Dad's devotion to work also affected our holidays because we never went away together as a family despite being able to afford to go on fancy trips abroad. Our holidays always involved Mum taking us off to Llandudno in Wales or St Anne's in Lancashire, which of course was much posher than Blackpool, for short breaks of maybe a week at the most. Dad would occasionally come to see us on a Friday night, Shabbat night, and stay Saturday and go home in the evening so he could be in the bakehouse for Sunday, which was a big day for the bakery. He had to be there to make the bagels; Bookbinder's bagels were very famous in Manchester at the time.

I think there may be an odd picture of us on the beach at St Anne's or Llandudno with Dad relaxing in a deckchair with his trousers rolled up and his feet in the sea. Llandudno was my favourite. We would stay at The Grand – a five-star hotel with a sea view – and Mum occasionally let me have a sip of her Pimm's or lager in the evening. I think having such a great time as a kid in Llandudno is actually one of the reasons why I eventually ended up living by the sea with my own family. I even have a love for seagulls because of Llandudno. I remember years later when we moved to Devon a neighbour was having double-glazing fitted because he couldn't stand the noise of them. I could never understand it because they are part of the charm of living on the coast.

Aside from being a workaholic and so committed to the bakery, I think the major reason Dad didn't ever come away with us was because he was terrified of leaving anybody else in charge, especially his brother-in-law, Uncle Bernard, who also worked in the business.

I can remember him saying, 'I know what'll happen, I'll come home and I won't have any bloody business left.'

The whole bakery business must have been difficult for Dad because he never wanted to go into it in the first place. It was purely because he was the only boy in the family – Dad had two sisters, Betty and Sylvia – that he was expected to take over Granddad's business. He told me that he had always wanted to be an accountant and that he had passed his 11-plus exam but wasn't allowed to go to the grammar school. He had to go to another school because Granddad wanted him to go into the business. Very sad really, so it's no surprise he seemed miserable so much of the time.

Dad was good with numbers and did all his own accounts and bookkeeping and that was in the days before calculators, although I do remember he used to use a ready reckoner. I certainly don't take after him – I was hopeless at maths, and in fact, I think I'm number blind. I did the odd stint in the bakery shop and struggled with pounds, shillings and pence, and before that, farthings. When I was fifteen I did a gig in Germany and discovered their currency was counted in tens. I was amazed because I could understand it, whereas at home, I was totally confused by our money.

I think Dad was a very disappointed man, which together with his upbringing made him a pessimistic so-and-so. It took me many years to get out of that way of thinking and to keep positive about things. In fact, my cousin Hilary told me a few years ago that my father was the most pessimistic bugger she had ever met in her life. While understanding that Dad probably didn't want to be running the business, I still believe he used to use it as an excuse not to involve himself in anything we kids did. A lot of it, I'm sure, was because he was just too tired. But I can also recall Mum telling me how she would occasionally go to the bakery and catch him standing around nattering, which made her wonder how he came to be quite so tired.

He was a very private person who didn't let anyone inside and had learned how to put on a facade for work. And, like a lot of men of that generation, he had great difficulty in showing his emotions. I can, however, remember some lovely moments when I'd greet him and he'd say, 'Come 'n' sit on me knee for five minutes, love.' He could be so sweet, but not often enough. The love and affection was there, but somehow he just wasn't able to show it then.

I once discussed this in a radio interview on *Woman's Hour* several years ago, saying that, while my brothers and I weren't deprived materially, our relationships with each other suffered because of how hard our parents worked and by the fact they weren't around very much. Of course, the *Jewish Telegraph* had a field day and printed a sympathetic, but totally misconstrued article on our 'deprived' childhood. My brother Ray, who had been listening to the broadcast, was incensed by how my words had been twisted and he challenged the paper.

I have no desire whatsoever to be disrespectful to my parents, but I have always been honest about them. They were of a generation that put work before everything else in order to provide for their family, which is commendable but can also have lots of negative consequences. I've worked hard over the years, but my values are just very different from theirs and because of my upbringing, I've always felt very strongly that you have to find a balance between work and family, which is probably why I went on to combine the two.

CHAPTER 4

SCHOOLGIRL ELAINE

While there were undoubtedly big question marks over my parents' commitment to the Jewish faith, I on the other hand, at the age of eight, was very determined to do the right thing and maintain the links to the family's heritage. So much so that on one occasion I took my Jewish studies just a little bit too far. As part of my weekly Hebrew class, I had to learn how to perform the Shabbat ritual, which involved blessing the bread, saying prayers, lighting candles and a little alcohol. The latter was nearly my undoing, if it hadn't been for my dear brother Ray.

Every Friday night, the man of the house is responsible for leading the *kiddish* ceremony, which involved saying a blessing over the bread and the wine. I can't remember the prayer for lighting the Sabbath candles now, but I can remember the one for the wine. As Mum knew I used to enjoy reciting the blessings she bought me a little pair of brass candles so that I could practise whenever I wanted. This particular day I decided that my practice should be a full dress rehearsal, after all a girl really can't practise enough, can she?

My rehearsal involved raiding the drinks cabinet and picking out all the bottles that were nearly empty. There was Tia Maria, cherry brandy and spirits. I got a tray, lots of little glasses, my candles and all the bottles and took everything out into the back garden and started my practice. Well, I don't know why but, being the conscientious student I was, I started to polish off all the booze and at some point later

I must have staggered around and collapsed on the lawn. Ray discovered me and carried me upstairs to bed. A few minutes later, I was as sick as a dog and had my first full-blown hangover at the tender age of eight. Luckily for me, Mum and Dad never found out, well if they did, they didn't do anything about it. Perhaps they thought the experience was enough of a punishment; it certainly felt like it to me.

This, however, wasn't my first encounter with alcohol – that actually came four years earlier at my granddad's funeral when all the grown-ups were sitting *shiva*. I went round the house drinking the dregs of everybody's whisky and got myself a little bit plastered. I didn't feel too great after that either and I obviously didn't learn anything from it, judging from my later experience.

While I was clearly an early starter where alcohol was concerned, I certainly wasn't with the opposite sex as I was too busy being a tomboy. Saying that, I do remember falling helplessly in love for the first time in 1953 with a boy called Sidney. My school had a pageant on Coronation Day and the class voted for a boy to be the Duke of Edinburgh and a girl to be the Queen. Sidney and I got the lead parts and I remember being very pleased because he was so fantastic-looking. He had blond curly hair and the most stunning blue eyes to go with it. I think he must have really stood out because he wasn't your average Jewish-looking boy. A normal Jewish boy, of course, would have had very dark hair, dark brown eyes and an olive complexion. Sidney definitely didn't look like that, and I thought he was gorgeous. I absolutely adored this boy for years, but I don't think I ever let him know how I felt. The fact that Sidney made such an impression on me makes me realise now just how sheltered my community was in those days.

Apart from that, and the marriage proposal from Sammy Portnoy, of course, my interest in boys didn't really develop until I was eleven or twelve. My enthusiasm for ballet and tap also waned and was replaced by other interests including the clarinet. I had been playing recorder and was quite good at that, making it into the school group, but one day I heard my school friend Annabel Clynes playing the clarinet and I knew I had to get one too, and after that, it was a saxophone and then the guitar. I was never very good at any of them, but trying to play them did teach me the rudiments of music and how to read the top line.

Bar mitzvahs were also very important in my singing development. It all began when I was about five with the rabbi getting me up to sing a few of my favourite songs at various festivities. From there I went on to sing at Ray's bar mitzvah when I was six and, after that, I think I started to get a bit of a name for it with my parents' friends which led to being asked to sing at their functions.

But even though Mum and Dad enjoyed my performances I still felt my brothers got more attention than I did. Dad never seemed to have any time for me. When he wasn't at the bakery, he was obsessed with football and his beloved Manchester United, and, when they weren't playing in the summer, it was cricket. He couldn't be bothered taking us out, but if Man United were playing, he was at the game, home or away, rain or shine. And, if he couldn't go in person, he would be watching it on the telly, in fact our television – one of the first in Cavendish Road – was totally and utterly dominated by football and cricket.

Dad did, however, take me to a cricket match once when I was about ten years old and I quite liked it, probably because he let me have half a lager. But despite this, neither he nor my brothers would ever let me play football or cricket with them, and being a bit of a tomboy I was always desperate to join in. On tour with Vinegar Joe years later the boys went to play cricket in a park on a gorgeous sunny day and they let me join in, which was great. To this day I've always wanted my own garden, large enough to play cricket, then no one would be able to tell me I couldn't join in.

As well as not letting me play football or cricket, my brothers used to pick on me. At times, they could be really horrible. One of the things that used to give them the most pleasure was throwing worms at me, which I hated; my reaction was over the top and no doubt that made the game even more fun for them. I had a thing about worms and snakes for years, and it wasn't until I moved to Devon and started a family that I managed to get over it.

As I never had anyone to play with at home, my parents decided to get me a dog for my eleventh birthday. We'd had a couple of cats, but I never thought of them as pets, they were there to keep the mice under control, which is probably why they were only allowed in the cellar. I used to love the cats but Mum and Dad must have known that I always wanted a dog. Dad went to Tib Street in Manchester and came home with a boxer. I named him Monty.

But Dad being Dad didn't buy a puppy, he got a nine-month-old dog thinking that it would be house-trained. The only problem was that Monty wasn't because the very first thing he did was to cock his leg on the chair by the telephone in the hall and pee everywhere. I think he had been pretty badly neglected because he was covered in eczema and was generally in a terrible state. Nevertheless, I loved Monty. I took him with me whenever I could, which was always fun because he was pretty crazy. He'd always be running into things with his head, even brick walls. When he spotted me coming home from school, he would charge like a complete loony to greet me. He was a great dog.

Monty helped to make my childhood happy, as did my cousin Hilary. Over the years Hilary has seen me through a lot. Her life is what my grandmother, and maybe my parents, would have liked for me. She went on to marry a nice Jewish boy and bring up her two children in a traditional Jewish way.

Hilary, who is only six months younger than me, is the daughter of my dad's sister Sylvia and her husband Bernard. They also had a son called Michael who I used to get on really well with – unfortunately he lives in Los Angeles with his wife Carolyn and I don't get to see him much these days. As Hilary and I were so close in age and got on so well, we spent a lot of time together growing up. And, with my parents being busy with the business, it was always Auntie Sylvia and Uncle Bernard who used to take us kids out at weekends. We often went to Ainsdale Beach in Merseyside, which was a very posh place at the time, and I can remember being horrible to Hilary, teasing her when we had ice creams. Hilary would eat hers quickly and I would lick mine slowly, knowing that she wanted mine because she'd finished hers. I would do the same when we had a packet of crisps too. No way to treat your cousin or your best friend, but that's what kids are like.

Unlike me, Hilary did well at school and passed her 11-plus with ease, so Auntie Sylvia and Uncle Bernard sent her to grammar school in Manchester. I didn't pass my 11-plus because, quite honestly, I couldn't understand the questions, which I suppose wasn't much of a surprise as I was in the B class and they didn't seem to teach you all the things you needed to pass the 11-plus. When I came to leave Sedgley Park Primary the choice of secondary school was restricted by your postcode and I was the only person in my year with a Salford postcode. So while all my friends went on to Hope Park Secondary Modern, I followed my brothers to the roughest school around – North Salford Secondary Modern.

I was terrified on my first day because I was used to mixing with nice Jewish boys and girls. Mum was obviously worried about me too. I remember her saying, 'You're going to a school where there are going to be a lot of children who haven't got nice things like you've got. Always wear the uniform; I never want to see you in anything else other than the uniform. Never let them see what you've got, then they won't have a go at you and you won't get bullied. Try not to stand out and remember it's everyone's first day, they'll all be just as frightened as you are.'

In those days they always sorted you by religion at school by asking you to stand up if you were Christian, Catholic or Jewish. Of course, I was the only Jewish one in the class and I felt odd because of it.

I remember all the girls saying, 'Ooh, we never knew you were Jewish.'

It never occurred to me not to stand up because I didn't know any different and couldn't see the potential problems it could cause. But, in all the time I was at that school, I never really got bullied. Maybe it was Mum's advice or maybe I was just able to get on with people from all sorts of different backgrounds.

For about six months after starting school, I was the only Jewish girl in the class, then two other girls came along. There was Maxine Sheff, an Orthodox girl who became my best friend at school, and Susan Mervyn, a pretty girl who I ended up having a bit of a fight with when she overheard me saying she was behaving badly because her mum and dad had split up. I also got on well with a very tall girl called Joan McVitie who looked about eighteen. Joan got pregnant when she was twelve, as lots of girls at North Salford Secondary Modern seemed too, and my mum, bless her, was always giving me clothes to give to Joan to help her out as she got bigger and bigger.

Despite having failed my 11-plus exam, I managed to get into the A-stream. I was also fortunate enough to have a brilliant form teacher called Miss Brown who was very good to me. She said she would try to bring me on so I could sit the 11-plus again. With her encouragement and help, I went from being bottom of everything to being top in English that year.

Maths, sadly, was another story. I'm not sure any amount of help would have made a difference with maths. I've just always been rubbish at it and still have a number block today. The only exception is phone numbers. I can remember the telephone number from Cavendish Road to this day and I memorise family and friends' telephone numbers because I think it strengthens my mind and helps me remember lyrics. It's fine as long as no one asks me to add them up.

Outside of school I was able to keep in touch with my friends from primary school who had gone to Hope Park County Secondary School by going to The Woodlands Jewish youth club every Tuesday or Wednesday night. We still got on well, so much so that I can remember my dad catching me on the phone gossiping with either Brenda Cohen or Rhona Stolberg and saying, 'You go on like a real Becky on the phone.' His way of saying I was being rather upfront and loud.

The youth club was also important for me musically because I started to sing with my first ever band. There was a boy there a year or two older than me, called Lionel, who really fancied me. Unfortunately, it wasn't mutual so his feelings for me were never reciprocated, but we did get on well as a musical partnership. We would practise every Sunday morning at his house and he would accompany me on piano while I sang my party piece 'Blue Moon'. We also performed 'Red Sails in the Sunset' and 'Blueberry Hill'.

Lionel played piano in a band called 'The Black Cats'. They used to wear blue Marks and Spencer sweaters with black cats on, and I thought they were wonderful, probably because I had a bit of thing for the guitar player. Eventually, I started a little relationship with him and we would go out to the pictures, but my parents were far from impressed; they thought he was no good and wanted me to stop seeing him altogether. As it turned out, they were right about him because years later when my son Jay booked a gig for me through him, we ended up in a dispute over quite a lot of money. I suppose the moral of that story is it's always best to listen to your mum and dad!

By then singing was starting to become more and more important to me. Thinking back, music was just an ever-present part of my childhood. The radio was always on at home and my brothers would be around it listening to people like Frankie Laine and Johnnie Ray. They also used to listen to the serial *Dick Barton – Special Agent* but I, of course, wasn't allowed to be involved because I was a girl. When Tony turned thirteen he got his first set of drums and became more involved in music, which proved to be something of a defining moment for all us Bookbinder children. I remember his thirteenth birthday very clearly because I sang 'Mr Sandman' at his bar mitzvah party with my grandfather's youngest brother's band, Nat Bookbinder and The Chapters. They apparently used to do pretty well and would often play on the American base at Warrington. In those days audiences used to be segregated, but Uncle Nat would only play to mixed, black and white, audiences so I imagine that caused a problem or two.

With his new drums, Tony would play along to records by Count Basie and His Orchestra, Louie Bellson, Gene Krupa and Buddy Rich. About the same time, Ray was given a trumpet and took his playing very seriously. He and Tony formed a little trad jazz band because that was all the go in the 1950s, inspired by jazz musicians Chris Barber and Ken Colyer.

I remember the trombonist Gabriel Jacobs, because he was one of my first crushes. He was very tall and thin and had acne: in fact he was completely covered in acne, but that didn't seem to put me off in the least. He was not what you would call a handsome man, but I was head over heels in love with him nevertheless. I was so mad about him I used to walk Monty near his house in King's Road every night just so I might catch a glimpse of him, and he didn't live anywhere near us at all. Years later, I wondered what attracted me to Gabriel. I've always had unusual taste in men, either going for amazing-looking guys or the odd, eccentric sort.

I was desperate to sing in my brothers' band, particularly as Gabriel was in it, but even though I was getting more and more passionate about singing they still wouldn't let me sing with them. I couldn't understand why they wouldn't accept me and remember feeling so upset because of it. At the time, I was too shy to tell them how I felt, not that it would have made any difference.

Despite never including me in their music, it was actually my brother Ray who sealed my musical fate when he gave me my first record on my twelfth birthday. It was Ella Fitzgerald's album *Lullabies of Birdland* and it was the first time I had ever heard her. In those days she was considered more palatable to the British audience than Billie Holiday or Sarah Vaughan. I absolutely loved her voice, so much so that I would rush home from school in my lunch break to play her on the early music centre we had in the living room. I memorised every track, 'Lullaby Of Birdland' and 'How High The Moon', I knew them note for note. Listening to her sing became an addiction; I just couldn't help myself. She was, without a doubt, my first and biggest vocal influence.

CHAPTER 5

FIRST AUDITION

I spent hours and hours trying to copy Ella's voice without much success because her voice was higher than mine. I always had great difficulty singing in her key and then someone told me you could change the key. I was so relieved as at that point I was getting pretty frustrated with myself. Part of my obsession with Ella was probably down to the fact that I hadn't heard many female singers I liked until I discovered her. She certainly changed that.

I was also crazy about rock and roll, which everyone else was into. The girls at school were all mad about Tommy Steele, Bill Haley, Marty Wilde, Billy Fury and, of course, Cliff Richard. I loved Cliff with a passion; not so much on a musical level, but definitely on a physical one. He was so incredibly good-looking. I was besotted with him for years, and had pictures of him all over my bedroom.

My school friend Sylvia Robinson, a Brigitte Bardot looka-like with NHS spectacles, took me to one of his concerts. The girls in the audience went wild, jumping up and down in the aisles. I'd never seen anything like it. I'd only ever been to the Ella 'Jazz at the Philharmonic' concerts, which were very civilised, the toe-tapping kind, so when I saw Cliff's gigs it was such a contrast. They were wild and teeming with deranged schoolgirls, all screaming at him as if there was no tomorrow. I liked Elvis's records too. Cliff, of course, had taken quite a lot from him. I liked both of them but I think they had great sounds rather than great voices. That's not to say that I didn't think Elvis was brilliant at what he was doing because he undoubtedly was. He was a white man singing black music, which was really quite something.

My love of music was fuelled by regular visits to the Free Trade Hall in Manchester, a venue that always had a good selection of artists performing. I remember seeing Count Basie and his band there. Tony had bought a ticket, but for some reason he couldn't go so I went, even though I wasn't particularly fond of the band because what I had heard was instrumental and I liked music that I could sing along to. Dad dropped me off and I went inside and found out that my ticket allowed me to sit wherever I wanted. As the Free Trade Hall was laid out in the round, I found a spot behind the drummer Sonny Payne. I ended up being enthralled by Sonny because he did something I thought was unbelievably cool: he came on stage carrying a pair of shoes over his shoulder, which he then put on especially for the performance. Not expecting any vocals, I was pleasantly surprised to hear Joe Williams sing. He had a beautiful Paul Robeson blues kind of voice, which I loved. I bought the album after that.

When Sarah Vaughan came to the Free Trade Hall I was beside myself with excitement. I had become passionate about her music through listening to Ella. Disappointingly, I got ill and wasn't able to go. I was mortified, but my brothers were sweet because they brought me a programme home. Luckily, I got to see Sarah years later at the Grosvenor House Hotel in London. She was performing on a double bill with Andy Williams for which my husband, Trevor, was the sound engineer. He got complimentary tickets for me and his mum and dad. Being at the Grosvenor House it was a sit-down dinner affair and we were seated above and away from everyone else, which I thought was great because if an artist is good I always like to be a good audience. Well on this occasion I was really enjoying myself, making up for that missed concert in Manchester all those years ago. I went a bit mad and one of the production crew came and told me to shut up so I told her I was enjoying myself and that she should go away. Well if I'm honest I didn't say it quite as politely as that. Anyway she must have got the message or perhaps she realised I was Trevor's wife because she didn't bother me again. I was a bit fiery at that time, and it didn't help that I'd just bought two bottles of Dom Pérignon, which I wasn't going to let go to waste.

I've always been fairly feisty, and still can be, if provoked. I think it stems from that determined streak in my character, without which I'm pretty sure I wouldn't have become who I am today. I can remember seeing Brenda Lee on the telly when I was about twelve and thinking to myself, 'I can do that'. I had this incredible determination to be a star and an overwhelming desire to be noticed by those closest to me. I wanted the attention – I think I still do today, to a point – and for them, for once, to see and acknowledge how good I was. Everything at home always seemed to revolve around my brothers and that upset me, probably making me such a resolute person. They had the private education at Grimes College which I suppose they needed in Mum and Dad's eyes because they would have to one day earn a good living and support their families, whereas I, being a girl, would just meet a nice Jewish boy and settle down and have everything done for me.

Not enjoying the same private education as my brothers didn't bother me. I was always off doing something I enjoyed, like skating, going to ballet, seeing the girls at the youth club and jiving, which my brother Ray taught me to do. However, it must have affected me subconsciously because I think I was jealous of everything they had. If I ever felt morose about it, I had Monty, my dog, and my Ella records. I would just put Ella on and sing away. That was what I really cared about.

Mum got me elocution lessons because she had the idea

I could become an actress. I had lessons with a wonderful lady called Maxine Keel who spoke with the most beautiful voice. Even though I didn't like the elocution bit, I adored the acting side. I entered one examination in my early teens in which I did quite well and all of sudden, Mum had aspirations of me going to the Royal Academy of Dramatic Art. That was going to be a tall order because I struggled academically which, as it turned out, was only to get worse because my teacher, Miss Brown, who had done so much to encourage me, died very suddenly. I was terribly upset at her death because I thought she was great. She had given me the extra help and confidence I needed and my grades had just started to improve.

Her death changed my life, and not for the better. I quickly fell back into my old ways, not doing very well at anything and I even started to skip school with my best non-Jewish friend, Beryl Heywood. Beryl and I were terrible. We used to write letters for each other to our teacher saying we had gone to the dentist and all sorts of things like that. We would abandon our school uniforms, dress up and go to the cinema. You had to be sixteen to get in. I was only thirteen but with make-up I could pass for much older quite easily. If that didn't work, we'd ask strangers to get us in, which wasn't the best of ideas, but in those days I didn't think about the consequences of what I was doing.

We got away with it for ages but eventually the headmistress, Miss Stone, an enormous 'two-ton Tess' of a woman with a bit of a beard, got wind of our antics and called us to her office for a good telling off.

I said to Beryl, 'Leave it to me. I'll do the talking. Don't say a bloody word. Let me go in first and I'll do it all.'

I told Miss Stone we were sorry and that we'd forgotten we both had to go to the dentist – a likely story I know, but it was all I had. I could see Miss Stone wasn't really buying it so I played my trump card. Knowing she was obviously quite partial to a cake or two, I told her my dad was making this new Black Forest gateau, which he had never done before because he was a Jewish baker.

I said, 'Would you be interested if I brought one of the gateaux in for you to try. I'd love to hear what you think of it, as my dad doesn't have very many non-Jewish customers because all his shops are in Jewish areas. I really would be very grateful if you would try it and let me know what you think of it.'

Luckily for Beryl and me, Miss Stone couldn't resist and she let us off. I guess saying 'no' to food wasn't one of her strong points. Every week after that I always had to bring in a big Black Forest gateau, or cream cakes, or the latest things Dad was making. I don't think I was ever going to do too well academically if I had to bribe my headmistress at thirteen, but the funny thing was that at the time Beryl and I were summoned to Miss Stone's office, Dad had been making Black Forest gateaux for ages and was supplying them to all the restaurants in the area.

During my time at school the only things that really interested me were Domestic Science, PE and, of course, music. School definitely taught me how to cook. I was always into cooking at school, but never at home. As it turned out, Mum didn't help me with cooking until much later in life. I don't think I was interested in learning from her at a young age and she expected that once married, I would have other people to cook for me.

Thank God I made a career out of singing because I ended up leaving school without any qualifications. I received a certificate from the rabbi for my Hebrew classes, a grade one in drama and a grade two in ballet, and those were all out-of-school activities. The only thing I got from school was the little prayer book that everyone was given. My last year was made worse by a string of illnesses. Between the ages of fourteen and fifteen, I was prone to colds and sore throats, but in my final year, what I thought was only a cold turned out to be pneumonia and, just as I was getting over it and getting ready for my exams, I got ill again. The pneumonia developed into pleurisy. After several X-rays it was discovered that I had major scarring on my left lung. I found out much later from Dr Lefever, who I used to go to see in London quite regularly, that I probably had had undiagnosed tuberculosis.

To get over the illness, our doctor Gerry Caplan, who was the son of Dad's great friends Uncle Maishe and Auntie Ada, told Mum she should take me away to Switzerland to get some fresh air. We went to Zermatt but Mum didn't think to find out what the weather was like there before we left and we arrived wearing high-heeled shoes, dresses and normal coats. The place was covered in about six feet of snow. To make matters worse, I got glandular fever, which ended up lasting for the whole time we were in Switzerland.

As a result I have a recurring problem. When I get very stressed or upset, I go down with the symptoms of pneumonia: terrible shivers and sweats. The illness also had an awful effect on my teeth. I went to the dentist so many times for fillings that he eventually realised that something else must be wrong. It turned out that the extended period of illness and the pills I'd been taking had rotted my teeth. Over the years I've spent a fortune on gold inlays and crowns.

I missed most of my final year being sick, so it was no wonder I left school in February 1960 at the age of fifteen with no qualifications and not a clue to what I was going to do with my life. The only thing I did know was that I wanted to be in the spotlight.

My parents, of course, didn't see my lack of academic achievement as a disappointment, because they had no expectations of me, other than marriage. They were, unsurprisingly, far more concerned for my brothers. Even a few years later when my career started to take off and I had a few successes behind me, I would come home from a tour and Grandma Bookbinder would ask me when I was going to settle down and find myself a nice Yiddisher boy.

Ironically, it was a Jewish connection that put me on the road to becoming a professional singer for one day I spotted an advertisement in the *Jewish Telegraph* saying that the music promoter and agent Don Arden was holding auditions at the Palace Theatre in Manchester for shows he was taking around the country. That was my chance, I had to go and sing for him. I didn't say a word to anyone and just took myself off to the Palace that Saturday and waited all morning for my turn – my chance to shine.

There were all sorts of artists there: jugglers, dancers and comedians and me, little Elaine Bookbinder. When my name was finally called I went on stage and did Cliff's 'Pointed Toe Shoes', which appeared on a November 1959 LP titled *Cliff Sings*. I also did 'Hallelujah I Love Him So', the Ray Charles song covered by Ella and Peggy Lee, but made famous to me by Eddie Cochran. I sang pop because I'd been so influenced by all the girls at school.

I was the last one that Don saw that morning, but by all accounts I blew him away because he told me I was marvellous and that I had to come back later that evening and go on the stage as part of his show. I just couldn't believe it so I rushed home and told Mum and Dad and my brothers what had happened. Tony was so excited, he couldn't wait to show off his little sister and even Mum and Dad seemed thrilled for once.

So that Saturday night I went on stage at the Palace Theatre for my big break in front of a massive audience. There I was with the pointed white shoes I had worn to the audition earlier that day and short black hair, which was the fashion – a very butch look. On reflection, it must have seemed bloody awful, but at the time Don Arden thought I looked wonderful.

After the show, Don went up to my parents and said he thought I was great and asked if I could come on the road with them to do the rest of the shows. I don't think they could quite believe it. We went off to the local kosher chip shop called Lapadis's, which was a couple of doors up from one of Dad's shops, to celebrate and decide what to do. I can remember sitting there, surrounded by all these people eating chips because he didn't do fish, just saveloys and pickles. Tony was unbelievably excited, I don't think I'd ever seen him so excited; he was so wonderful. As for me, I was just thrilled that I'd finally been noticed. The chips must have been pretty good because Mum and Dad decided that I could join the tour.

We went home and Mum packed me a case full of my bat mitzvah dresses because she didn't want me going on stage again looking as awful as she thought I did that night. The next day they took me back to the Palace Theatre to get on the tour bus. So there I was, barely fifteen, about to go off round the country with all those famous musicians and the furthest I'd ever been away from home on my own was Taunton with my cousin Hilary and my girlfriends from the Jewish youth club.

CHAPTER 6

ON THE ROAD

Stepping on the tour bus at 10 a.m. that Sunday morning in 1960 was one of the most daunting things I've ever done in my life. Not only was I going away from home for the first time, truly on my own, but I was in the company of about twenty men, most of whom were well known at the time up and down the country. There was Conway Twitty, Johnny Preston, the guys from the backing band called The Echoes, including a man called Laurie Jay who I would meet again much later on, Wee Willie Harris, and a drummer called Tony Crombie who was one of the best jazz drummers around at the time.

As if getting on the bus wasn't challenging enough, after a while the other musicians started to come over and talk to me. They were saying funny things that I didn't really understand. Now I realise they were being rude and suggestive, but a fresh-faced fifteen-year-old little Jewish girl from a nice part of Manchester, didn't have a clue what they meant, let alone know how to handle the situation. When we eventually got to the theatre in Nottingham that evening I told the tour manager, a cockney man called Henry Henroid, what had happened and he said to Don that he didn't think it was right that I should be left alone on the bus and in the dressing rooms with all those men.

However, it was a huge cast and dressing rooms were few and had to be shared. Nevertheless, Don took heed of what Henry had said because that evening rather than having to be in with the scrum he made sure I had my own dressing room at the theatre. Well, actually I shared a dressing room with him but as he was on stage most of the time compering the show, I pretty much had it to myself. Originally a comedian and singer, Don had turned to promoting shows and acts after realising it was more profitable, but at this point it must have made good sense for him still to be part of the show. Despite having my own dressing room I quickly formed a strong dislike of backstage facilities – a feeling which has stayed with me, mostly because they were for a long time dirty, disgusting, horrible places that were neglected simply because they weren't on show to the public.

I got a nasty surprise when I came to get ready for the show and opened my big suitcase to find that Mum had packed me nothing but my bat mitzvah dresses. Worse still, I didn't have any practical things whatsoever; I hadn't got a towel or a piece of soap and there sure as hell wasn't anything like that at the theatre, so I ended up having to find a shop to buy myself some soap and a towel. The other thing I found odd about the theatre was that there only seemed to be one toilet. A teenage girl among all those men, I was naturally very shy, and didn't want to have to share a toilet with them. I kept on trying to find the ladies' room but there just wasn't one.

I can also remember wondering what and when they all ate. Don soon answered that question because he appeared with a big bucket of fried chicken, which was the first time I had tasted it in my life.

Don said, 'Come and have some chicken.'

I was absolutely starving so I had a couple of pieces. Having been brought up on traditional Jewish food I'd never tasted anything like it before. Afterwards I thought I must start trying these fast food places, which I think must have only just arrived in England. But by far the biggest thing that happened that night was going on stage under a new name. Don had decided it would be better if people didn't know that I was Jewish.

He said, 'You can't call yourself Bookbinder.'

I asked, 'Why not? What's wrong with Bookbinder?'

He replied, 'It's too Jewish-sounding. You can't have that.'

So just as Elaine Bookbinder had made her debut on stage in Manchester, so she disappeared to be replaced by Elaine Mansfield. Don told me that when we had driven from Manchester to Nottingham we had passed through Mansfield and that's when he decided I should be called Elaine Mansfield. I sometimes think he had called me Mansfield as a bit of a laugh because he was promoting the actress and singer Jayne Mansfield's British tour, and you couldn't really find two more opposite women.

It didn't make any sense to me, as that's all I'd ever known and it seemed totally normal. But then, unlike today, it was quite common for people to try to conceal their Jewishness in order to succeed in public life. In fact, that's what Don had done himself. When I read his autobiography *Mr Big* years later, I understood a lot more about him and realised why he was the way he was. He was actually hiding his own Jewishness. Born Harry Levy, he was brought up in a strict Jewish family in Manchester's Cheetham Hill. I think he had learned to sing at the synagogue just as I had done, so we probably had quite a bit in common, although I think my family was very well-off compared to his. At a relatively young age, Don decided that he had to change his name if he wanted to get on in show business. It must have worked because he did become very successful.

Despite what he thought, I've never had problems with my Jewishness and I still don't, but others definitely have over the years. I wasn't about to argue with Don about changing my name that night because he put the fear of God into me despite having given me my big break. He hadn't actually done anything to make me feel that way, he just seemed to have that effect on me. It probably wasn't helped by that first night in Nottingham when he saw me about to go on stage wearing a shocking pink, flouncy bat mitzvah dress with diamanté straps and loads of petticoats underneath.

He said, 'What's with the frock?'

I didn't have much of an answer, or anything else to wear! So I went on and sang dressed up and looking like a dog's dinner. From his point of view it must have been very strange because all of a sudden I was totally different from the girl with the very distinctive look who had wowed him just a couple of evenings before.

After the show Don said he was driving back to London and that I was to go with him and stay with his family at their house in Brixton. I remember sitting in the back of his car all the way to London; I wouldn't sit in the front because I was so frightened of him. When we got to his house I was made to feel welcome by his wife Paddy, a big lady with very red hair who used to wear lots of jewellery. I found out much later that her real name was Hope and she was called Paddy because her father was Irish.

In the morning I met Don and Paddy's children, David and Sharon. David was a couple of years younger than me and Sharon must have been about six or seven. Sharon, of course, went on to marry Ozzy Osbourne of Black Sabbath – the heavy metal band that her father used to manage – and become one of the most famous women rock music managers in America and Britain, starring in *The Osbournes* reality TV show as well as being a judge on *The X Factor* and *America's Got Talent*.

Paddy offered me a bacon sandwich, which I naturally passed on. She then asked if I'd like some cereal instead. This proved to be my first ever experience of cornflakes.

In the short time I was at the Arden's house, there seemed to be a constant flow of people coming to see Don, along with some very interesting language, the like of which I wasn't used to. I particularly remember a big black woman who was full of life and who must have lived nearby. Don spoke to her as though she was one of the family, which I thought was odd because that didn't happen in Manchester. The only black person I'd met at that time was a girl called Eileen Atkinson who I knew at school, and she was only half black. Eileen was 5 ft 8 in at thirteen and a terrific runner. I always wanted to run like her, but my legs weren't like that. Don was wonderful with people but I was too young and naive to appreciate it. I wish I'd met him later on in my life because I'm sure we would have got on much better.

The following night the tour went to Bristol, but I got ill, probably due to the stress of the situation, and the tour manager Henry put me on the train back to Manchester.

I can remember saying to him on the way to the station, only having done two gigs, 'If this is show business, I don't want to know.'

I obviously hadn't taken to all the men and the dodgy dressing rooms very well. Henry was caring and tried to comfort me, 'Don't think all show business is like this. We aren't all like that. You've just had a bad experience. Have another go.'

When I got back to Manchester I remember being in the back of our car and somehow the c-word just slipped out of my mouth. I think I must have been saying something about how Don referred to people. Well, Mum and Dad went up the wall. Suffice to say they were far from impressed with my little showbiz adventure. That was just the way Don and Paddy spoke, everything was effing this and effing that. Recalling that episode I'd like to have been there a few days later when Mum got a phone call from Don saying that he wanted me to go back to London because he thought he could get me some auditions. Apparently, he told Mum he knew that I didn't like him. Well, that wasn't quite true, I was a bit frightened of him.

Despite the recent additions to my vocabulary, my parents weren't opposed to the idea and a few days later Mum and I travelled to London on the train. Don started to get me lots of little auditions in all kinds of different places. At first Mum and I used to stay at hotels. I think we went to the Cumberland Hotel a couple of times, which was quite nice, but as more and more auditions came up, he suggested we rent a flat because it would be cheaper than staying in hotels all the time. So for a short period, taking Don's advice, we rented a little furnished flat, off the Brompton Road in Knightsbridge, of all places, for about £7 a week. Money obviously wasn't an issue, Mum just wanted to stay in Knightsbridge. While I've criticised my parents for not noticing me or giving me the attention I so desperately wanted, they were always very generous in supporting me. I think it's fair to say they paid dearly for me to succeed in the music business.

As well as the auditions, I sang in lots of small floorshows for the American bases, which Don organised, here and in Germany, so I would often perform with dancers and comedians. I remember a comedian, a great guy called Bob Bain, who I thought was ever so funny because he was always putting on an American accent but was actually as Scottish as you like. We used to be taken everywhere by Don's driver, Peter Grant, who had a little VW. Peter went on to do very well for himself and became Led Zeppelin's manager.

One of the floorshows I successfully auditioned for was at the Astor Club in Berkeley Square. I later discovered that it was regularly frequented by the Kray twins. So I suppose it's possible that I might have performed in front of them. One of the well-known artists who performed there regularly was Kathy Kirby. I couldn't believe this woman when I saw her. I thought she was even more beautiful in person than she was on TV. She was also the first person I'd ever seen with shiny lips. After meeting her I felt very self-conscious.

I couldn't help but wonder what the audience made of me when they were used to watching this gorgeous, willowy blonde woman in a wonderful mink stole and high heels.

I remember auditioning at the Astor alongside Anita Harris who I think had already started to make a name for herself. I wasn't too confident about my audition, but fortunately the owner Bertie Green and the agent Michael Black liked me and booked me for a week.

As I was going to be there for that long Don suggested that I stay at his mother-in-law Dolly's place at Clapham Junction. Dolly used to run theatrical digs and the walls of her place were covered with photographs of all the artists who had stayed there. When I went, it had become a place for students.

Dolly was a wonderful woman but her accommodation left a lot to be desired, to say the least. The place was filthy and, to make matters worse, there wasn't any hot water so I only had a bath once a week. Every Friday night, I used to boil several kettles of water so I could take a bath. And, if all that wasn't bad enough, Dolly was one of the world's worst cooks, if not the worst. Her cooking was so bad she made my grandmother's food seem tasty.

One of the men staying there said to me, 'Dolly gets the food all right, but it's what she does with it that's the problem.'

The food was so terrible I ended up living on chocolate. Mum and Dad would send me money to cover the rent and some extra to live on, but I'd spend it on going to the pictures and buying chocolate which meant I became very, very chubby and quite spotty. The other problem was getting my washing done; there weren't any launderettes around in those days. This meant packing my suitcase full of all my dirty clothes and taking them back home every couple of weeks.

When Mum came and saw Dolly's house, she was dumb-struck. She thought it was disgusting and insisted on getting me out. Strangely, I quite liked living there because I loved Dolly. I suppose the combination of Dolly's company and the excitement of being in London somehow managed to make me forget about how bad my living conditions were.

It was performing at the Astor that provided a way out because there I met Ann Roule who I think was either Bertie Green or Michael Black's secretary. When Mum came down she got talking to Ann and told her how she didn't like 'her Elaine' staying at Dolly's in all that dirt and grime with no hot water and that she had to try to get me somewhere else to live. Ann said I could stay at her place in Stockwell on a temporary basis. When I saw her flat I thought it was fabulous. But best of all, she had hot water and a lovely bath and shower to go with it! Ann was great because she would only let me pay rent for the time I was actually there. She didn't charge me whenever I went home or was away doing an audition or a floorshow.

One of the times I had to go away was when I was booked by Don to perform at two American bases in Germany at Frankfurt and Wiesbaden. This was the first time I'd been abroad on my own so it was incredibly exciting. I was booked with three dancers, the band The Echoes and the comedian Bob Bain whom I liked. My worst memory of the trip has to be the ferry crossing to Ostend. I'd never been on a ferry before and I was really, really seasick. I felt dreadful. I was so relieved to get off that boat and into a vehicle for the drive to Wiesbaden.

Germany presented me with my first encounter with a duvet. I thought to myself, 'What am I going to do with this? Where are the bloody blankets?'

We didn't have anything like a duvet at home and I just didn't have a clue what to do with it – did I sleep on top of it or underneath it? I somehow managed to get by, probably by copying the other girls who I shared a room with. I guess that experience pretty much summed me up. I was super-confident singing, way beyond my meagre fifteen years, but when it came to everyday stuff I definitely wasn't. If I'm honest, I was probably a bit immature. Nevertheless, from time to time, Don did manage to shake my confidence; he had the ability to scare me half to death, almost certainly unintentionally, although I was never entirely sure. I remember him asking me once how I learned my songs. I told him that I got the sheet music and then learned them from records.

His reply was, 'Can't you read the music?'

I said, 'No,' and he laughed.

However, that wasn't quite the truth; I could read the top line but as I couldn't read the bass line, it was easier to confess total defeat. That one conversation had a profound effect on me because it stayed with me for many years. In fact, I believe it eventually proved to be the catalyst for my learning to play the piano. I suppose you have no idea at the time how a little comment like that might affect you in the future.

I think it's because of such instances that I try very hard to build up people's confidence rather than just knocking them down all the time. I felt at the time that Don's attitude towards me was like that. However, in hindsight, and in fairness to him, it was also probably because I was so young and introverted, and didn't have the first idea about how to speak to adults, let alone someone like Don. And that was way before he got his reputation for being the music industry's loose cannon and managing bands like the Small Faces, Electric Light Orchestra and Black Sabbath – I think the papers used to call him the 'Al Capone of pop'. I suppose I was also just a kid that had got a bit over-confident from singing at home and at bar mitzvahs who, all of a sudden, was totally overawed by all the very professional music people around her. I can remember feeling that perhaps I wasn't actually quite as great as I thought I was.

Strangely, the emotional hold Don Arden had over me

never disappeared because when I saw him again years later I felt exactly the same. He was breaking in a new female artist with my then husband, Pete Gage. I found myself staying out of the way in the background. I just couldn't bring myself to speak to Mr Big and I can't really explain why. There I was in my mid twenties, still unable to communicate with him.

Whenever I watch Sharon Osbourne on TV, I see so much of Don in her. She has that same sort of rudeness, that same bolshie and bullying attitude, which her dad had. To be fair, she can be very supportive too, something that I can honestly say I never witnessed in her father. In her defence, she must have had a tough life with him.

While working with Don, I got to know Sharon and her brother David quite well. In fact, they were part of one of my most vivid memories, an experience that unsurprisingly also had a lot to do with my incredible fear of their father. On the day in question, I took Sharon and David to Battersea funfair. I've always loved funfairs and theme parks, but that definitely wasn't the case that day. We had great fun together, enjoying all the different rides until they made me take them on this thing called the Dive Bomber. It was totally terrifying because the straps were weak and it felt as though the three of us were going to fall out at any moment. Thank God we didn't. After we got off they wanted to go on again. I couldn't believe it. There was no way in this world that I was ever going to go through that experience again.

As if the ride wasn't bad enough, there was the terrible thought of being responsible for the death of Don Arden's children. I can't begin to describe my relief when I finally got the pair of them home to Brixton.

CHAPTER 7

THE ERIC DELANEY BAND

I was probably one of the few artists Don Arden really liked but never actually signed. He always knew what to do with girls like Brenda Lee, but even though he recognised my talent, he couldn't see what to do with me because I was so different from them. In fairness, I was singing pop and jazz and the auditions he got for me just weren't right. It was also probably something to do with my insecurity and lack of confidence. I can remember feeling confident and positive about my ability but at the same time, inadequate and nervous. I never had a problem with confidence on stage but off stage was an entirely different matter. While that was partly due to my relationship with Don, it wasn't completely his fault. I guess what it comes down to is that, at fifteen, I just didn't know how to deal with a character as strong and formidable as Don Arden.

My self-doubt had its positive and negative side. On the one hand, I believed I was the best; on the other, the realisation struck me hard that I wasn't actually the greatest. There were plenty of artists with much more experience and talent than me. I had a lot to improve and it wasn't going to happen overnight, it was something I would have to work at very hard.

When I came to leave Don it was easy because I didn't have a contract, he just let me go. The career break I so badly needed came along around the time of my sixteenth birthday in 1961. It was my brother Ray who provided it. As much as I say my brothers held me back in a lot of ways, they also knew what I wanted to do and were very support-ive. Ray used to buy *The Stage*, the trade newspaper for the entertainment world, regularly and one day he spotted an advertisement for an audition with the Eric Delaney Band, one of the most popular big dance bands of that time.

He said, 'Come on, I'm going to take you to the audition.'

We went along to a Top Rank dance hall type of place with a huge dance floor and a stage where the band played.

As soon as Eric Delaney saw me he said, 'I've seen you before haven't I? I've seen you at the American bases in Germany. I remember you, you're Elaine Mansfield. You can only sing rock and roll, can't you?'

I said, 'No, I can sing all sorts. I can sing ballads. I'll sing a ballad for you called "Misty".'

'Misty' is a beautiful song with a good vocal range. It was a big hit for Johnny Mathis but I didn't listen to his version, I knew it from hearing it sung by that great hero-ine of mine, Sarah Vaughan. I sang 'Misty' for Eric and he thought it was wonderful, and asked me to join the band. I think he was totally amazed that I had the ability to sing that kind of song at the age of sixteen.

Singing with the Eric Delaney Band, whose music is best described as up-tempo dance hall music, was to be fantastic for me because I not only gained great experience, I also got to perform with some great artists.

It was also here that Elkie Brooks was born. I'd never liked being called Elaine Mansfield and I always felt that Elaine Bookbinder was far from being catchy so I decided to become Elkie Brooks. When I was just a teen, I went out with an eighteen-year-old Jewish boy called Jackie Lubo, who came from somewhere in Eastern Europe. He explained that Elaine was Elkie in Yiddish. I don't know if he was right or not but I liked it far more than Elaine and it always stayed with me. I just came up with Brooks as a kind of shortened version of Bookbinder.

The start of my time in the Eric Delaney Band, however, proved to be pretty tricky because I soon found out that I was replacing Marion Williams who was a beautiful black singer with a powerful voice, very much of Sarah Vaughan's ilk. In fact, she was a close friend of Sarah's and whenever they got together, so the story goes, they would get stupefyingly drunk. The rest of the musicians in the band told me she had wonderful pitching and that she was always in tune. I had a rather big pair of boots to try to fill. I had no option but to give myself a good talking to.

I can remember telling myself, 'Come on, you can do this. You're not bad. You're actually quite good.'

Luck, however, proved to be on my side because it turned out that I knew a lot of Marion's songs and I also sang in the same key as she did which meant Eric didn't have to pay for any costly new arrangements. One of the songs I did have to learn though was Dakota Staton's song 'The Late, Late Show'. I quickly came to love this number and I thought I sang it, and the rest of Marion's material, pretty well, but whatever I did and no matter how good it was, I always felt I was being compared to my predecessor and that really bothered me. In a way though, I suppose it was good because it made me try harder and really think about my singing and pitching. The band put Marion on a lofty pedestal; it seemed like she was the most amazing thing that ever walked and she should have been a megastar, but from what I can gather, she also had emotional problems and was quite a morose person, which probably explains why she never hit the heights she could have in the business.

It might also explain why she left the band. Eric was a real tough cookie and I imagine that wouldn't have helped her state of mind. He was a brilliant drummer and a great showman, fantastic with the audience but as soon as he was off stage he became as hard as nails. I remember he had these completely emotionless eyes, which made him seem very uncaring and distant. He didn't socialise with the rest of the band. I don't think anyone ever really got to know Eric.

He was also pretty tight with money. He used to pay us in dollars – I think it was about $25 a week. This was, of course, pretty good money for a young girl like me but the rest of the band didn't think so, especially as the conversion was about three dollars to the pound at the time. They persuaded me to ask Eric to give them more money because they thought I would have more chance of getting something out of him. Obligingly, I went to Eric and said that I didn't think it would be a bad idea if we all got a couple more dollars a week, but he wasn't having any of it.

He just said to me as quick as you like, 'A girl of your age shouldn't be doing this for the money.'

I guess that's the way he had to be if he wanted to make any money and keep going. In fact, I wish I'd been a bit more like that with some of my tours. I sometimes think I was too much of a soft touch with my crew and band in the past.

It's fair to say, you were never going to get rich as a member of the Eric Delaney Band. I think the most I ever got paid for a gig was $5, which would generally work out to be between $20 and $25 a week, out of which we had to pay for our own accommodation. The only thing Eric paid for was the coach, which left from Allsop Place in London, behind Baker Street station.

Talking of accommodation, my first gigs with the band were at airbases in Germany; one in Frankfurt and one in Wiesbaden. Because I'd been there while I was with Don I said to my mum when she asked where I'd be staying, 'Don't worry, I know the hotel there. I don't need to book. It'll be fine.'

Well it turned out to be one of life's important lessons because when we arrived there were no rooms. But, as I was standing there in the hotel reception wondering what the hell to do I got talking to two boys who were a bit older than me and who spoke perfect English. They said they had a friend just round the corner who had a bedroom in somebody's house and that I could stay there. I thought this was great so I jumped at the chance, got in their car with them and they dropped me off at their friend's house. I thanked them very much for their help and I stayed holed up in the room all night, too terrified to go out even though I was starving. I hadn't eaten since breakfast. Fortunately, the night passed without event and I survived unscathed. When I think about it now I can't believe how stupid I was. You don't just get into a car with two complete strangers and go off to somebody's house. I must have been a total idiot. I suppose that's what a bit of misplaced confidence does for you. I thought because I'd been singing at the bases and clubs when I was with Don that I knew what to do, but nothing could have been further from the truth. I was getting a little bit more streetwise, but I was still a long way off full speed.

It wasn't just the accommodation Eric was tight-fisted about. All the time I was in the band he never paid for any new arrangements, so I ended up singing to poor arrangements of the latest pop songs and doing the same old standards all the time, which always seemed to me to be a shame. Well his methods must have worked because he went on doing the same thing quite successfully for years and years. In fact, he came to see a gig of mine in 2008 and he looked really well and said he was still playing. Sadly, though, he died in 2011.

As well as being shrewd with money, Eric was also always pretty good at choosing his musicians. When I was with him we had a great group of guys who were able to make the most of the music they played despite the arrangements. The people who stood out for me were the brilliant trumpet player Tony Fisher, the other vocalist Gene Williams, who I clicked with, and the saxophone and vibraphone player Jim

Lawless who introduced me to Billie Holiday. Jim kept telling me that I had to hear her, so one day I sneaked into the PX (the Post Exchange) store on the airbase – you were only allowed to go in if you were in the services but I managed to get in around the back – and bought a couple of her albums. When I listened to them I couldn't understand what Jim was going on about. I was so used to listening to singers with big ranges and great technical ability, and I didn't think Billie had either. It took quite a few months for me to understand what she was about, but once I got into her music, I wouldn't listen to anyone else for about two or three years. To this day I don't think she had an incredible voice. It was her phrasing and her empathy with the lyrics, mixed up with the drugs and alcohol, which made her music so amazing. In terms of technical ability Ella had it for me. Before I saw her live in concert, I had pictured her as a willowy blonde. I always found Ella's sound very white in her singing but I suppose her first influences were more white than black. Even though Ella was my first influence and technically the better singer, it is Billie Holiday who I feel I have greater affinity with.

Gene Williams, the other vocalist in the band, was a black South African who spoke beautifully; I just loved the sound of his voice. He was a wonderful singer and I got on with him really well, so much so that I eventually felt he was like a brother to me. We had a great time performing together. Where a lot of singers in those days just sat down and waited for their turn to sing, Gene and I would stand behind the band and clap our hands to the rhythm of the music or play tambourines until our next song. Gene taught me to count bars and gave me some fantastic advice about making sure I knew the keys of my songs. He told me to copy the words of all my songs down in a book then get the piano player, when he had a few moments, to find my key so that I could write it next to each song.

He said, 'When Eric says he wants something medium tempo all you have to do is say to the piano player, "'Give Me The Simple Life' and give me a G".'

After that I made it my business to learn lots and lots of standards and write them down in a little red pocket book Gene gave me. Hanging out with Gene all the time, I suddenly started to meet lots of black people which, for a white Jewish girl from Prestwich who had only ever known one black girl at school, was great fun. He and Jim would befriend the American airmen and their wives and families, and they would buy us drinks. This is how I came to try my first ever cocktail. My favourite then was Vodka Seven, made with Seven Up lemonade and lemon or lime juice and served in a very tall glass. I thought it was fabulous. Did I enjoy them! They were like lemonade and I would knock them back as if there was no tomorrow, but I never had a hangover; the next day I would be up with a completely clear head. I had another favourite, cherry brandy cocktail that I used to go crazy over, and one called Sloe Gin Fizz. There I was, just sixteen, sipping away at all these amazing cocktails on an American airbase where you had to be over twenty-one to drink alcohol. I don't know how I got away with it; I guess they thought I was older because I was in the band.

I also loved the way they danced. The Twist was just coming out and I felt I was pretty good at it but the GIs just seemed to have a different way of doing it, which I'd never seen before. Oh, the way they moved, I just thought it was brilliant. I was impressed by the music they were into and that's how I got turned on to Smokey Robinson, Chuck Berry and Little Richard. I used to moan to Gene about Eric and the rest of the band for not being willing to introduce some Motown and R&B music to our set.

I remember saying to Gene, 'This music is great. Why can't the band see it?'

But like a lot of jazz musicians that I've met over the years they had tunnel vision and couldn't see anything beyond jazz.

After our stint in Frankfurt we went back to England and played at lots of large dance halls and hunt balls. I found the hunt balls very strange, as I'd never seen these big country houses or met those sort of people before. They were very toffee-nosed and, because of that, I thought they were horrible. We played all the same music as we did in Germany so the 'gentry' could enjoy dancing in their stiff and non-rhythmic way. These gigs didn't go on for too long and we soon found ourselves heading back to Germany to do another residency at an airbase in Baumholder.

While we were there I decided to bleach my hair blonde. The hairdresser in the little village was great and gave me the best bleach I think I've ever had. Because I had such short hair at the time the roots would start to show every couple of weeks. I must have looked a right sight. When I went back to my natural colour my hair started to fall out. I had great big bald patches and it took about a year for it to grow back. I was mortified, but I did get some good wigs and in any case, it was the done thing to wear wigs then.

Although we were generally away for long periods I never got homesick. As long as the music was right I was a happy bunny and I think I'm still like that to this day. I was enjoying myself and for the first time I felt that this was the life for me. I was with a good group of people and part of a team and I loved being in the spotlight.

The last show of our six-week stay in Baumholder was one of the most memorable, and I was definitely in the spotlight that night. I'm not quite sure how the idea came about but there was a nice, small young man called Tony who let me wear his uniform so I could go on stage dressed up as an American soldier. When I was all kitted up the rest of the band strapped a big bass drum to me and I came out for the last number beating in the rhythm. I got a massive cheer from the audience, which made me feel great, but I'm not sure what Eric made of it because he didn't know a thing about what we had been planning.

After Baumholder we went home and did a few more dance halls and hunt balls, but the work started to slow down. I was just about to hand in my notice when we were offered a two-month residency at the NATO base in Naples. I thought, 'Great, steady work and a chance to go to Italy.'

Even though I was away a lot of the time I was still living at Ann's place in London when I was back in England. However, one night, despite it being a fantastic escape from Don Arden's mother-in-law's place, it all became too much. Ann had told me that she would be away for a couple of days, so I thought I had Saturday night to myself. After I'd cooked something to eat, I left the pots until the morning so I could just sit and enjoy the TV. Ann, however, decided to come home early and had a complete head fit when she saw all these dirty pots piled by the sink. After that confrontation I vowed never to share a flat with anybody else again in my life, and I never have.

By the time we went to Naples my beloved friend Gene had left the band and had been replaced by an American singer called Herbie Goins. Gene ended up becoming a solo artist on the German cabaret circuit. He came to see me do a show at the Dominion in London when I'd just done 'Pearl's A Singer'.

He was still quite an attractive-looking man and I remember my husband Trevor saying, 'Oh, he's one of your old boyfriends, isn't he?'

Just as I had done with Gene, I started to hang out with Herbie who was also a great bloke; I guess us singers like to stick together. We must have looked quite odd because he was about 6 ft 5 in and as skinny as you like, and there was little me with my short, bleached blonde hair. He introduced me to some interesting American airmen, one of whom was to become my first serious boyfriend. He was twenty-one, a gorgeous, muscular guy who I adored at the time. We spent loads of time together as you do when you're young and in love. We got on so well.

Our time in Naples came to an end too soon and I found myself back in England. In between missing my new boyfriend and all the Delaney gigs, an opportunity of a job in Manchester came up at a club called the Whisky A Go-Go, which was owned by Billy Charvin. The club was an eatery and a cabaret with, as I later discovered, a gambling house upstairs. I went along to the audition and there must have been fifty girls there, all with their music. I, of course, didn't have anything at all so I just quietly shuffled to the back of the queue and waited.

When it was my turn to sing the piano player asked, 'Where are your dots?'

A year or two earlier, a question like that would have completely thrown me but because I had had all this experience with the Delaney band, I said, 'Just play a twelve-bar blues in B flat.'

He asked what tempo and I said, 'Slow.'

Luckily, my new-found confidence was followed by a good performance and the band – the Dave Ellis Trio – were apparently so knocked out by my performance they told Mr Charvin they wanted me.

As it was a quiet period for the Delaney band I was able to work at the Whisky pretty much every night. It was a great gig because Dave Ellis, the piano player, and the other guys were fun to work with. He and his girlfriend, and Ronnie Pearson, the drummer, would come over to Mum and Dad's on Sunday, and some evenings after work, and we would learn about fifteen new songs a week which, thinking back, was quite an achievement.

Sometimes they came after the show at two or three

in the morning and I would cook them steak and things under the grill. My speciality, a bastardised version of Steak Diane, always went down a treat with them. If we didn't do that we would go to a club called The Athenaeum in Moss Side, which, like it is now, was a really rough area. We would often play there until five or six in the morning and still have enough energy to go back to my place afterwards. I would end up rolling into bed just before my dad got up for work. I suppose you can do that when you're eighteen.

By working at the Whisky I got to know Michael Parkinson. He was a newsreader on Granada TV then and would sometimes come to the club after work. He did me a big favour because after hearing me sing he arranged for me to sing on Granada one night. I think I gave a pretty decent performance of Ella's 'Love For Sale' but my lasting memory of the occasion was wearing a very low-cut dress with loads of padding inside my bra – well, that was the look then and I wasn't strong in that department and needed a bit of artificial help to get anywhere near it.

Between working at the Whisky and doing stints with the Delaney band I was pretty busy. Then, all of a sudden, Eric asked me if I would go back to Naples for a residency at the airbase. Well, even though I was having such a great time at the Whisky, I wasn't going to turn down a paid holiday in Italy with my boyfriend, whom I had missed so much. It couldn't have been better, because when I told Dave Ellis about the offer, he got Mr Charvin to keep my job open until I got back.

Naples was fabulous. I was desperately in love and my month there all too quickly disappeared. Fortunately, I was only home for a few weeks before we were heading back again for a two-month stay. Not long after returning to England from the second trip, I got the bad news that my boyfriend had to go back to America. Our love was consigned to letters, which meant the inevitable happened – we drifted apart and eventually lost contact.

Just before Christmas 1963, I was getting ready for a night at the club one evening when my mum came into my room clutching the newspaper.

She said, 'You'll not be working tonight,' and she showed me the paper. The Whisky A Go-Go had burnt down.

Having left the Eric Delaney band to work at the Whisky full-time, where I was having the time of my life singing almost every night with a great group of guys, I suddenly found myself out of a job. But, as the saying goes, when one door closes another one opens, and before long I was in London mixing with some of the biggest pop names of the 1960s.

CHAPTER 8

BRIGHT LIGHTS

The opportunity to go to London came from Billy Charvin. He owned another Whisky A Go-Go club in Soho's Wardour Street. He told the Dave Ellis Trio and me that he would try to get us work in London if we went and stayed for a week. Without a job and now more determined than ever to make it as a singer it was an easy decision for me, especially as I'd already spent some time in the city in my Don Arden days.

Finding accommodation at short notice wasn't a problem either. Jimmy Savile, who we'd got to know from working in Manchester, fixed us up. Jimmy, probably the flashiest DJ around at the time, was based at the Top Rank dance hall and was big news but his recommendation of digs left a lot to be desired. When he was working in London Jimmy said he stayed at a really nice hotel in Paddington and insisted we should stay there too. What he failed to tell us though was that he had the best room in the place, a penthouse-type affair on the top floor with a shag pile carpet and an en suite bathroom, and the rest of the place was vile. The rooms were horrible, cold, cramped, dark, dirty and smelly with one toilet between us all down the hall. It was the stuff of nightmares.

Our week in London proved to be very similar to our accommodation – awful. The London Whisky was nothing like the Manchester one. The London venue was a disco club, and probably one of the first in the country to boot, which meant that we couldn't just walk into jobs there.

Nothing worked out, and Dave Ellis and the other guys quickly got disheartened and decided that London wasn't for them after all. I felt pretty much the same except that I was introduced to a wonderful place right underneath it called The Flamingo Club.

I fell in love with The Flamingo and it quickly became my reason for returning to London time and time again. It reminded me of performing at the American bases that were alive with rhythm and blues. On average, I would spend a couple of days there every other week and I kept that up for about three months. I never actually worked at The Flamingo but I got to jam with some of the best bands who did, including John Mayall and the Bluesbreakers, Georgie Fame and the Blue Flames, and Chris Farlowe and the Thunderbirds.

Georgie's band was my favourite. He wasn't what you'd call a schooled musician but he had great feel and I have to say I'd never heard a white man play like that before. His music was a fantastic fusion of R&B and jazz; it was incredible. My love of Georgie's music and our jamming sessions soon blossomed. To be honest, I think I fell in love with his playing more than him as he certainly wasn't the best-looking bloke around, especially as his teeth kind of crossed over each other, which I remember thinking was cute. When he was working in Manchester, I took him home to meet my parents.

Mum, of course, wasn't too impressed with my choice and said, 'What the bloody hell do you see in him? He's got horrible teeth. He needs them straightening out. You should tell him to get them done.'

She also described him as a 'bloody drink of water', which is a Northern expression meaning she thought he was a bit of a wimp. That didn't bother me because I was just so into the man. I really shouldn't have been because he was living with a half English, half Spanish woman called Carmen. To be blunt, I think I was just a little something on the side for him. He and Carmen were a team and over the course of the six months Georgie and I saw each other I was never able to persuade him to give her up.

I don't think my feelings towards him were ever really reciprocated. For instance, I once arranged to go over to his flat in North London and cook him a meal, but things didn't turn out quite as I had expected. I asked him what food he liked and then went out to buy some beautiful T-bone steaks and loads of scampi before heading over to his place. When I got there, however, I was left banging on the door of his empty flat. He'd gone away without telling me. I was so furious I left the food outside his door. He phoned me a couple of days later and said he'd had to go and do some gigs. He also mentioned he'd found rotting food on his doorstep.

I thought, 'Serves you bloody right.'

Georgie introduced me to drugs, albeit only weed. I tried it, like you do, but I couldn't see what all the fuss was about: it just didn't do anything for me. While I didn't really smoke much weed then, I made up for it later, but it still didn't do much for me. It made me giggly and silly which might explain why I was attracted to harder stuff.

After being stood up and realising that Georgie was never going to take me seriously, we parted. To make sure I didn't see him, I went to The Scene Club, which was where The Animals played. Going there regularly I got to know the band, well mostly the keyboard player Alan Price actually.

From the Newcastle area, Alan was a man who had an awful lot to say for himself. You could talk to him about anything because he was one of those Geordies who had an opinion on everything. Saying that, I thought he was a very intelligent bloke and I found him interesting. I also admired his musicianship because he was one of those natural, self-taught musicians – like Georgie – who didn't need the 'dots', he could play by ear.

I quite liked him and it wasn't long before he seemed to be all over me like a rash, but like my relationship with Georgie, as fast as I fell for him, he seemed to lose interest in me. Looking back on it now, I think Alan only went out with me because I knew Georgie and he really wanted to meet him. It wasn't long after I'd introduced them that Alan seemed to cool things off with me. My instincts were right because he and Georgie formed quite a successful partnership and made two albums together.

While my relationship with Georgie didn't go anywhere, it did however lead to meeting a record producer called Ian Samwell. Ian, or Sammy as he was known, was a guitarist whose claim to fame was writing 'Move It' for Cliff Richard. After hearing me sing a few times he said he'd like to manage me and that he would get me a record.

He had a collection of up-to-date R&B stuff and he told me there was a great song called 'Something's Got A Hold On Me' by a lady called Etta James that he thought would suit me. He then managed to persuade Rick Gunnell, who owned The Flamingo, to pay for me to record it at IBC Studies in Great Portland Place, opposite the BBC, and together they sold it to Decca Records.

The arrangement for the record was done by a man called Earl Guest – I think his real name was Reg but that wasn't very 'showbiz' – and one of the session guitarists was none other than Jimmy Page, of future Led Zeppelin fame; I doubt he even remembers doing it now. My B-side was Barbara Lewis's big hit, 'Hello Stranger'.

There I was, all of a sudden, making my first record. It was amazing and I couldn't quite believe it. One minute I'd been having the time of my life jamming with all these great musicians but not really earning any money or furthering my career, and the next, I was cutting a record and thinking I've got the break I'd always wanted, and that I was finally going to be a star. Not bad for the quiet Jewish girl from Prestwich.

Well that wasn't quite how it turned out, but it was definitely the start of something. There was some TV promotion on *Ready, Steady, Go!* and *Thank Your Lucky Stars* and the record was pretty well received by the media, but it didn't chart. It didn't help that Lulu recorded 'Shout' at the same studios a few days before me, and Decca promoted it heavily. That wasn't a surprise because Lulu is what I call an entertainer, very showbiz with a very marketable act, and I wasn't. But it wasn't just Lulu I was up against, there was Dusty Springfield and Cilla Black. I felt I didn't quite fit in.

I still desperately wanted to be a successful recording artist but I had to earn a living so when Ian came up with the idea of going to America as support for The Animals I jumped at the chance. It was when 'House Of The Rising Sun' was top of the American charts and The Animals had been booked for two weeks at the Paramount Theatre in New York. I think Don Arden may have been in the picture, but I didn't ever see him. He might have promoted it, I don't know. The only problem was that Ian said if I wanted to go I would have to pay both my airfare and his because he couldn't afford it. As always, my parents came to the rescue. They didn't want me to go on my own so they didn't mind paying for Ian as well.

In the summer of 1964, I embarked on my first trip to America. When we arrived at Kennedy Airport I found myself in a tricky but funny situation because the people there didn't realise I was part of the show, instead they thought I was the press officer which meant they all kept coming up to me and asking all these questions about The Animals.

All I could do was say, 'I don't know. I'm part of the show.'

That wasn't the only tricky thing about the trip. Not only were Alan and I not speaking after the end of our little relationship, but almost as soon as we got off the plane my manager and chaperone, Ian, disappeared leaving me alone in very, very hot New York. I didn't see him again for the whole two weeks I was there. I did, however, have the last laugh. During my stay I bought a record player so I could play all my American singles. English turntables were different from American ones. So as a payback for being abandoned, I made Ian carry it all through the airport. It was heavy and awkward to carry and it amused me watching him struggle with it.

I hated America, well at first anyway. We stayed at the Manhattan Hotel, which was good, but of course, I had to pay all my own bills, which wasn't so good, especially as I wasn't being paid very much for my appearance on the show. Musically, the experience wasn't that great either because I wasn't happy with what I was doing. But as if to make up for the shortcomings the line-up for the show was impressive. Chuck Berry was top of the bill with The Animals and a female group called The Dixie Cups and the R&B singer Dee Dee Sharp.

There were also three American girls who I had to share a dressing room with called The Rag Dolls. I didn't think much of them vocally or personally; they were bitchy, vain and, despite what they thought, they couldn't sing if their lives depended on it. They gave me a hard time in the dressing room about my hair because they were convinced I was wearing a wig, which of course, I was, because my hair was still recovering from being bleached in Germany. I wasn't very good at backcombing and styling it so it was a lot easier to wear a wig, but I sure as hell wasn't going to give them the pleasure of knowing that. They wouldn't leave it alone and kept on and on at me saying they were sure I was wearing a wig. My way of dealing with it was to try to get out of the dressing room as fast as I could. That experience left an indelible mark and I still have a problem to this day with people who are vain and have an awful lot to say about themselves, especially if they aren't as talented as they think they are.

As I got older and a little more experienced in life I became far more direct with people who got on my nerves. In fact, one of my managers, Alan Seifert, summed it up quite well saying, 'You do sometimes lack a little charm, Elkie.'

To which I, of course, responded, 'Thank you.'

The gigs at the Paramount were incredibly long; they used to start at 9 a.m. and go on all day. What I found strange was never having the chance to get to meet any of the other performers. I think it was just how they were then, so despite being on the same bill as Chuck Berry, I wasn't introduced to him. I eventually got to meet him years later when I was at Newcastle City Hall with Vinegar Joe. Knowing what it feels like to be isolated, I've always made a point of saying hello to people on the same bill as me.

One person I loved meeting in New York was Horace Shytel Glover. Horace was a wonderful, big black guy who was a dress designer. I met him through The Dixie Cups because he made all their dresses. Horace and I hit it off straightaway, which was great because being left on my own I needed a friend.

One day he said to me, 'Come on, I'm going to take you to the Apollo.'

I was so excited because the Apollo to me was this legendary place where Billie Holiday and Ella Fitzgerald had played. I think Ella actually did her first audition there. Top of the bill was Mary Wells, who personified the Motown sound of the early 1960s, and American soul singer Joe Hinton. It was an amazing gig, but I struggled to take it in because I was so overcome by being at the Apollo. It was a very, very emotional thing for me but Horace couldn't understand why it was such a big deal.

A day or two later he took me to his mum and dad's place in Harlem. Wow, what a culture shock that was. I couldn't believe it, there were three or four people living in a tiny one-room flat. It was strange though because while the room was minute, the refrigerator and television were absolutely enormous. But for a sheltered white, middle-class English girl obsessed by black music, Harlem was a thrilling experience. I stayed in contact with Horace after my New York adventure and he became a close friend to me and went on to make lots of stage outfits for me. It was funny though because when the outfits arrived from America they would always be a bit too big because he'd made them without ever fitting me, so I would then have to have them altered.

After the gig at the Paramount I flew back to Britain and was offered a two-week autumn tour around England supporting The Animals, which meant the challenge of being around Alan again, who still wasn't speaking to me. The other support acts for the tour included American blues singer Tommy Tucker, who had a big hit with 'Hi-Heel Sneakers', and rockabilly musician Carl Perkins. Tommy and his wife were lovely, and Carl was an excellent, funny bloke, who was also a great guitar player.

Carl came to see me at a show many years later and when we met he said, 'You don't remember me, do you?'

I took one look at him and said, 'Yes, of course, I do, Carl.'

When you are stuck on a tour bus for a couple of weeks you need some good friends, especially when your ex is ignoring you. Fortunately for me, the Nashville Teens were on board; they were great to be around and I always enjoyed their company. Scottish singer Barry St John befriended me. We got on famously and stayed in touch for a long time. She even sang backing vocals for me on a short tour I did and introduced me to Aretha Franklin's music, which I've loved ever since.

After The Animals' tour finished I started performing in cabaret shows – a tough type of gig, if there ever was one. Having been around a crowd of good musicians for long periods, on the cabaret circuit I felt alone and would often turn to a glass or two of brandy to get myself through.

I wasn't what I'd call a heavy drinker, I would mostly drink socially, but when you're on your own you start looking into yourself and thinking about everything that's going on. I would get pretty upset wondering why I hadn't been more successful. I knew that part of the problem was me and the fact I wasn't a very showbiz-type person and anyone who knows me will tell you that I'm still not that way inclined. Also, my stint with the Delaney band made me realise that I was only truly happy when I was singing the stuff I wanted to sing. It's still the same today, it has to be right musically, or I'm not happy.

Up until then, I'd sung what had been put in front of me, as you do at the start of your career, but I knew deep down that pretty much anybody could have done them and there wasn't much of me in them. 'Something's Got A Hold On Me' was on the right track but the songs I recorded with Decca – although I was never signed to them – weren't, they were just too pop for me. I sang 'Nothing Left To Do But Cry' and 'The Way You Do The Things You Do', the Temptations' hit in America in the same year. My B-side to that was a song I wrote with Alan Price called 'Strange Though It Seems' which was a fabulous, bluesy piece. In fact, thinking about it, that was the best thing to come from our relationship.

Things started to change for the better when Jean Lincoln became more involved in my career. Jean was an agent who record producer Ian Samwell used and she was the person who presented me with the biggest gig of my career to that point, supporting The Beatles on their 1964 Christmas Show at the Hammersmith Odeon. I'd met and appeared with The Beatles a couple of years earlier on *The Talent Spot* radio programme at the BBC's Paris Theatre when they were just starting to get big.

I thought they were wonderful and very talented but I was never in awe of them: to me, they were just a load of

Liverpool lads who played in the same clubs as my brother Tony. Tony had started to do very well for himself as the drummer with Billy J. Kramer and The Dakotas and who, for some reason, also decided to call himself Mansfield as I had done briefly after being discovered by Don Arden.

Poster for The Beatles *at the Hammersmith Apollo*

The show was two very full-on weeks at the Odeon with just two days off for Christmas Day and Boxing Day. I had a very nice dressing room with a big TV, which was just as well because I only turned it off to go on stage as no one ever came to see me. The Beatles, of course, being at the height of their fame, had a constant stream of people going in and out of their dressing rooms. I was in my dressing room alone and nobody gave me a second glance. I think they thought I was a bit stuck up, but I was actually just painfully shy and didn't want to go anywhere where I felt I might be imposing. Saying that, I was never invited to join them anyway. All this meant that my average day consisted of drinking half a dozen Guinnesses and watching loads of telly before going on stage to perform. And when you went on stage all you'd get was the girls screaming incessantly. It wasn't only me who suffered, it happened to everybody else on the show too including The Yardbirds who, of course, featured none other than Eric Clapton. They only had eyes and ears for The Beatles. What was sad though was not getting to know Eric Clapton. Having read his book, he sounded great and I think we would have had a lot in common musically.

While I was always in control and managed to sing very well on stage, my drinking no doubt played a part in a very embarrassing rehearsal episode with The Beatles. The Christmas show was a big panto-type affair with Jimmy Savile compering so we had to do several silly things as extra entertainment for the crowd, one of which involved me jumping over a long skipping rope. In rehearsal Paul and someone else, I forget who, were holding the rope that I tried to skip over it, but me being me, I fell over horribly on my arse in front of everyone, much to their amusement. I was so embarrassed I just wanted the ground to swallow me up.

A lovely letter from Bob Dawbarn

Between being bored stiff and drinking far too much Guinness every night, I was relieved when the show came to an end. Afterwards, a lovely thing happened, I received a letter from *Melody Maker* journalist Bob Dawbarn, which I still treasure to this day. He said if talent was the criterion for The Beatles Christmas Show I should have been getting the biggest applause. Fantastic praise I know, but I'm not sure all those screaming girls would have agreed with him.

CHAPTER 9

CABARET

While I hadn't really enjoyed doing The Beatles Christmas Show I knew it was the kind of exposure I needed and I realised that it was Jean Lincoln who had organised it, not my manager Ian Samwell.

Having been abandoned by Ian in America on The Animals tour, I started to see the way ahead more clearly, so when Jean suggested to me early in 1965 that she sat in the manager's seat, I didn't hesitate. Shortly afterwards, I told Ian that we'd gone as far as we could together. Ian didn't seem that bothered by my decision, which was fine by me. I'd first met Jean through Ian just after the autumn tour with The Animals. She was Kenny Lynch's manager and, I think, secretary to Maurice King when he had an entertainment agency. Ian was using her as an agent to get me gigs and it was obvious from the beginning that she was the one who had the connections.

Very quickly she managed to get me a recording contract with EMI and I did a few singles for them that, quite honestly, anybody could have done. 'He's Gotta Love Me', 'All Of My Life' and 'Baby Let Me Love You' were pop songs that were just not me. Making records was, unfortunately, only a very small part of my regular life. Little cabaret gigs, which Jean got me up North, were my bread and butter. I had to do the clubs because nothing was happening for me on the recording side of the business. I hated doing them. They were horrible – the pits of the world with hideous names like 'Fiesta'. I was made to sing material like 'On A

Wonderful Day Like Today' and 'On The Street Where You Live', show tunes, which I loathed. My bad memories of touring the clubs probably contribute to why I hate musicals so much and why I have always refused to sing in them unless an enormous amount of money was offered, which of course, it never was.

I used to take myself to these gigs in my first car, a little Mini which Mum and Dad bought me for my twenty-first birthday. I absolutely adored it. I think I appreciated it even more because it had taken me so long to pass my test. Hilary and all my school friends seemed to pass their tests easily, I on the other hand, had to work hard for my treasured licence. And, if it hadn't been for my cousin Michael, I don't think I would ever have passed. He was the only person that would take me out to practise: I think everybody else was too scared to get in the car with me. I can't say I blame them. Even today, I have to put my hand on my heart and say I'm still not the greatest driver.

Jean would sometimes come along to my cabaret gigs for the first couple of days, but most of the time I would be on my own. My parents and my brother came to a couple of shows and I remember once, before I'd passed my test, them bringing me back in the car and I was bursting to go to the toilet.

I said to them, 'Just stop here, I'll go behind the hedge.'

They were stunned at my request. It didn't bother me, I had to go, but I guess they were wondering what had happened to their lovely little Jewish daughter. Luckily, they didn't know the half of it; I always played my cards pretty close to my chest.

Generally though, I would drive myself to the club with my frocks and my dots and get there in time for the band call at four or five o'clock – bands that were largely second-rate and couldn't read my music – then I'd to go and find my digs and head back for the show in the evening. I'll never forget spending my twentieth birthday alone on the Isle of Man in digs so squalid and damp that there was water running down the walls. It was a horrible birthday.

Suffice to say that working the cabaret circuit quickly became the unhappiest period of my career and, to get through it, I did what a lot of people do; I started knocking back the booze. I didn't think anything of drinking during the day. I would walk into a pub and have quite a few pints of Guinness then go off and find myself something to eat, have another few jars, and eventually make my way to the club for the show.

The experience made me question all over again whether I was in the right business. I started to think that maybe I should be doing something else like teaching cooking or PE. It was a really upsetting time for me and I became more and more disenchanted and very, very low. I was on my own, singing songs I didn't want to sing, with bands that couldn't play the music. Drink became my best friend. I think it helped to make the bands seem better – it's a bit like when you go out and see someone who's not very attractive and then you have half a dozen pints and all of a sudden they start to look fantastic. Well that was my philosophy with these bands, although in truth, I don't think I could ever have drunk enough to make them seem good.

It wasn't long before I progressed from drinking pints of Guinness to downing lots of cheap brandy because it didn't make me feel so bloated. Fortunately, I never got into smoking – I smoked a little bit but I wouldn't call myself a real smoker, probably due to my enduring respiratory problem. Drink was my vice and it very nearly got me into big trouble one night after a show in Rotherham. The band that night had been worse than normal – loud enough to make anybody cry – and I drove back to Manchester having had at least a half-bottle of brandy. As luck would have it, I got stopped by the police for speeding. I was as charming as I could be and incredibly, they let me off without even giving me a speeding ticket. This was just before the introduction of the breathalyser test, in which case, it would have been a different story. I was so upset afterwards I headed for my favourite curry house on the outskirts of Manchester, which I knew stayed open late. I sat down as quickly as I could and told them to take their time preparing the curry so I could have a drink. I ended up having about three or four pints of lager before the curry. I don't know how I did it but I do remember getting in the car and feeling even more upset and crying all the way home. How I managed to drive home – pissed and crying – I'll never know. How stupid can you get? I had just escaped getting done for drink driving and then went and topped up with more booze because I was upset. Utter madness.

All I can say is that I went out there to live and I did, but it's no good doing it through a bottle, and that's what I was doing then. Luckily, I learned from the experience and eventually moved on. Perhaps these things help to make you into the person you become. Things are very different now and I can safely say that I've not had a drink before going on stage for more than thirty years.

Life started to change for the better when Jean got me a gig on an RAF base in Germany: a job that was to prove to be the beginning of a lifelong friendship with an incredible musician. It all began at London's King's Cross railway station. We were taking the train to a military base near Basingstoke so we could fly out on an RAF plane to Germany. At the station, I met the other performers who'd been hired for the stint. The first people I met were Peter Goodright the comedian and the amazing Les Dawson, who I liked the moment I met him. He was an incredibly talented man who could just talk about anything and make you laugh: a truly wonderful person.

On the train I met Humphrey Lyttelton and was

completely captivated by him and, as it turned out, he with me. I knew of Humph because he'd had a big hit with 'Bad Penny Blues' in 1953 and I'd been taken to see him do his *Here's Humph* TV show at Granada Studios in Manchester when I was twelve. It was a very good show with Maxine Daniels – Kenny Lynch's sister – and singer Lita Roza of 'How Much Is That Doggie In The Window?' fame. I liked Humph straightaway and felt as if I'd known him all my life. The way he talked to me and listened to what I had to say was so refreshing; there was no side to him whatsoever, he was upfront and honest.

'Here's Humph' invitation

When we got to Germany, he said to his manager Susan da Costa, 'You will like Elkie. She's great.'

Susan, of course, couldn't understand what he meant and said to him, 'She's so odd. She doesn't say anything. She just sits and looks out of the corner of her eye at everybody. I don't think I've ever seen anyone quite so wary.'

What Susan didn't realise was that I was as pissed as a parrot at the time so I was keeping fairly quiet in an attempt to hide the fact. Coupled with being a bit of an introvert in situations where I didn't know people well, I probably didn't make the greatest first impression.

Humph endeared himself to me even further at rehearsal for our first show. Because I was shy and didn't go out making a big entrance, Bobby Jay, who was a BBC producer, was being very patronising in the way he directed me. He made a big deal out of showing me how to present myself and how to bow to the audience.

Humph pulled him up, 'You shouldn't do that.'

Humph knew I was very upset with what Bobby had said and asked Susan to get me an enormous schnapps, which I'd never had before – and I loved it. I had the drink and went on and did a Billie Holiday blues song, and was absolutely fine. In fact, Humph came up to me afterwards and said he thought I did a great show, and that I was amazing. But then disaster struck because as I got up to give him a hug I managed to knock a pint of beer all over him. If that wasn't bad enough he didn't have a change of clothes so he had to travel home soaking wet and reeking of beer. There was one more mishap, however, that brought a smile to my face. Bobby, who liked a drink even more than me, got his comeuppance when he walked straight into a lamppost and knocked himself out cold.

After our engagement in Germany Humph invited me to sing with him any time I wanted to at The Six Bells in Chelsea and at The Bull's Head in Barnes – a place he ended up playing at for more than thirty years. That's how my long and special relationship with Humph started. I went there a few times and that soon turned into every other weekend, and before long I was at one or other of the pubs all the time.

This led to Humph saying to me in late 1965, 'You might as well come on the road with us.'

We did all sorts of shows, some in theatres and some playing for dances. But one thing quickly became apparent – I loved it. It took me back to my days singing with the Eric Delaney band, but was much better because I was enjoying the music more. I earned about £20 per gig with Humph, but I wasn't bothered whether that was good or bad because I was happy. Humph always made sure that I was okay and he spoke to me as an equal. That was the fantastic thing about Humph: he never talked down to anyone.

I think Humph admired my talent – he said some wonderful things about me in his book 'It Just Occurred To Me… The Reminiscences and Thoughts of Chairman Humph' – and I definitely admired him, which is why we got on. He was very good to me in those years and it was down to him that I regained my confidence and started to get myself back together again. I don't know what would have happened if I hadn't met him; probably death by drink. Humph was the best and he made me feel that I was the best.

By 1966 life was great and that year turned out to be quite significant in more ways than one. Ever since Jean Lincoln had started as my manager she'd been going on at me about having my nose done to remove the Jewish bump. I eventually gave in and shortly after my twenty-first birthday I had surgery, costing a couple of hundred pounds at a Harley Street clinic, to straighten and shorten it. At first, I was very pleased, especially as I'd spent years dressing around it with long fringes and wearing my hair partially over my face, but as the years have gone by I've come to regret the decision. Looking back, I now believe that Jean's nagging was more to do with her paranoia and obsession about looking beautiful. She was gorgeous and for her, success depended in part on appearance. The funny thing is that while my old Yiddisher nose was banished forever it resurfaced on my younger son Joey who is a stunning-looking young man.

My nose wasn't the only thing to be operated on that year. I had to undergo a throat operation to remove nodules on my vocal cords that had developed due to misuse. I ended up having two procedures. The first was an operation to remove a nodule on the outside of the vocal cords but afterwards it still wasn't right so I had another procedure which involved freezing the one on the inside rather than having it surgically removed.

The surgeon told me not to speak for six weeks so my parents paid for me to go to Portugal with Humph's manager Susan to recuperate. Susan is half Portuguese and had asked me to join her on the trip to visit her relatives. We had a fantastic time together, especially as I hadn't seen the sun since I was in Naples with the Eric Delaney band. The trip was funny because the locals presumed I was Portuguese because of my olive skin but because I couldn't speak, they thought I was deaf and dumb. Susan and I had quite a laugh playing on that.

I went back to see the surgeon after six weeks and he was pleased with the results. I started to talk a couple of weeks later but the amazing thing was that when I eventually was fit enough to sing I'd gained two tones in my register. Previously, I could manage top A at best but after the operation I was able to reach top C. The highest I can hit now, on a good day, is D and I comfortably sang a top C sharp on my 2010 album *Powerless*. I believe a lot of the vocal problems I suffered in the past were due to the smoke in cabaret clubs and not being able to relax when I was singing, probably because I was singing material that I didn't like or that didn't suit me.

Jean Lincoln was responsible for the next chapter in my life in late 1967. I'd been singing on and off with Humph and his band for a while but it wasn't regular; it was more a case of Humph ringing and saying where he was and asking if I was interested. Sadly, in order to pay the bills, cabaret shows were still a constant part of my musical life.

Aware of my intense dislike of the cabaret circuit and realising that I wasn't cutting it as a recording artist, it dawned on Jean that I needed a backing band for my shows. I liked the backing band idea but there was never enough money for me to pay three or four musicians. Despite this, Jean thought we should take a chance and we started to put out the feelers to find the right people. It was my old Delaney band friend Herbie Goins who provided the introduction I was looking for when he got in touch on a visit to England from his new home in Spain.

Herbie insisted that I meet Pete Gage. He had just left The Ram Jam Band and was looking to put a band together. The Ram Jam Band was an R&B type of group with singer Geno Washington, an American serviceman, as their front man. Pete had met Geno at a gig at one of the military bases when they were in need of a new singer and soon enough they'd become Geno Washington and The Ram Jam Band. They were very popular on the club circuit and had two successful live albums in the charts.

The story of how Pete and I met is quite amusing because we had a bizarre exchange on the doorstep of my flat after he had rung the bell.

When I opened the door he said, 'Where's Elkie?'

I naturally replied saying, 'I'm Elkie.'

With an element of surprise in his voice he said, 'Oh, fine.'

After that odd introduction we chatted for a while and I have to say that I instantly found him very good company. That night Pete, his friend Jean and I went out to a club. I remember thinking how refreshing it was to meet someone that knew how to organise things and who had his feet firmly on the ground. Some time later, Pete recalled our introduction explaining that he'd thought I was the maid and a pretty good-looking one. I found it amusing and it endeared him to me. I suppose it also helped that he found me attractive.

Not long after our first meeting Pete said, 'If you're thinking of getting this band together I'd better come to see you at one of your cabaret shows.'

After the show, he said he liked me and thought I was a reasonable singer, but he didn't feel it was going to work with him getting a band together to do cabaret gigs. Later he admitted that he didn't think I was very good at all, but he changed his mind completely after he saw me perform at a jazz gig with Humph. I think he realised that cabaret didn't bring out the best in me; it made me seem average. Yet despite being convinced of my talent, he still didn't think the time was right to get a band together because of financial reasons. Nevertheless, something had started to happen between us and we were spending more and more time together.

Pete wasn't what you would call good-looking. He was quite short with blond hair and blue eyes but he was a very clever bloke; he passed his 11-plus when he was nine and I think he must have had a very high IQ. After leaving school he formed a rock and roll band called The Zephyrs and it was this group that went on to become Geno Washington and The Ram Jam Band.

Our relationship was difficult because Pete was dealing with the death of his wife Pauline in a car crash three months before we met. The accident happened when Pauline fell asleep at the wheel as the two of them were on the way back from a Ram Jam gig in Manchester. They had only been married six months so it was incredibly tragic. She and Pete had lived together in a flat in Catford, but after she died he couldn't bear to be there anymore.

When we decided to set up together he arranged for us to do a house swap with his mum. She moved into the flat and we took over the bottom floor of her house at 116 Springbank Road in Lewisham. Pete's sister Pam and husband Ian and their baby daughter Tamla had the upstairs flat. The place was in a right state when we moved in. His mum was crazy about cats and she'd not done a very good job of cleaning up after them. To be honest, I don't think she'd even tried.

While we were unbelievably happy creating our first home together, Jean on the other hand was furious when she heard I'd given up the Chelsea flat she'd found for me to go and live south of the river!

CHAPTER 10

DADA

It wasn't just where I lived that Jean had an opinion about, she was also pretty adamant that I shouldn't have been seeing Pete at all. This came to light quite dramatically one night when Pete, Jean and I went out together to a dreadful cabaret gig. After the show, Jean took it on herself to phone my parents to say that she didn't think it was good for me to be going out with Pete. Funnily enough, Dad didn't react the way I thought he might. I think he was relieved at the prospect of not having to keep giving me money. Finally, he thought I had met somebody who was capable of looking after me. Good old Dad, ever typical – thinking of the money first.

This incident caused my relationship with Jean Lincoln to break down. After that we never spoke again. Sadly, the next time I heard of Jean was in 1969 when I took a call from a journalist who told me she had been found dead in her fiancé's apartment in New York. She could only have been in her early thirties as she was about ten years older than me. She had been living in New York with Rik Gunnell, owner of The Flamingo Club in Soho and manager of Georgie Fame and Geno Washington. She had been crazy about him. Chris Farlowe told me some time later that he had found her on the floor in Rik's apartment. She'd been drinking a cocktail of Black Russians mixed with sleeping pills.

Her funeral was a very odd occasion. Pete and I went but we decided to keep a low profile. Singer-songwriter Kenny Lynch, who I knew from The Flamingo, was there as he'd known Jean very well; she had been his manager but we didn't get the chance to speak. I saw him a few years later at a Jimmy Tarbuck charity show and we had a chat about Jean's death as it had affected us both quite badly. She was such a beautiful woman: it was tragic that she died so young.

After all my horrible experiences of the cabaret circuit and anxious about what next to do with my singing career, living with Pete in our own home in Lewisham was fantastic. I was enjoying life. The worries and responsibilities of going out on the road and being self-sufficient had disappeared. Pete was taking care of me. I was keeping house. I was happy.

We were also putting our mark on our new home, quite literally, as we'd decided to decorate. Pete went to town, painting the walls in these amazing, psychedelic colours. One wall was pink, graduating in intensity to bright red. At the time, I thought it was great, but I don't think it would work for me anymore. I've always encouraged people to enjoy themselves when painting because it's not something I ever do. Pete responded well to my encouragement. By the time he'd finished we had an astonishing selection of brightly coloured walls, their modernity somewhat offset against the old-fashioned furniture from my flat which Mum, bless her, had bought for me many years earlier. It might have looked a bit out of date but it was good quality because Mum would have only bought the best.

The house consisted of two front rooms – one of which was our bedroom – and behind that was the kitchen; the tiniest kitchen you've ever seen but it sufficed and I can remember cooking some very interesting meals there. While I was keen on cooking, I'm not sure what my family would make of my cooking if I served them up one of my Springbank Road meals today. Our lounge was one of the back rooms and in it we had a nice little black-and-white TV, a table and chairs and my old sofa that turned into a bed.

When my mum and my brother Ray came to visit for the first time I think they had quite a fright. It was, without doubt, a change from my plush Chelsea flat, but the important thing was that Pete and I liked it. In fact, we thought we had the funkiest little place going. I have some really fond memories of living in Lewisham. I remember walking round the department store admiring the beautiful china, just like the stuff my mum used to have, and thinking one day I've got to get china like that. Eventually, I did, when we moved into our beautiful house in North Devon. I bought an entire Royal Doulton service from Banbury's in Barnstaple, which is very similar to the department store in Lewisham. The house had a garden, which was something of a novelty for me because I hadn't had one since I was a child living at Cavendish Road in Prestwich. It was only a tiny garden but I loved it because I could sit out whenever I wanted and enjoy the nice weather.

For Pete though, the house wasn't just home, it was also a base for his music, which was everything to him. He taught himself to play the guitar at a young age but struggled with music at Eltham College in South London and ended up leaving at sixteen, partly because the course was so classically focused. Actually, I think he was thrown out of music class for playing modern chords.

Music was his obsession and the front room of 116 Springbank Road became his little studio where he created lots of demos. He was constantly playing guitar and inviting fellow musicians over. It seemed like I was forever answering the door to musicians who would come round to jam. He also started doing some gigs with the R&B reggae band Jimmy James and The Vagabonds, which was signed to the same label as his old group, Geno Washington and The Ram Jam Band.

I, on the other hand, wasn't doing much singing at all. I would do the odd gig with Humph and occasionally Pete would get me to perform here and there at a club with a few of his friends backing me. Pete also spent quite a bit of time teaching me to play the piano. Being a guitarist, he taught me to play the piano as you would a guitar. So instead of learning just one way to play a chord, he showed me different inversions, or patterns, which made my playing more versatile, especially when accompanying myself.

Other than that, I was just keeping house and going through my hippy phase. But all that changed when almost by accident, I started singing with some of Pete's friends who had been coming round quite a bit. My rehearsal partners were: Tim Hinkley, a keyboardist; Ivan Zagni, a guitarist; Martyn Harryman on drums; and a bass player whose name I can't remember. At about the same time I also started playing the vibraphone, which I found enjoyable, although I didn't think I was much good at it. All this did me the world of good and I was soon right back into my singing, which didn't go unnoticed by Pete and I think he began to see me in a different light. All of a sudden, he saw real passion in my singing, something which he hadn't seen much of before. While we never did any gigs, I think we made a pretty good sound together, but this wasn't to last. Ivan was jealous of me and I think he had me thrown out of the group.

Our rehearsals proved to Pete that I really did want to sing with a group. It wasn't long before Tim, Ivan and the bass player were off the scene, and Pete, Martyn and I were rehearsing with a new group of musicians. There was Don Shin on organ and bass pedals and Paul Korda, Jimmy Chambers and me on vocals. We added Barry Dougan on alto sax, Malcolm Capewell on tenor, and Ernie Rauchan on trumpet and flugelhorn.

And this was how we came to form our first group, Dada, towards the end of 1969. We signed up with Atlantic Records who agreed to pay us a retainer to rehearse and make an album. This was a landmark moment for me. I loved being part of a band again. I had been happy singing with the Delaney Band and the Humphrey Lyttelton Band. Even though I'm best known as a solo artist, I've always worked better when part of a team. I think that's still true today because any solo artist has to have a good support team so they can be at the top of their game.

The best way of describing Dada is to say that we were a rock fusion band because we were a mix of classical music, jazz and R&B. Pete and Paul Korda wrote all the material, which was pretty good but we didn't ever make up our minds on what we were or what we stood for. This lack of clear direction would be a problem. Additionally, we discovered it was hard to keep a large band together and expensive; too expensive as it turned out for the record company.

Most of us got on pretty well, especially as the brass section was nearly always out of it on dope. My relationship with Paul Korda, however, can best be described as a clash of personalities. When he decided to leave the band shortly after we finished recording our one and only album, *Dada,* in 1970, I was far from heartbroken. They say things happen for a reason and I believe that was the case with Paul's departure because it was to prompt the beginning of something truly beautiful.

Ahmet Ertegün, one of the founders of Atlantic Records, knew he was shedding money on Dada at a rate of knots. The album cost them a fortune to make because they'd been paying to keep all of us together as well as buying all the equipment we needed. I guess the writing had been on the wall for Dada for a while. In the short time we were together, little had happened for us commercially and we were burning a hole in the record company's pocket. Ahmet heeded the advice of his good friend Chris Blackwell, the owner of Island Records, and broke down the band to make it more manageable.

We went to watch Robert Palmer sing at a club in Hanley in Stoke-on-Trent. At the time he was the lead singer of a band called The Alan Bown! Although his name was Robert Allen Palmer, his parents and friends in Scarborough used to call him Allen, so to avoid any confusion between him and Alan Bown he decided to use his proper first name, Robert, instead. I thought he had a nice singing voice but I wasn't that thrilled about it. Some people aren't the greatest singers but they have distinctive voices, and, in my opinion, Robert was in this category. I think it's quite rare to get someone with a distinctive sound who is also a great technical singer. Robert was definitely a good singer but he was also eye candy for the girls and they went crazy for him.

I think we were all agreed from the moment we saw Robert and heard him sing that he would be perfect for Dada. After a good meeting we left him with the tape of our album. But even though our meeting had been positive, we didn't hear anything from him for ages. Then one day, late in 1970, about six months after we first met, he phoned and said he'd like to join the band. His decision came at the perfect time because we had just been invited to go on tour in America to support a psychedelic rock band called Iron Butterfly.

I don't have too many memories of the tour other than it was a much more pleasurable experience singing alongside Robert than Paul Korda. The one memory that does come to mind relates to our tour manager, Brian Lane of Hemdale Management, who also managed Yes. Being an unknown British band in America was tough but things became increasingly difficult as the money started to run out. One night after we came off stage it all got too much for me and I decided to take out my frustration on Brian by throwing all our beer cans at him when he came into our dressing room. With so many drinkers in the band, my barrage went on for quite a while. It didn't improve our situation, but it did make me feel better at the time.

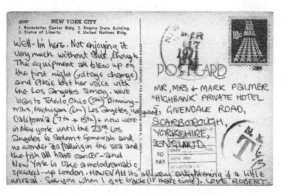

A postcard from Robert Palmer

On the tour Phil Carson, the managing director of Atlantic Records, asked us if we would like to fly out to the Cannes Film Festival in his private plane to do a corporate gig. Pete and I thought this would be great so we said yes, but we were soon regretting it because we'd taken 'private plane' to mean 'private jet'. There was nothing 'jet' about it. Phil's private plane was a tiny fragile-looking machine with little wings and a piddly propeller. We were so envious of the rest of the band who had flown out to France on a scheduled flight in what must have been sheer luxury compared to the all-round discomfort of Phil's little plane.

To make matters worse, when we eventually landed and made it to customs Phil caught a glimpse of my passport, which was still in my real name of Elaine Bookbinder, and he started laughing like a drain. This got right on my nerves, but I quickly realised how I could shut him up. I'd known Phil for a while because he'd been coming over to our house to make demos with Pete in the front room as he fancied himself as a bit of a singer so I'd got to know that his name wasn't Phil Carson at all, but Phil Pratt.

I said, 'Well it's better than having a name like Pratt, isn't it?'

Suffice to say that he very quickly stopped making fun of my name!

Back at home, money became even tighter and Pete,

being the type of guy he was, decided that we should sell our house so we could support the band. After a couple of years at Springbank Road, just before the formation of Dada, we'd moved up the property ladder and bought a three-bedroom house in Sidcup Road that I'd had my eye on for a few months. Sidcup Road was in a well-manicured, suburban part of Lewisham; I think it's fair to say that we were a right couple of hippies and didn't exactly fit in to the suburban English middle-class model! At the time we didn't have enough money to buy it, so my parents came to the rescue yet again, and gave us the money for the deposit. I think they lent us the money in the hope that if we had our own proper home together, Pete would pop the question. He did, and we got married on 3 February 1971.

Pete's mum knitted for me a copy of a 1940s wedding dress in emerald green and purple wool. I wore a pair of platform shoes made to match a pair that my mum had from the same period that were all the rage again in the 1970s. Mum wanted to buy me a smart coat to go over the dress but I chose a second-hand velvet jacket instead that looked more hippy to complete my outfit; not surprisingly Mum hated it. The ceremony was at the local registry office in Lewisham and afterwards we went to a bistro nearby for a small reception with Mum, Dad, my brother Ray, Humph's manager Susan, a guy called Big Wally who was a friend of Humph's band, Pete's mum, his sister Pam and her husband Ian, and the best man Stuart Morgan.

Pete and I had been together for four years and getting married seemed like the right thing to do. I also think that Pete felt obliged to make our situation legal after my parents had put up the money for the deposit. That also caused another issue for me because I discovered later that Dad had told everyone that he'd lent us the money for the deposit; I thought it had been a gift. Years later my husband Trevor and I paid him back with interest.

So while I was understandably a bit deflated about moving from a house to a little council flat at 51c Burlington Grove, Fulham, after only eighteen months, I wasn't exactly heartbroken either. But even the drastic measure of selling the house wasn't enough to save Dada from the inevitable. There have been quite a few bands since that have taken the rock fusion idea and succeeded with it, but it obviously wasn't meant to be for us. And so the brief Dada era came to an end, but rather than everything suddenly coming to an abrupt halt, Dada transformed into something new and, as it turned out, something far more exciting – a band called Vinegar Joe.

CHAPTER 11

VINEGAR JOE

I suppose it must have been late 1971 when Vinegar Joe officially came into being. While it seemed on the surface that Dada just became Vinegar Joe, I discovered some time later to my horror that my place in the band had by no means been a certainty. Chris Blackwell, the boss of Island Records who had been instrumental in introducing us to Robert Palmer, was almost as successful in getting rid of me. He saw the band as having one front singer with a rear section. Fortunately for me, Robert made sure I still had a role because he convinced Chris that I was a great singer and that I should share lead vocals with him. It's frightening, looking back, to think that I was so close to not being part of something that subsequently proved to be so important and influential for me.

With the arguments out of the way, the initial line-up of Vinegar Joe was very much the old members of Dada: Robert and me on vocals, Steve York, Pete and Robert on guitar. The only new members were Tim Hinkley, who I used to rehearse with in our house at Springbank Road, on keyboard, and drummer Conrad Isidore who recorded the first album only with us.

Chris Blackwell influenced the musical direction that Vinegar Joe took. Both he and Ahmet Ertegün of Atlantic Records thought we would be much more marketable if we were more clearly rock and roll and suggested that we put aside the bizarre mix of hippy, classical and jazz music of our airy-fairy Dada days. It was Chris too who came up with the name Vinegar Joe because, for some reason, he'd been reading up on General Joe Stilwell of the American forces who had been given the nickname Vinegar Joe because of his sour puss personality. Although he was known for being very caustic, General Stilwell was apparently also the sort of guy who would drink and eat with the men. I think he was what you'd call a man's man who liked to be a part of the real stuff that was going on.

Chris told us the story and said, 'Why don't we use that as your name.'

We had nothing better to offer, despite all the intelligent boys in the band, so we decided to go with it, after all if the record company boss thinks it's good, there might be more chance of them promoting you. Sadly, that wasn't to be the case, but we had a lot of fun along the way. There was a great feeling of unity in the band and with our new musical direction, Vinegar Joe very quickly built a big following on the live music scene, regularly packing out places like the Marquee club in London. We would be there every week and sometimes we'd get residencies, which was quite something in those days. I remember Humph and his manager Susan coming to see us there and saying afterwards that he thought we were a great band and how wonderful it was for me to have found something so good. That meant a lot to me.

But while residencies were fine, our bread and butter was playing the university circuit, as well as at other popular live music venues. We also did quite a few TV shows in Germany. The live gigs brought us some amazing publicity and some critical acclaim via great reviews. Our music was often described as 'an hour of get up and boogie'. We had a very lively, exciting and vibrant feeling, which is what the audience liked. This energy also had an effect on me and I started to get a reputation for, shall we say, my 'overexuberant' performances. I underwent a bit of a personality change during my time with Vinegar Joe. Gone was the nice but naive little Jewish girl from Prestwich who was terrified of Don Arden and sang what she was given; in her place was a raunchy rock 'n' roll artist who would abuse her audiences if they weren't getting into the music enough. Having endured the cabaret circuit, which I hated with a passion, and then getting hooked up with a group of people who thoroughly enjoyed their music, I couldn't accept an unresponsive audience. Looking back, I think it's probably because they were too stoned but I didn't see it that way at the time. One of the music papers once said, 'If Elkie Brooks is on stage and the audience aren't giving enough of a response she'll tell 'em to get off their f'ing arses and start boogying.'

I couldn't argue with it because that was my favourite saying in those days. With the benefit of hindsight, I think my antics were born out of sheer frustration because I truly believed the band was great and I loved being in it. I have to hold my hand up and admit I shouldn't have done that, but that's just the way I was then. Today, of course, I know how to conduct myself and I've been very well behaved on stage ever since those Vinegar Joe days.

I enjoyed working on my new image. Whenever I had the chance, I'd head for the second-hand shops and the antique market on the King's Road, near our flat in Fulham, to buy my stage outfits. I remember buying a bikini-type top which I liked so much I embroidered 'Elk' on the front in diamantés just to make sure that no one mistook me on stage. I think it's fair to say that in Vinegar Joe I found myself and became pretty damn uninhibited and outgoing.

My energetic performances also led to an incident, which involved a picture of me in the *Melody Maker* with my arms up in the air alongside an article describing me as the original 'understains lady'. It didn't bother me because I've always paid a lot of attention to my appearance and used anti-perspirant to avoid comments like that. Pete, on the other hand, was very upset, so much so that he ended up writing to the editor to complain. At the time, the editor was Ray Coleman, who turned out to be a huge fan of mine. In fact, ever since I got to know Ray through Pete's letter, he's been very helpful to me; he always ensured we got good coverage and he even wrote a nice piece for the programme of my second tour in 1980.

Live gigs were definitely what Vinegar Joe was all about and because we did so many, I don't think the record label ever went to town on promoting our albums. Our first album *Vinegar Joe* was what I call a 'shirt button' album because it cost nothing to make and the record company never put any money behind it. Even the album cover was done on the cheap, albeit very effectively because Robert got a friend to make plasticine figures of all of us sitting in a bowl of snack food. I was seated in the middle surrounded by the long-haired boys – Robert, Pete, Steve, Tim and Rob Tait – all very surreal.

In performance, Robert and I took it in turns to sing lead vocals. We hardly ever sang together; on Robert's songs I'd just do backing vocals and vice versa. It worked best for us that way. It was our style. My best tracks on the *Vinegar Joe* album were the ones Pete wrote, the blues songs like 'Early Monday Morning', 'Ride Me Easy Rider' and 'Live A Little, Get Somewhere' which I still play on the piano when I practise. I also love 'Avinu Malkeinu', which is a setting of the Hebrew prayer, 'Our Father, Our King'. It remains a great favourite and I recorded it again in 2002 with my son Jay on the *Shangri La* album. I also did 'Circles', which was Robert's song, on my 1995 album of the same name. *Circles* was quite a retrospective album; on it I re-recorded several Vinegar Joe tracks including Jimi Hendrix's 'Angel' which was on our second album, *Rock 'n' Roll Gypsies*.

Our third album *Six Star General* was named by Chris Blackwell to tie in with the General Stilwell theme. Of course, there's no such thing as a six star general, but it worked because there were six of us at the time. We were all pictured on the cover with a star behind our heads. I started writing when we were making *Six Star General*. I finished off a song called 'Lady Of The Rain' that Pete Gavin, the drummer, had started. It's not a great song but it got me going. Before that the only song I'd been involved in writing was 'Strange Though It Seems' which I did with Alan Price. When we were off our heads in the back of the van with me singing outrageous lyrics that I'd make up as I went along, Robert always used to say to me, 'You come up with these things, but why don't you bloody well write them down.'

Over the years, every time I thought of a lyric, I would remember what Robert said and get a pen and paper out. Now it's become a habit and I do it all the time. I've written lots of songs since then, but I've never thought of myself as a songwriter. Robert certainly convinced me to write my ideas down and to take myself a bit more seriously but generally I left the song writing to Pete, Robert and Steve as they had a flair for it.

Despite having some excellent songs, many of which I think still sound pretty good today, we weren't success-ful as recording artists, which is where the money's made. Consequently, we were just a working band making our money from gigging, which as you can imagine was hard work, but it was a lot of fun. The average earning for the band was about £100 a night, which was good but not when you split it six ways, after paying for a driver and someone to look after the gear. I think the most band members ever got paid was £28 each a week.

Talking of drivers, we had several along the way: there was Norman Dugdale – our road manager – and then, at the tail end of Vinegar Joe, our old drummer John Woods, who was such a beautiful bloke, ended up doing the job as the band didn't want him to play anymore. Sounds terrible,

I know, but he eventually went on to better things working as Robert Palmer's personal road manager when he went solo. We got through a few drummers over the three years; the ones I remember were Conrad Isidore, Rob Tait, John Woods and, finally, Pete Gavin. There was another guy who we kept for only a month. One night he nearly stopped the band because he dragged so much, he was so slow. Someone else who didn't last was bass player Mick Shaw who took over from Steve York after he had a car accident in America. I really liked Mick but no else did so he got the boot. We also had four keyboard players: Tim Hinkley, Dave Thompson, John Hawken and our last, Mike Deacon.

Spending so much time together group members can get pretty fed up with each other. There can also be a fair amount of competition. We used to play Monopoly in the van on the way to gigs. I have vivid memories of one of our keyboard players John Hawken, who married a Playboy bunny, being staggered that I was still in the game after he'd gone bankrupt because he thought I was thick. The person I clashed with the most was guitarist Jim Mullen. He came to us from the Brian Auger Band. We'd got to know him because he'd been sitting in on a lot of our London gigs and Pete thought it would be great to get him on board permanently. Pete felt his own playing wasn't that good at the time and he wanted to bring someone in who was really amazing at solos so he could just concentrate on playing rhythm guitar, but I knew from the moment he suggested it that it was a bad idea.

Jim was, without doubt, an amazing guitar player with a fantastic background. Artists who are used to working with top-flight musicians can be a bit difficult to deal with and this was certainly true of Jim. If he'd been more modest, it might have been okay but the trouble was, he had to keep letting everybody know how great he was. For me, that made him a first-class pain in the bum. Although he was getting on my nerves, I decided to be grown-up in the way I dealt with him. I believe that if you give a person enough rope, he'll eventually hang himself. And that's exactly what Jim did. Strangely, it was the fact that I wouldn't argue with him which was his undoing. He was always goading me, trying to get me into an argument, and I would never oblige.

I thought, 'What's the point: where's this going to go?'

It all came to a head when we were on the road in Belgium. We were in a restaurant and Jim ordered *moules marinière*, which is something I used to enjoy many years ago until I had food poisoning. Jim, as always, was trying to get me to argue but I just kept on ignoring him and he ended up getting so frustrated he started crying into his mussels out of pure exasperation. Despite my feelings for Jim we carried on working together and he came on tour to America with us in 1973 when we were supporting Wishbone Ash. When you're touring you get really tired and you've often got a very short fuse and this is how he got me to argue with him. It wasn't a massive argument, I just told him bluntly to 'eff off' which I think let him know how I felt. That was the final straw for me, so when we got home at the end of the tour I gave Pete an ultimatum, I said, 'Either he goes or I do.' He went.

Touring used to take its toll on all of us and that's why I took coke, it kept me going. It was a bit like having a cup of coffee. I certainly did like the odd toot but I never really got off on it in the same way the rest of the band did. Today Pete is a clean-living guy who works as a music teacher in Australia, which funnily enough was what his mum did.

While I could cope with the coke, the same couldn't be said for hash brownies. Unknowingly after a gig in Glasgow at a friend's house I ate one and it proved to be a real trip. We were having a couple of drinks, as you do after most gigs, when these brownies appeared. I tucked in not realising they contained hashish, so I was seriously confused when I started hallucinating. That really scared me and I've never done it again since.

I had another terrible experience while celebrating after a gig at the Marquee with all the band and friends. This time though, it was a legal substance that was the cause of my woes; none other than the Janis Joplin tipple, Southern Comfort. I thought if it's good enough for Janis, it's good enough for me and I should give it a try. My trouble in those days was that I didn't do things by halves and I ended up polishing off most of the bottle, possibly with a line of coke for good measure. On the way home to the flat in Fulham I was dying for the loo so I made Pete stop the car but I was so desperate I decided to get out before he'd come to a stop. Luckily, he was going quite slowly because I fell out on to the pavement and wet myself. I was wearing this big gypsy skirt and it got completely soaked. Not a good look I can assure you. What's more, it took me two days to get over the hangover. Suffice to say, I've never touched a drop of Southern Comfort again. Just the smell of it takes me back to that night in 1973.

That was the start of a series of falling episodes. After a great gig at the Black Swan in Sheffield we travelled back to London to do the all-nighter at the Roundhouse in Camden Town where bands like Yes regularly performed. Having done two great performances I came out of the gig and fell from the top of the Roundhouse steps all the way to the bottom. The steps, as anyone who's been to the Roundhouse will know, are incredibly steep and are made of solid concrete. How I didn't break my neck or my back, I don't know. Today, after having learned how to break a fall by practising the martial art aikido, I don't think I could survive such an accident. I guess I must have been extremely relaxed from being rather inebriated at the time. Amazingly, I didn't even have a bruise the next day.

My next fall came at one of our weekly residencies at the

Marquee, and this time it was a result of my determination to give an energetic stage performance. Even though it didn't seem as dramatic as the others, it actually has had a nasty, long-term effect on my body. I had a terrible habit, when the spirit got me and I was lost in the music, of repeatedly banging the microphone stand up and down on the stage. The ends of the stand were heavy and rather short, which was why I liked to do it. At the Marquee, this was not a good idea. There were one or two glass footlights embedded near the centre of the stage where I happened to be positioned. One leg went right into the lights, breaking the glass, and I fell very ungracefully backwards, arse over tit. Being the determined person I am, I managed to get back up quickly and carry on singing without suffering too much ridicule from the audience. It wasn't until the band broke up that I discovered how badly I'd injured myself. Resting from injury, my body seemed to seize up. I was in such a bad way that I was on all fours, unable to straighten up. Pete took me to a chiropractor, who after giving me an X-ray and examining me announced that my pelvis was out of line and that the prolonged inactivity was undermining my recovery. If you look closely at me today, you can see I'm still lopsided. The chiropractor set me various exercises to do, which I've done religiously for the last thirty years, and he also gave me the most valuable piece of advice that anyone has ever given me: keep mobile and do lots of walking; proper walking, not just walking to the shops. As a result of following his advice, I hardly ever get bad backache: the only time I suffer is when I'm immobile for long periods like on long car journeys or on aeroplanes.

The fact I'd hurt myself quite badly on several occasions in the course of the Vinegar Joe journey and managed to come out the other side perhaps made me open to a very unusual proposition. Towards the end of 1973 when publicity for the band was waning, Pete thought we needed a stunt to get us back in the papers. He came up with a plan that involved me getting mugged on my way back home to the flat in Fulham in the alleyway that leads from Putney Bridge underground station to New King's Road. The long coat I was wearing would be ripped; my bag, all my money and credit cards would be stolen; and his friend – an ex-boxer (Pete knew a lot of rather dubious characters from south London) – would punch me in the face to make sure it looked real. After all, nobody would be stupid enough to be punched in the face just for some publicity, would they?

Everything went smoothly, although I have to admit I was scared stiff at the time. I met the ex-boxer as planned and before punching me, he put on a leather glove so it wouldn't mark my face too badly. He also told me to exhale fully when he hit me. I know it's going to sound strange, but I thought he was a really nice bloke. After being 'mugged' I ran back to the railway station and asked them to call for help. An ambulance came and took me to the nearest hospital, but on the way there I began to feel really naughty. And, after being checked out by the doctor, I started laughing uncontrollably, much to the disgust of our agent John Sherry, who was there with me and in on the whole thing.

He said, 'For God's sake control yourself because there's going to be a guy coming in from the press at any minute.'

When I saw Pete later he said, 'With that kind of bottle, you'll definitely be a star one day.'

For all our efforts and the risk, we were gutted to get only a couple of small newspaper articles. The other problem I had was that Robert smelt a rat and despite feeling shaken I had to do the gig that night to make sure he'd believe what had happened. When I got there he took one look at my bruised face and instantly swallowed the story. Not since my nose job have I had such terrible bruising. To make matters worse, the coat, which I loved, was all ripped to shreds, and it was a real hassle getting my credit cards back.

I never did tell Robert the truth. If he'd found out, I'm not sure how he would have reacted. You could never quite tell with Robert, which probably had something to do with his competitiveness. Robert was far more competitive than me; I just loved being in the band and that was enough. He, on the other hand, could be quite unpleasant when he felt threatened by somebody else's success. After seeing me on the front page of the *Melody Maker* with the headline 'Jeans and sweat band Vinegar Joe and the face of '73 is Elkie Brooks', Robert walked into the dressing room and sarcastically said, 'How's your jeans and sweat tonight?' He would also mock me for looking in the mirror all the time to make sure I was looking okay. When I walked into the room he used to announce to everyone, 'And now we have Elkie Brooks on mirror.'

Despite intermittent tension we got on very well and had a lot of fun together. Clearly, none of our disagreements were noticed by the fans because the girls were convinced that Robert and I were an item. A beautiful photograph taken by showbiz photographer Gered Mankowitz of us holding hands, me wearing a see-through body stocking, added to the illusion. Nothing could have been further from the truth since Pete and I were married.

But, boy, could he make me mad, especially on those nights when the audience were unresponsive. That was when we needed him to be on form and to be giving 100 per cent. Instead he'd be half-heartedly going through the motions. He'd act like the band had got nothing to do with him, but on the nights when he did dare to join the band we were extraordinary. I don't think any other members of the band would say anything different. Robert wasn't a team player and, had he been, we might have been a very rich and successful band, but we weren't.

I've always felt that Robert viewed Vinegar Joe as his rehearsal band. So you can hardly blame me for feeling outraged when the fans blamed me for the break-up of the band. Everyone thought it was me who wanted to go solo but it was actually Robert. He had plans for a solo career a year prior to telling us. He'd got all the material together and Chris Blackwell had lined up a few members of the New Orleans band Little Feat who Robert really liked, to record his debut album, *Sneakin' Sally Through The Alley*.

He did his first solo show at The Apollo in Hammersmith, and all the band went except me because I was still too upset with him. Afterwards they told me he was very disappointed that I wasn't there. I did, however, see him when Steve York had a party at his flat in Regent's Park just after he'd finished his first album. He came over with his wife Sue and, fuelled with drugs and alcohol, I told Robert that he had never taken a long, hard look at himself in the mirror. I was grabbing and pulling him towards the mirror, but he just wouldn't look at it.

He said, 'It's all right for you, you can look at yourself, you're very down to earth. You can see yourself, but I can't look in the mirror like that.'

I'm not sure if there was anything significant in what happened that evening because we were both pretty out of it, but I've always believed that Robert never really confronted his fears. I don't think he ever actually looked at himself in the mirror in that wider sense and I think that's what I was trying to get him to do that night in 1974 which was, as it turned out, the last time I ever saw him.

CHAPTER 12

LIFE AFTER VINEGAR JOE

Vinegar Joe had been everything to me and life without it was hard. I was like a fish out of water. I'd been a member of Dada and part of Vinegar Joe for a good four years and in all that time I constantly believed in what we were doing, all along hoping we were going to be hugely successful. To find that we weren't was deeply upsetting.

I was very disappointed that Pete and Steve didn't want to keep the band going, either with just me, or by getting another singer to share the lead vocals with me. They'd obviously talked about it and come to the conclusion that it wouldn't be the same without Robert, so that was that. I'd always dreamed of being happy musically and Vinegar Joe had fulfilled that dream. I'd also dreamed of having a good relationship with a man I cared for greatly and I felt I had that with Pete. However, shortly before the band folded in late 1973, I noticed a change in him. I still loved him but somehow things weren't quite the same as when we'd first met.

There was also the issue of children, which played on my mind at times. I really wanted to have a baby when we started Dada but Pete just didn't want to know; there always seemed to be some reason why it wasn't a good idea. Perhaps our lives would have been different if we'd decided to have kids. Saying that, I believe things happen, or don't happen, for a reason. Everything eventually turned good for me on that front.

I was fortunate that a few projects came my way to save

me from wallowing in my sorrow at the prospect of losing Pete. In December 1973, I was asked to sing for two nights in a live version of The Who's rock opera album *Tommy* at the Rainbow theatre in London. I took the role of Tommy's mother, Mrs Walker, a part that previously had been played by Maggie Bell. It was a fun line-up featuring Roger Daltrey as Tommy, Bill Oddie, Jon Pertwee, David Essex and Merry Clayton as the Acid Queen. I shared a dressing room with Merry and Maddy Prior of Steeleye Span. It was funny because I kept calling Merry 'Mary' because I couldn't understand why anyone would be called Merry; I thought that was just a word that was used at Christmas or when you'd had a few. I remember Keith Moon coming into the dressing room wearing a great big wolfskin coat. I think I sang on five of the songs and joined in at the end. It was good experience but I didn't get a sense that 'Tommy' would go on to be a successful musical. The show gave me an opportunity of meeting up with Don Arden's son David Levy. I hadn't seen him since I took him and his sister Sharon to Battersea funfair on that terrible day when I thought we were all going to die on that horrendous ride. I enjoyed catching up with David and it was great to see what a smashing bloke he'd become.

My first proper project after the break-up was in spring 1974 and, as it turned out, it was the thing that kept me going. It was a BBC TV play called *Masquerade: Something Down There Is Crying*, written by Adrian Mitchell. I think it was loosely based on the story of Vinegar Joe. I played the lead role of a female singer who accepts a gig singing for some rich stockbroker types. The event turns out to be not quite what she expected. We rehearsed for a week in London before filming. All the other actors were seasoned professionals so I was quite up against it, not having done any 'drama' since leaving school. I took it all very seriously and approached learning the script as I did memorising my lyrics. When we came to filming, I thought I did very well, but I've never been offered any more parts since, so I guess I wasn't quite as good as I imagined. A couple of years later I saw Helen Mirren, before she was famous, play my role in a stage version of the original television play called *Teeth and Smiles* in Chelsea.

Not long after my acting debut and finale, I met up with Steve Marriott of the Small Faces and Humble Pie who I'd got to know in London in the early 1960s through my former manager Ian Samwell. When I was first introduced to Steve, it couldn't have been very long after he'd come out of *Oliver* in the West End. I liked him immediately. I thought he was a very natural musician. He would quite often come up to my flat and we would just jam together; we had some great evenings and I was fond of him, in a completely non-romantic way I might add. He was just like my little brother and when I say little, I mean it, because he was so tiny, he only came up to my shoulder, and I'm not exactly tall.

Our re-introduction came through a great bass player friend Boz Burrell who played with King Crimson before forming the supergroup Bad Company with Paul Rodgers of Free fame. I originally met Boz, who sadly passed away in 2006, when I was doing the cabaret circuit. My manager Jean Lincoln would occasionally get his group the Boz People to be my backing band when they weren't performing on their own, but I got to know him better through Tim Hinkley, the Vinegar Joe keyboardist. Boz had said that he knew Steve Marriott quite well and that he'd mentioned my name to him. He suggested I came down to his studio for a bit of a get-together.

It was great to see Steve again. We had plenty to talk about since I last saw him, and we'd both been managed by Don Arden. I was thrilled he had done so well in his career, he'd gone on to great things with the Small Faces, but I have to say it was quite a shock seeing him again because he had become very, very fat, and being so short, he looked quite strange. I think he'd got that way because he was trying to get off coke and was drinking heavily as a result. It was very upsetting to see him like that but something more upsetting happened after our recording session in his studio. I was singing particularly well that day and we recorded a fabulous duet of an old Ray Charles number. Steve, I think, must have felt I was outsinging him because I later found out he had erased the tape: what a great moment in time to have destroyed.

At about the same time, Pete and Steve York did a stint as a backing band for a South African singer and her husband. The press picked up on it and made it sound as if we were re-forming Vinegar Joe, which was pretty sad to see, knowing full well that nothing could be further from the truth. Pete was also busy creating a different musical path for himself as a producer. He produced one for me: a song called 'Rescue Me'. It was released by our old label, Island Records, but didn't do anything because it wasn't promoted.

After that he started working with Joan Armatrading on her second album, *Back To The Night,* for A&M. This gave me an opportunity to pursue one of my other passions. Knowing that I was keen on cooking and that our friend Lyn Taylor was also a very good cook Pete asked the two of us to provide the catering for the album, which was being recorded at Rockfield Studios near Monmouth. I'd got to know 'Big Lyn', as I call her, from the Vinegar Joe days as she was an ardent fan of the group. She lived round the corner from us in Fulham. As Joan used to come over to the flat to see Pete quite regularly, we both knew her, which made the catering gig simpler. I remember being very impressed when she arrived at the flat on an enormous motorbike; I thought that was very cool. Joan was great and we had a wonderful time cooking for her and the ten or so other musicians and technicians every day for about a month. I'm still very much into my cooking today, much to the delight of my family who are all good eaters. The catering job also gave me a chance to write a few songs between meals as I'd brought my little piano with me. I think Joan came to like my singing too because years later I was surprised to hear that she'd been seen in the audience at one of my London gigs. I felt that was quite an honour.

These 'bits' of work had kept me ticking over through most of 1974 and towards the end of the year, just as I was beginning to worry about what to do next, I got an offer to go to America to do backing singing for a band called Wet Willie. The opportunity came via Frank Fenter at their record label, Capricorn Records. I'd met Frank when I was in Dada and he was in charge of Atlantic Records; evidently he'd gone on to join brothers Phil and Alan Walden at Capricorn in Macon, Georgia. Frank knew I was out of work since Vinegar Joe split so he got in touch. I thought it was a great chance to get away from it all and put the bitterness and disappointment I still felt about the demise of Vinegar Joe behind me.

Wet Willie then was a big, high-energy band on the southern states circuit and was made up of brothers Jimmy and Jack Hall; Jimmy was the singer and Jack the bass player. I got my opportunity when their backing singer got pregnant and had to leave. The other singer in the band was Jimmy and Jack's sister Donna who I ended up getting on with really well.

The whole band took me under its wing and I had a great time staying at their home in Mobile, Alabama, for about three months from Christmas 1974. They were all good musicians and I liked them, but I got on particularly well with the guitarist, Ricky Hirsch, who is the only southern Jewish guitar player I've ever met! He was a great guy and we still keep in touch now by email.

The experience of being a backing singer was very differ-ent from what I had been used to. As a lead singer I was responsible for making sure that the audience was having a good time; I didn't have that pressure with Wet Willie. While I was there Pete came out to see me and tried to nego-tiate a deal for me with Frank Fenter and Capricorn, but he wasn't interested.

When I came home in the spring of 1975, I met up with Alan Seifert, who had heard about me from the Vinegar Joe days. He was putting together an album called *Flash Fearless versus the Zorg Women*. It was based on a cartoon character featuring lots of artists including Alice Cooper, James Dewar, John Entwistle, Maddy Prior and Keith Moon. I didn't know much about the album, I just saw it as work. What it did do, however, was turn Alan on to my singing. He liked it so much he paid for me to do four or five demos with keyboard player Kirk Duncan. I had quite a bit of material because in between singing with Wet Willie in America I'd been writing more songs, all of which were pretty similar to those I'd been singing with Vinegar Joe. Almost immediately after doing the demos, Alan said that he wanted to manage me and straightaway delivered the goods by getting me a deal with A&M Records, a label formed by Herb Alpert and Jerry Moss.

The managing director of A&M in England, Derek Green, loved the demos and came up with the idea of sending me out to the Record Plant Studios in Los Angeles to make my first solo album *Rich Man's Woman,* working with flavour-of-the-month producers Kenny Kerner and Richie Wise. They had just finished an album with Gladys Knight. While this seemed a good idea at the time it didn't turn out well. I suppose I wasn't to know, I just wanted to succeed in the music business and it seemed like a great opportunity.

Not long after, Alan and I went out to LA where he had arranged a band for me, but as soon as I started to work with them I knew things weren't right. I felt like a singer in a session with a group of guys who didn't know me and weren't into my music. I think this was reflected in the recordings we ended up with. I've always believed that the songs on *Rich Man's Woman* were nowhere near as good as the demos, and I think Derek Green felt the same way when he heard them. After an initial week of publicity, which involved me doing a stint at Ronnie Scott's club, promotion for the album dwindled. A&M were not impressed. Derek was disappointed with the album and, I have to say, I think he was right.

It was a rocky album and A&M wanted to produce a sleeve with impact and one that moved me away from my hippy Vinegar Joe image to something a bit sexier. Well they definitely succeeded because we did a photo shoot with me wearing very little. All I had on was a length of fluffy material covering the all-important areas. By standards today, the cover was nothing to get excited about, but in the early 1970s it was considered to be very risqué. In fact, I remember being interviewed by a woman in New York who said it was dreadful and that I should be ashamed of myself for being photographed half naked. She thought I had a great singing voice but that I looked like a showgirl on the sleeve, which I suppose I did. She said I would never be taken seriously as a singer if I kept on doing album sleeves like that. Her remarks took me by complete surprise because I didn't see anything wrong with it.

I was bitterly upset the music hadn't turned out as well as I'd hoped. The track I was most proud of was 'Where Do We Go From Here' which was a song Pete wrote. It was released as a single, along with 'He's A Rebel', but neither of them made much impact. I honestly believe if we'd made *Rich Man's Woman* in England with the musicians I wanted, we would have ended up with a much better album. And that way, I wouldn't have been saddled with criticism over a 'controversial' cover shot! I was also annoyed for not asserting myself enough with the producers. Because they were experienced, I thought they knew what was right for my voice but looking back on the experience, they clearly didn't, and the album suffered as a result. I have to say that it's taken me many years to be able to stand up to producers in recording sessions and express my feelings honestly.

Despite the disappointment of my first album failing commercially and everyone involved, including me, losing faith in the product, Derek and A&M turned their attention to making a follow-up album. This time Derek's idea turned out to be right on the money. He wanted to get producers Jerry Leiber and Mike Stoller involved. I, however, wasn't keen because I thought they were a lot older than me and very dated in their attitudes. Saying that, I did like a lot of the songs they'd written for Elvis Presley and I certainly admired Jerry Leiber's ability as a writer.

Despite my initial reservations, Jerry and Mike were brilliant people to work with and they got some fantastic musicians involved including Jean Roussel on keyboards, who became a great friend and who I've worked with throughout my career. Jean did all the musical direction and was amazing all-round; we very quickly developed a great respect for one another.

We started rehearsing for what became the album *Two Days Away* in the spring of 1976. We spent three weeks in our drummer Trevor Morais's studio in Little Chalfont, Buckinghamshire, which was very enjoyable. We then went to do the initial recordings at CBS Studios in Oxford Street. I remember going in each day, sweltering on the train in England's hottest summer ever: what a summer that was. We did all the basic tracks in London and then Jerry and Mike decided they were going to take a holiday so we switched location, at great expense, to the Electric Lady Studios in Greenwich Village, New York, where we did all the vocal backings as well as a few of my lead vocals. The consequence of the shift was that we didn't complete the album until the tail-end of 1976.

While I was in New York I got a call from Jean Roussel who was in Philadelphia working with Cat Stevens. He said Cat was looking for someone to sing the middle section duet and backing vocals on '(Remember the Days of the) Old Schoolyard'. Jean had suggested getting me to come over at the weekend because Leiber and Stoller only worked 10 a.m. to 6 p.m., Monday to Friday, and Cat had agreed. The recording went well and Cat seemed happy with the result. It was great working with him as he was already a well-established artist; I can also remember thinking how stunningly good-looking he was.

I didn't see Cat again for years until one day, when I was coming out of a hotel in London, I bumped into him. We had a good catch-up during which my son Joey was happily chatting away without the slightest clue who he was talking to. When I told him afterwards that he'd been talking to Cat Stevens he was blown away.

I knew I was singing well when we were recording the tracks for *Two Days Away* and I had a feeling deep down that the album was going to be good, but I don't think I really had any idea of how important it would be for me. Even though I knew I was on form, I did find it fairly hard going at times, especially in those confusing moments when Jerry told me to sing a song one way and then Mike said to do it differently. I remember going to the loo and having a snort of coke, and coming back saying I'd do whatever they wanted, knowing full well that I was going to do what I thought was best. It seemed to work, as they were both happy. I suppose I must have compromised, but it's always difficult working with two producers, which is why I prefer these days to work with just one, my son Jay.

At one particularly memorable rehearsal I remember

Jerry Leiber saying, 'I want to play you this song, I don't think you're going to like it, it's too countryish for you but I'll play it anyway.'

It was a song by Ralph Dino and John Sembello who were two well-known session musicians in America.

I said, 'Go on, I've got an open mind, I like a lot of country.'

I listened to it and told them I liked it but that they needed to write a middle section.

To which Jerry said, 'No problem.'

And with that he disappeared and came back half an hour later with the completed version of 'Pearl's A Singer'.

When Derek Green heard it he thought it was fantastic, which was just as well because the album cost hundreds of thousands of pounds to make. Top producers like Leiber and Stoller do not come cheap and the recording costs for the musicians and engineers were eye-wateringly expensive. The bad news for me was that because of the way my music contract was structured I had to pay for all of these costs, which meant I ended up owing A&M lots of money for many years after. I got an advance but the expenses and costs in the end all come out of your cheque – a practice which was very unfair for the artist.

Derek Green knew that he had a good record on his hands and was very keen to make sure that we had an album cover to match; one that wasn't likely to cause controversy. The shot they chose was sexy but it was much safer. In fact, it was to be the start of a whole image change. Alan Seifert and Derek were trying to steer me away from my rocky Vinegar Joe look towards something much more middle of the road and classy. Being a raunchy rocker at heart, I initially resisted but very quickly realised that they were serious, so I did the sensible thing and conformed to their wishes.

It was decided that 'Pearl's A Singer' would be the first single from the album, so they dressed me in a beautiful, long gown for the promos. I say beautiful but I didn't feel that way about it at the time. I remember thinking that this was how people were going to see me from now on, as an evening gown diva. All of a sudden I was mainstream, and I didn't like it; deep down, however, I knew they were right. This was, without doubt, a decisive moment in my career because I would have to live up to the new image, and anyone who knows me will tell you that's really not me. It is, nevertheless, what my fans have come to expect, so I always make sure that's what they get at my gigs.

When the album was released, A&M pulled out all the stops on publicity with the knowledge that finally they had something good to work with. They advertised it in the papers and promoted it everywhere; they made sure it worked and it did. 'Pearl's A Singer' was released as a single on my thirty-second birthday, 25 February 1977. To my delight it took off straightaway, reaching number 8 in the charts and establishing me as a solo artist. After all the false starts, at last I had a hit record. It was obviously just meant to be.

CHAPTER 13

A NEW MAN

With 'Pearl's A Singer' reaching number 8 and *Two Days Away* getting to number 16 in the album chart and spending twenty weeks there, my musical life had never been better.

It's funny how a little bit of success makes the phone start ringing. One minute I'm struggling for my big break, the next Bryan Ferry's management are asking me to do a duet with their star. Being open to the idea, I went along to Bryan's expensive London flat where he played me a recording of him singing a song called 'I Can't Stand It'. I remember the original version by The Soul Sisters in the 1960s so as soon as I heard Bryan's attempt I knew he had bastardised it and, in my opinion, ruined it. I told him I would love to do it if we did a new backing track with musicians of both our choices because the feel was all over the place.

I said, 'You've also got to get the lyrics to the song right. At the moment it's not for me.'

I could see Alan my manager going quietly mad, but for me the music has to be right. We didn't hear any more from Bryan, and I don't know if he ever did anything with the song.

I caused Alan even more grief when he fixed a meeting with Andrew Lloyd Webber and Tim Rice to talk about me doing the lead role on the *Evita* album. They played me some of the songs but as always, when the subject is music, I can't keep my mouth shut. After listening for quite some time I suggested doing something differently on one of the songs.

As soon as I'd opened my mouth I could tell that neither of them liked it. Not long after we said our polite goodbyes. I never even got to sing a note. Alan told me later that they thought I had too much to say for myself, which was true enough. I suppose I talked myself out of a really successful part but I've never really liked musicals so I didn't cry tears over it. Julie Covington got the gig and I was pleased for her.

While things on the music front were great – aside from not hearing from Bryan and upsetting Andrew and Tim, my personal life took a sudden turn for the worse when Pete announced he'd met someone else and didn't want to be with me anymore. We'd had a similar confrontation around Christmas 1976 which we'd managed to get through but this time we both decided that there was no going back. It didn't come as a big surprise to me because I knew we had grown apart since Vinegar Joe ended, but his timing could have been better as it was just a few weeks before we were due to start rehearsing for my first solo tour, and Pete, of course, was very much part of my live set.

My love life, however, changed for the better one memorable day in the summer of 1977 when I went to see Diana Ross in concert at the Victoria Palace Theatre. Alan Seifert had offered me some tickets. I wasn't a fan but I'd always thought she was very glamorous. Diana had a great sound. And having read her book I can understand why record producer Berry Gordy went for her as the lead singer of The Supremes; she has a distinctive, very girly sound, which was fabulous.

And strangely, it was this incredible sound that changed my life. I have to say that Diana was brilliant that night. The spectacle of the show was amazing but it was the quality of the sound that really impressed me. Despite having a very small sound system, a huge orchestra with a great big rhythm section, loads of dancers and singers, you could hear everything clearly.

I hadn't experienced anything like it before, so at the interval I decided to go and see who was responsible for the sound. I was so impressed I wanted to meet the sound engineer and shake his hand. I went up to the desk and this tall, stunning-looking, twenty-something guy comes over and shakes my hand.

I said, 'I've just got to say that this sound is fantastic, you're amazing, what is your name?'

He said, 'My name's Trevor Jordan. Who do you work for?'

I replied, 'You probably haven't ever heard of me, I'm Elkie Brooks, I've got a record out and I'm about to go out on tour. I'm going to tell my manager all about you, you're amazing.'

The next day I phoned Alan and told him he had to get this guy to do the sound for my tour. Alan duly arranged a meeting for a few weeks later with Trevor and his colleague Huw Richards, who he was training up, and me. While I was instantly attracted to Trevor, I wasn't looking for anything because only two weeks earlier Pete had moved out of our flat on Burlington Road to live with his new love, Pamela.

We began the meeting in Alan's office in the King's Road, but because it was so small we moved down to the Alibi coffee shop, which was directly below. We had coffee and something to eat, and I tried very hard to pay attention to what was going on but I couldn't stop thinking, 'I really like this guy'. It was strange because I'd been so very sure that I didn't want another relationship. I suppose though that's often the way life works, when you're not looking for anyone, you fall head over heels in love.

Luckily, Trevor had just finished the Diana Ross tour so he was available to work for me. We had a few more meetings to tie up all the loose ends and started rehearsing about a week later. It was odd because Pete was there with me every day as musical director of the backing band and there I was, growing keener on Trevor by the day. I've always thought that work is a great healer, and it definitely proved to be so in our case because Pete did a brilliant job and the rehearsals went from strength to strength. Pete and I got on perfectly well; in fact we are still good friends today.

While rehearsals were going smoothly, one session proved particularly important for me as it brought about a major lifestyle change. During the course of rehearsing we would have one or two coffee breaks but being musicians, these often turned into coke-snorting opportunities. On this occasion, Pete, Steve York, Tim Hinkley and the crew decided to chop several lines on the lid of Trevor's sound mixer. As well as doing the sound Trevor had been hired to supply some of the equipment, which was why one wing of his precious Mavis mixer that he'd built with a friend for Pink Floyd came to be in the rehearsal hall. He subsequently told me that it was the first quad board; I'm not sure what that is but it sounded important. Anyway, as the guys were cutting the coke, I could tell from looking at Trevor that he wasn't happy, though for some reason he didn't say anything. It must have been a funny sight, all of us lined up like kids in the dinner queue at school but in this case waiting for their snort of cocaine.

When it was my turn Trevor looked at me and said, 'I don't understand why you're doing that. You don't need to do it.'

Having been getting up early all week to do my hair and make-up to impress Trevor, I had no option but to say, 'You know, you're right.'

I went off and got myself a glass of water and I've never touched a line of coke since. Over the years my sons Jay and Joey have seen musicians and members of the crew do drugs and witnessed first-hand the effects of it. They made up their minds early on not to go down that road.

Without the distraction of cocaine, I concentrated on making the most of the rehearsal, and trying to get close to

Trevor. I never wanted to rehearse later than six or seven in the evening, so at about that time every day we'd all head off to the pub. It very quickly became apparent that Trevor felt the same way about me as I did about him. There was, however, one slight problem, his colleague Huw – he was always there. Huw, who has gone on to be one of the country's best sound engineers, was Trevor's shadow. He stuck to Trevor like glue, which wasn't convenient for a girl looking for some quality time with a bloke she fancied. Trevor, of course, was far too nice to exclude his friend from anything. Fortunately, Huw sussed out that I had my eye on Trevor and asked me one day if I wanted some time alone with him.

He said, 'I tell you what I'm going to do, Elk, when the question of going for a meal comes up I'm going to say that I've got to go home because my mum and dad have a special family gathering.'

And that's how Trevor and I got together. One night in the pub at about eight o'clock, just as he'd promised, Huw announced that he had to go home for a family get-together. Trevor offered to give him a lift and I asked if he'd mind dropping me off as well. We got into Trevor's fabulous red Jensen and headed for Huw's place.

After we'd dropped him off I played my trump card saying, 'I'm hungry, shall we go and have a Chinese?'

We went to Mr Chow's in Wardour Street, not far from the Marquee club, where they served fantastic Hoi Sin duck, which I was quite partial to at the time, having been introduced to it by Alan. Not only did I find Trevor great-looking, I found him terrific company too, and it was even better now that we were alone together. We had so much in common that it was no surprise we hit it off straightaway. In fact, I don't think I'd ever met anybody quite like him because I'd only really been around musicians. He also made me laugh which I found refreshing.

After the meal we took a walk by the river. I couldn't

believe what was happening. I thought I had it all worked out and wasn't going to get involved again and there I was falling in love before I was even divorced. The evening just swept us away and one thing led to another, and before we knew it we found ourselves at the Holiday Inn in Swiss Cottage where we had a wonderful night together. The next day, however, I had a crisis because I couldn't find the ring that Mum had given me for my birthday. I'd taken it off before going to bed and somehow it vanished into thin air. We searched everywhere for it, but couldn't find it. So, as it turned out, the night was memorable in more ways than one. Whenever Mum asked me why I wasn't wearing her ring, I somehow always managed to come up with an excuse so she never found out what really happened.

Our relationship got more and more serious but by being very careful we managed to keep our affair under wraps for the rest of the rehearsals. During the tour, however, Alan realised what was going on, but he seemed pretty cool about it because he liked Trevor and thought it was only going to be a passing fling. The tour was a success and I was packing out gigs everywhere. But, more importantly, my relationship with Trevor blossomed and we had the time of our lives getting to know one another better.

At the end of September 1977, the tour gave me the chance to perform at the Royal Albert Hall, which I felt was quite an achievement and recognition of my newly found success. The gig went well and at the customary after-show drinks with everyone we all got quite merry. Still trying to be discreet about our relationship, Trevor had booked a room at Blake's where he thought we would be able to get away from it all for the weekend.

Walking there, Trevor said, 'When you get your divorce from Pete, I think you ought to consider marrying me.'

Well, I didn't believe him because we'd both had a few so I said, 'Ask me again in the morning.'

If that wasn't eventful enough when we got to Blake's the funniest coincidence happened. We checked in and went to our room where we had a few drags on a joint and just before leaving the room to go down for a drink, I went to the bathroom where my bathroom turbulence set us both off into uncontrollable laughter. We had just about calmed down when on opening our door to go downstairs we bumped straight into Pete and a PR girl from A&M coming out of their room. We took one look at them and burst out laughing again. It was so surreal. Of all the hotels in London, we had both somehow managed to book into the same one trying to avoid each other. Matters were compounded when we lost one of our roadies who was booked in at the same hotel.

Trevor said, 'Where is he then?'

Pete replied, 'He should have been down ages ago.'

After a while the two of them went up to his room to investigate and when they knocked on the door they could hear a voice calling for help! When Pete told him to let them in they heard him shout, 'I can't, go and get a pass key.'

With a key from reception they opened the door and found him stark naked with hands and feet handcuffed to the bed. He'd been there for hours waiting for some professional female entertainment. In anticipation of her arrival he'd been experimenting with the equipment, unsuccessfully. The rest of our stay was very normal, yet very enjoyable. The next day we drove down to see Trevor's parents, who I'd met the previous evening at the Albert Hall.

On the way I said, 'Now you're sober, are you going to say the same thing you said to me last night?' And he did, so I knew he was serious.

We met his mum and dad in a country pub in Ashwell, just north of Stevenage where they lived, and Trevor told them our news. I think they were genuinely pleased for us. I got on famously with his little brother Robbie who was only about nine. He had an Emu puppet and to this very day I always remind him of how I used to sit him on my lap with Emu and we'd have cuddles.

Not long after our decision to get married, which we made about three months after first meeting, Alan Seifert came up trumps by finding me a flat at 109 Hammersmith Bridge Road overlooking the river. I was desperate to get out of the Fulham flat to start afresh somewhere else with Trevor. Fulham had too many memories and I couldn't contemplate being there with him. I thought Alan's find would be perfect for us as our first place together so I discussed it with Trevor and he agreed. With my recent successes I was able to afford something a bit more luxurious. The flat was superb, but it was at the top of the building and there was no lift. The bedroom was downstairs, the lounge, dining room and kitchen were open plan; the best thing about the flat was its sliding roof, which was great fun until it broke.

Unfortunately, just before we were due to move in Trevor had to go to New York because he was committed to do a week and a half with Canadian singer Gino Vannelli. This would have worked out fine with the second part of my tour but the Vannelli tour got cancelled and Trevor was seconded to the longer Jack Bruce tour, with Ginger Baker and Eric Clapton.

Just before he went away he asked me to look for an engagement ring as we hadn't had a chance to buy one together. I ignored him, thinking that if he really wanted to get engaged he'd have to come back and look for a ring with me or find one on his own in America. Having not been given an engagement ring by Pete, I was determined to do things properly this time.

Trevor, however, ended up coming home early, fed up with all the antics on the tour and saying he missed me desperately, of course. He flew back to meet up with me on the last night of my tour in Glasgow where I had champagne waiting. It was great to have him back, especially with the prospect of living together in Hammersmith.

When he moved into the flat he was fantastic because he threw himself into decorating and getting little things to make it seem more homely. And it wasn't long before I had the engagement ring I so badly wanted. We started the search in Petticoat Lane, looking for a second-hand antique ring, but soon decided that a new one seemed more appropriate. We went to Asprey's in Bond Street, a shop that I had heard so much about, and chose a beautiful diamond and sapphire ring that was not too over the top.

We very quickly settled into our new life together in our lovely Hammersmith pad, having a lot of fun along the way. The place we'd rented was one of two apartments, side by side, owned by the same man, a racing driver. Living in the other flat were two brothers, Nigel and Chris Warren-Green, who both played for the Royal Philharmonic Orchestra. We got on brilliantly with them. Bizarrely, Trevor had worked with them several years before. They were the first classical musicians I'd ever met. I'd always envisaged that it was only pop and jazz musicians who were heavy drinkers – Nigel and Chris certainly put me straight on that score.

It was pretty entertaining living next door to a violinist and a cellist. They practised at home at strange times of the day and in quite strange places. The bathrooms of the two flats backed on to one another, which quite often meant that our first trips of the day to the loo were accompanied by the sounds of a cello being played from the neighbouring toilet. While the sound of a cello being expertly played is beautiful, it has to rank as one of the oddest bathroom habits I've encountered.

I think, though, Trevor and I probably deserved being subjected to this as we certainly put Chris and Nigel through some things in our time there. On one particularly memorable occasion, Chris and Nigel ended up taking some unnecessary flak from another neighbour because of us. Not long after we'd set up home together Trevor and I bought a whippet that we named Winnie. On the evening in question I think we must have had one or two drinks too many, or maybe it was a puff or two too many, and we both ended up naked, chasing poor Winnie around the flat, making a bit of racket in the process. This seriously enraged the two guys who lived in the flat below us, who to be fair used to make a fair amount of noise themselves, if you get what I mean. Our capers that evening got to a stage where one of them felt he had to do something about it, so he came upstairs to complain, but he mistakenly knocked on Chris and Nigel's door instead of ours.

All of a sudden we heard lots of shouting from the hall-way and, after finding our dressing gowns, opened our door to see the German member of the couple standing there in some bizarre costume that was probably best kept indoors, having a right go at a totally bemused Nigel.

Trevor, never one to worry about getting involved, asked what was going on. The German guy told him they'd been making a noise. Trevor quickly put him right, saying, 'No, that was us, we were chasing the dog around.'

The guy then proceeded to vent his anger on Trevor, which is never a good thing to do, complaining that he and his partner were trying to work. He didn't really look like he was working unless, of course, he was making a dodgy film. Trevor didn't react very well to this complaint, prob-ably because they'd made so much noise in the past, and promptly gave him a bit of a kick that sent him tumbling down the stairs, back into his flat.

This wasn't the only time that Chris and Nigel got roped in to our problems. On another occasion, Trevor was trying to get a Chesterfield sofa we'd bought up to the flat. His first attempt on the stairs had failed so he decided to get it up through the window with ropes. He had recruited

Chris and Nigel to pull on the end of the ropes in our flat, but they were quite rightly petrified about hurting their hands.

I remember Trevor shouting, 'Don't worry about your bloody hands, just pull.'

But as they were about to pull it in through the window the rope snapped and it went crashing down on to the railings below, which the poor lady owner had only just finished painting. Amazingly, the sofa survived pretty much intact. We eventually managed to get it up to the flat and it proved to be really rather comfortable. I suppose it was worth all the effort, although I think our female neighbour would probably have seen it very differently.

Thank goodness Chris and Nigel weren't around on the day that Trevor tried to get my upright piano into the flat! This time he got Huw to help him and they managed it without any trouble; unfortunately the same couldn't be said when the pair of them came to move us out of the flat sometime later. They'd almost made it all the way down, with Huw at the top and Trevor at the bottom, when Huw lost his grip. Trevor somehow managed to jump out of the way but the piano went whizzing off down the stairs just as our friend Rod, who lived on the ground floor, opened his front door. The piano went flying into his flat at a rate of knots, but remarkably didn't hurt him or cause any damage whatsoever.

I can honestly say that the only ups and downs we had as a couple living in that flat together involved getting furniture in and out, so when my divorce was finalised we both felt secure in our relationship and in February 1978 we didn't waste any time setting a date for our wedding.

Since I was a divorcée and Jewish we could hardly have a church service, so we decided to get married a month later on 1 March at the Old Registry Office in Trevor's home town of Stevenage. We only wanted the immediate family there as neither of us had a lot of money, which meant a big bash was out of the question. We opted for a reception for ten guests at Sopwell Manor, St Albans. We also wanted to keep the wedding quiet so the only person outside of the family we told was Alan.

Before the ceremony we enjoyed a quiet drink at Trevor's parents' home and then set off for the registry office. When we arrived we were greeted with an unpleasant surprise. Alan, not wishing to waste a publicity opportunity, was waiting with a press photographer. We dealt with it, but the cat was well and truly out of the bag and our news was in the national newspapers the following day. To make matters worse, Alan insisted on staying for the meal, and, to top it all, turned round to Trevor's mum and said, 'I give this six months.'

She was really upset, but we all tried not to let it ruin the day. Anyway, I'm pleased to say that Alan's prediction was spectacularly wrong because we're still together more than thirty years later.

CHAPTER 14

WALHAM GROVE, FULHAM

Two days after the wedding we flew to Las Vegas for our honeymoon. Sadly, though, this wasn't the usual romantic honeymoon, it was a working one because Trevor had already agreed to a three-week stint doing the sound for Andy Williams at Caesars Palace, and Trevor, being a man of his word, honoured his promise.

Andy looked after us and put us in a luxurious suite. I had met him in London and on that occasion he took us for a meal and a ride in his limousine, after which we went to Stringfellows club. He couldn't get over how shy I was. I remember Trevor advising him that I was not like that at all. If I'm honest, I think I was just a bit in awe of being out in a club with Andy Williams. It was fine for Trevor because you could see how well he and Andy got on; there was such a respect between them.

I saw Andy's show at Las Vegas several times and enjoyed his singing. I was thoroughly impressed by his ability not just to sing but to chat to the audience and put them at ease. He had a very gruelling schedule – two shows a night. Having done a few myself, I can't even begin to comprehend how he managed it.

While this was tough for Andy, it was good for Trevor and me because we had the days to ourselves. We made several trips to Lake Mead and other tourist sites. On one of our visits we hired a little motorboat and went whizzing round the lake admiring the huge houses and expensive yachts. They must have looked at us in horror, but we didn't care. At one point we found a little island and decided to explore. Trevor got off to pull the boat ashore and I fell over backwards into the boat. I couldn't stop laughing so he had to drag me out somehow. I wasn't laughing quite so much when the boat broke down later and the expensive gold medallion I'd bought him in Asprey's fell into the water as he was frantically pulling the cord to restart the engine.

Halfway through our stay, I was struck down with pneumonia. I think the humidity of the hotel was to blame, but, whatever caused it, I was in a terrible state. This time both lungs were affected and I was so ill I went down to seven stone. Trevor had to take me to hospital, which meant carrying me out of the hotel through the casino to the car. After being diagnosed and getting the right medication I recovered pretty quickly, which was good because I had a very busy time ahead.

Before we left for home we tried our luck on the slot machines and won $20, which we exchanged for silver dollars. I've still got them today as a memento of our honeymoon.

On returning home we managed to get a small deposit together to buy the Hammersmith Road flat. We also sat down and had an important conversation about our careers. Trevor felt that if we were going to make a success of our marriage one of us would have to sacrifice a career. After talking about it for a while we decided to focus on mine because we felt I had the greater earning capacity.

Trevor immediately cut back, deciding to work only for Diana Ross and Andy Williams, and even those he was trying to limit. Not long after making this decision, Trevor got a call from Diana Ross's manager Don Peake, who invited him to do the sound for a Diana and Frank Sinatra show at the Forest Hills tennis stadium in New York. Trevor said he couldn't do it and Don said he'd talk to Diana. We thought that was the end of it but a day or so later we got

Starting at the very beginning with a snap of my mother holding me as a baby.

Those Bookbinders kids: with my brothers, Ray (left) and Tony (right).

Auntie Betty (left) and a colleague outside the Bookbinder bakery in Manchester.

With Mum in Llandudno, where we went every year and stayed at the Grand Hotel. It was my favourite place to go on holiday as a child.

ABOVE: Mum, Dad and Grandma Gochin with an assortment of Bookbinder children (from front left): my cousin Michael, me, cousin Melinda from Israel, Tony, cousin Hilary and Ray, looking like he'd rather be somewhere else.

LEFT: With my best friend and cousin Hilary at Manchester Ice Palace – I'm a powder puff and she's a cowgirl!

ABOVE: Singing at my brother Tony's bar mitzvah, aged eleven, accompanied by Uncle Nat's band.

LEFT: Attending a family event as a teenager in my first posh frock, handmade by my mother.

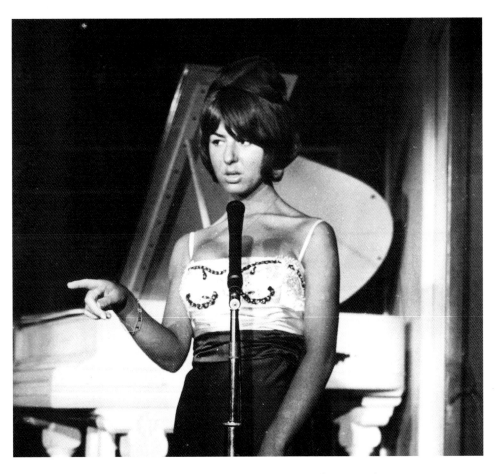

ABOVE: Taking to the stage in my early twenties at the Whisky A Go-Go club, owned by Billy Charvin.

LEFT: I may not have got my talent for singing from my parents but it's clear where I got the dancing gene. Here are Mum and Dad on the dance floor at a family wedding.

ABOVE: With Georgie Fame in 1964, toasting his twenty-first birthday – dodgy teeth but a great smile.

BELOW: Getting married to Pete Gage in 1971. Someone should have told him I'm allergic to flowers.

A truly beautiful shot of me and Robert Palmer, taken by Gered Mankowitz during the Vinegar Joe years.

OPPOSITE: What a rocker! On stage with Vinegar Joe in 1972. The outfits may have changed but I'm still a rock 'n' roll girl at heart.

ABOVE: Making headlines as *Melody Maker*'s hot tip for the Face of '73 – a fantastic way to end the year.

ABOVE: Vinegar Joe's last line up (from left): Steve York, Mike Deacon, me, Pete Gage, Robert Palmer and Pete Gavin.

LEFT: Signing the register with Trev on our wedding day, 1 March 1978.

Life on the road during our first tour in 1980. At the back is Geoff Whitehorn giving the Vs, next to him is Duncan Kinnell and Tim Hinkley has baby Jay on his lap.

Thanks a million: Alec Leslie (left) and Derek Green (right) of A&M records presenting me with my gold disc.

Trev and me with baby Jay, enjoying being parents in the back garden of our first house in Walham Grove.

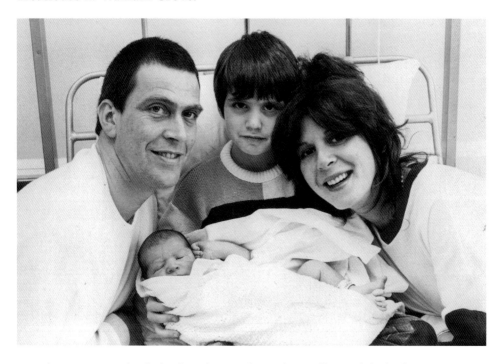

Jay always wanted a baby brother and much to all our delight he got Joey for his seventh birthday.

Trev and Winnie getting ready to take a flight over Woolacombe. Their hang-gliding escapades made the front page of the *North Devon Advertiser*!

The band (from left to right): Melvin Duffy, Lee Noble, me, Steve Jones, Mike Richardson, Andrew Murray and Brian Badhams.

ABOVE LEFT: Flanked by Jenny Herniman (3rd Dan) and Morgan Mills (2nd Dan) – we're all looking a bit worse for wear after several hours of training. I owe so much to them for their patience over the years.

© By kind permission of Ornella Hawthorn Gardez

ABOVE RIGHT: With Soke Eddie Stratton (9th Dan), posing at the opening of his dojo in Barnstaple in the early 1990s.

The lovely Lulu and I taking the opportunity to catch up at a tribute concert for Don Black at the Palladium in 2008.

WYNDHAM ROSE HALL
Montego Bay, Jamaica

ABOVE: All the family out for dinner in Montego Bay, Jamaica, where I was doing a show. Both the boys have grown up such a lot since then.

LEFT: With Wilf Pine, bouncer, promoter, self-confessed gangster and mine and Trev's 'godfather'.

An intimate moment with the legendary Humphrey Lyttelton.

Doing what I love best. Live on stage in 2009.

Photo by Phil Slaughter

another call from Don asking how much he wanted to do it. Trevor said no again and the numbers kept on going up and up, eventually reaching a figure he couldn't refuse; not because of the money but he felt it was beginning to look as if he was ridiculing them. In fact, one evening, Diana had called him into her dressing room and asked what was stopping him coming over.

He said, 'I'm married now to a singer called Elkie Brooks.'

Diana replied, 'Why didn't you say you wanted to get married, Trev? I'd have married you if you'd have asked me, if it meant getting you back on tour.'

As it happened, that was the last time Trevor ever worked with Diana.

The start of 1978 had been an incredibly busy time – a number 16 hit with 'Lilac Wine', getting married, going to Vegas and rehearsing for yet another tour. Before getting married, I recorded the *Shooting Star* album partly at CBS Studios in London and partly at the Workshop in Los Angeles with David Kershenbaum, the house producer of A&M Records. It was a bit like working with the producers I'd had on *Rich Man's Woman* because I felt like a session singer rather than a solo artist. However, this time I had my good friend Jean Roussel as my musical director and some other great musicians including Andy Newmark on drums and Jerry Knight on bass and backing vocals who went on to become a huge star in the rap and hip hop world but tragically died young from cancer. The production area lacked spark and I confess that I'm not that proud of many songs on the album. Only a few turned out the way I hoped they would, songs like 'Too Precious', which I started writing some years before but finished off with Trevor in mind, and 'Just An Excuse' which I played piano on myself, with Jean. Even though A&M didn't push *Shooting Star* in the same way they had *Two Days Away* it still somehow managed to make it to number 20 in the album chart and my cover of

Neil Young's 'Only Love Can Break Your Heart' struggled to number 43.

Not only had the music not turned out as well as I had hoped, the album cover was dreadful. Alan had gone ahead and produced it without any input from me. I remember him showing it to me for the first time at our local pub, the Blue Anchor. I took one look at this horrible illustration of me that made me look about two stone heavier than I was, and ripped it up right in front of him. Despite this dramatic reaction I didn't throw it away and, for some reason, I still have it today.

However, the tour we did to promote the album was, without doubt, a musical high, if not a financial one, as it transpired. We'd begun rehearsing almost immediately after getting back from Las Vegas. Our first performance was on 30 April and we continued throughout May. The highlight of the tour was playing at the Palladium from 15 to 20 May. I think I was the first British female singer to do a one-woman show there. I got a rush when I saw my name up in big lights with 'Sold Out' slashed across it. It was such a great buzz being on the same stage as all the famous people I'd grown up watching on TV as a little girl, especially the incredible Shirley Bassey. On the last night I have a wonderful memory of looking up at my mum and dad in the royal box. That was quite something.

Trevor remembers it well too, but for quite a different reason, as he got told off by none other than Yul Brynner, who was there rehearsing for *The King and I* during the day. One morning while the cast were on stage rehearsing Trevor and Huw were in the auditorium making a right old racket sorting out things for my performance that night and Yul shouted at them to be quiet.

After my week there, in line with the tradition for headline artists, I was given the gold plaque from the No. 1 dressing room with my name on it. I gave it to my parents as a souvenir.

Both Alan Seifert and A&M boss Derek Green also gave me gifts to mark the occasion. Alan presented me with a black Porsche watch, which he knew I really wanted, and Derek gave me a beautiful gold necklace, with a diamond in the centre. I still wear it.

When my mum saw it she said, 'Couldn't he have given you a bigger diamond?'

It was at this time, just as I was beginning to enjoy real success, that Alan hit me with a financial bombshell, which related to the two *Shooting Star* tours I'd done. I was already pretty unhappy with the second, European stage of the tour, which started in Amsterdam on 23 November 1978 and finished in Zurich on 7 December, because, without my knowledge, the promoter Andrew Miller had persuaded Alan to make me do two shows a day on several occasions which, as any artist will tell you, is crippling. There was also an issue about a show in Frankfurt, which I was forced to pull out of for safety reasons when Trevor discovered the stage was full of holes. When Derek Green heard he went mad, and sent me a snotty telegram and followed it up with a personal visit to tell me that I had to behave myself unless I wanted to lose my contract.

As if these problems weren't enough, Alan told me the tours had lost money and that I owed Andrew Miller £48,000. Trevor and I were devastated. Financially, it hit us pretty badly as I was left with just £100 in my bank account and Trevor had to fight to get his salary as the sound engineer, which of course they were reluctant to pay. Luckily though, we got the money and it kept us afloat. I just couldn't believe that I could do a sell-out tour and not make any money. Trevor and I very quickly became convinced that profits had been blown on champagne that we had not been drinking.

Fortunately, Derek and A&M agreed to bail me out by paying Andrew Miller back, but the deal involved signing a new recording contract with A&M for another eight albums, which I had no option but to do. This proved to be one of the worst times of my new solo career. I'd struggled to make a success of my singing, only to get knocked back down. Little did I know, but I was to pay dearly in years to come for agreeing to this new contract.

While life seemed pretty bleak on the money front, musically things were going quite well. My cover of the Peter Allen and Carole Bayer Sager song 'Don't Cry Out Loud' did well in the charts, getting to number 12 at the end of 1978.

In the spring of 1979 I was due to go to LA to record my fourth album *Live and Learn*, but not long before I was supposed to leave I started to feel peculiar; I seemed to be on some kind of big, chemical-free high. Wondering what was wrong, I went to see Dr Lefever, my local doctor in London, and he told me I was pregnant. Trevor and I couldn't believe it. He very much wanted a family and we'd even talked about adopting if I didn't get pregnant. Being seven years older than Trevor, in my thirties, I had started to think I'd left it too late and that I would never have children so I was delighted with the news, as was Trevor.

We decided to keep it a secret for a while so we only told Trevor's parents. Based on the reaction I'd had when I told my parents we were getting married, we didn't bother telling mine. I knew they would be more interested in what number my record was in the charts. I eventually plucked up the courage to tell Derek Green halfway through recording the album in LA. He had asked Trevor and me to dinner while he was over doing some business and checking out my new tracks.

I said, 'Derek, I've got some news for you, I'm going to have a baby.'

Well, I've never ever seen such a look of complete and utter horror and disappointment on anybody's face in all my life. I think he thought I'd thrown in the towel and that it was the end of my career. When I came to tell Alan I got a very similar reaction. He left me with the impression that I could kiss my career goodbye.

Breaking the baby news to Derek only seemed to make my LA recording experience worse. Even though A&M had gone back to Jerry Leiber and Mike Stoller in an effort to try to recreate some of the *Two Days Away* magic, things didn't feel right with the session musicians we had working with us.

When we first came to record I was excited because we had a lot of black session musicians who I thought would be fantastic. Sadly they didn't ever throw themselves into the music and it seemed to me that they were just going through the motions. I was left feeling disappointed. Experiences like this help explain why I care so strongly about team spirit in my band today. Since about 2005 I've been working with a brilliant group of musicians who give their all every time we do a gig.

If it hadn't been for Jean Roussel we may not have achieved anything decent on *Live and Learn* at all. There were some great tracks like 'He Could Have Been An Army', which I tend to start my shows off with today, and 'Not Enough Loving Left' and 'Who's Making Love', but everything else seemed pretty flat to me in terms of production.

Despite the disappointment of the recording experience I had a good time in LA. One day in particular stands out though. I was in the green room at the studio when this rather round woman looked over at me. She said, 'Elkie, you don't recognise me, do you? It's Sharon Levy, the little girl that you took to Battersea funfair.'

Well I have to say, I didn't recognise her. Not only was she grown up – nearly twenty years had gone by since the funfair at Battersea – but she'd become a major player in the music business. I couldn't believe she was the same person.

We had a cup of tea together and a good chat about what we'd both been up to. She told me that she was a music manager, which I suppose wasn't surprising as she'd grown up watching her father Don Arden manage so many successful artists. It was good to see her again after all those years. Nowadays, as Sharon Osbourne, I think she looks terrific.

Away from the studio, life was good because Trevor was very often with me as he was still doing the odd bit of work with Andy Williams in Las Vegas and Reno, and with someone else in New York, so he would fly over to see me whenever he could. We had some great fun together and several memorable experiences, which are inevitable if you spend any time with my Trevor.

On one occasion I remember him driving me to the studio in a stunning silver Mustang, which he was particularly pleased to have hired. He was on his way to go hang-gliding, which is his great passion, and he was looking at the map and chatting to me at the same time. This proved to be his undoing because he drove right into the back of a woman who'd stalled at some traffic lights. The woman went mad, and the nightmare was exacerbated by the complications of having a hire car and an English driving licence.

We had a lot of fun the day we went to a famous hang-gliding site at Torrey Pines in San Diego; a place Trevor always reminds me is the oldest hang-gliding site in the world. After Trevor had done his flying thing we went down to the beach. There we were, looking very English – me in my Marks and Spencer's pregnancy bathing suit and Trevor in his trunks – enjoying the California sun, when all of a sudden he turns to me and says, 'Elk, look at that bloke over there with his surfboard, I don't think he's got anything on.'

As the guy came closer we saw that he was indeed stark-bollock naked, although I have to say it wasn't exactly easy to tell. Very soon we noticed several other naked people, which quickly made us realise we'd stumbled on to a nudist beach. Despite being two fairly liberal members of an industry known for its open-mindedness, we were pretty taken aback. But, not to be intimidated by the situation, we went for a swim, which would have been fine except that as we walked in, I got caught by a wave that sent me flying. Fortunately, both bump and I were okay. The nudists obviously didn't put us off because a week or so later we went back again, but being English, we decided not to follow suit, or should that be 'birthday' suit?

After being knocked over by a wave, my next adventure came when we went to Disneyland. Trevor was desperate to go on all these outrageous rides, which were signed 'unsuitable for pregnant women'. Finally, we found one indoor roller coaster that didn't carry any such warning. It was dark with flashing lights and there was only a single safety bar holding us in which was pretty useless because on the first corner I disappeared into the inside of the car. I guess we must have missed the warning sign. I love roller coasters but it's really best not to go on them when you're pregnant.

Having scared myself at Disneyland, I scared loads of people at the studio when I put on the flashy roller-skates that Trevor had bought as a present for his younger brother Robbie. Seeing a heavily pregnant woman roller-skating evidently freaked out everybody and according to Trevor they were speechless as I whizzed off down the road. I had been a pretty good skater as a child in Manchester and felt confident on my wheels despite my bump.

With the exception of the roller-coaster ride, I took good care of myself throughout my pregnancy, doing all the exercises and even remaining vegetarian through the entire term. Trevor and I decided to go vegetarian when we first got together and we carried on with it for about eight years. All in all I had a wonderful pregnancy; my only slight problem was my iron level, which dropped. I got over this by drinking a pint of Guinness every day, although I should add, that my pregnancy black stuff was the only alcohol I did drink. I made sure I stayed well away from the hard stuff, which of course I was quite partial to.

When we came home from America I did a photo session for the album sleeve. This time Alan played it safe. I guess having witnessed my extreme adverse reaction to the last cover he thought it would be best to go for just a close-up shot of my face. Good decision!

Rather unsurprisingly, when the album was released A&M didn't promote it very much, and it only made it to number 34, staying in the charts for six weeks. Neither of the two singles – 'He Could Have Been An Army' and 'Falling Star' – did very well either.

Things started to improve when we decided to let Alec Leslie, who we'd met via Alan Seifert, promote the *Live and Learn* tour. Alec was totally different from Alan and Derek; he was very positive about my pregnancy, which I found refreshing. I coped well with the physical demands of the tour and found a way to make clothes work for me too. I wore lots of tracksuits for rehearsals and some big flouncy frocks for the shows including the one Bruce Oldfield designed for me for the *Lilac Wine* tour. The tour was a great success and Alec proved to me that you could make good money from touring, something Alan, of course, had always told me was virtually impossible.

The returns of this tour enabled us to buy our first house together. I'd been working on several songs for the album with Jean Roussel at his house at 48 Walham Grove in Fulham. I'd taken a shine to the house so when Jean mentioned that he was looking to sell, Trevor and I instantly offered to buy it. It was a fabulous, three-storey place, which he'd bought from Cat Stevens.

We managed to do the deal with Jean without having to sell our flat. Trevor then decided he was going to renovate the place so that it would be perfect for me when I came home with the baby. With a Christmas due date, time was against us if Trevor was to have it finished for baby's arrival. He recruited Huw, his dad and lots of friends to help. Amazingly, for once in our lives, everything went to plan.

I went into Queen Charlotte's Hospital on 20 December 1979 after going to an office party Alan had thrown. I had to go to the party on my own because Trevor was too busy working on the house. He probably wouldn't have gone anyway because, by that time, relations with Alan had become too fractious. The hospital wanted to induce me because the baby hadn't turned due to the damage I'd done to my pelvis falling on the stage at the Marquee club. I was pretty freaked out at the thought of having a breech birth but when they came to check me out they said everything was fine.

That night I had the most dreadful time with what I thought were wind pains that hit me regularly every hour. In fact, I'd started to go into early labour naturally before I was due to be induced the next day. They never tell you what it's really like when you go into labour. I now know that it's like having chronic wind pains because I had them for nearly twenty-six hours.

The birth itself though wasn't too bad, mostly because I had an epidural. The pains I had the night before were far worse. It was a fabulous experience because Trevor was there with me. He had just finished work on the house when he got the call to come to the hospital. He turned up wearing his builder's gear, which Mr Simms, my gynaecologist, thought was hilarious. He seemed to enjoy seeing Trevor get all dressed up in a hospital gown. It wasn't very long after that our son Jermaine Jerome Jordan, or Jay as we came to call him, was born at 6 p.m. on 21 December 1979 just as it started snowing. He was a beautiful little chap, weighing 8 lb exactly.

The next day I had to try to get myself together because Alan, of course, had arranged for a photographer from the

Daily Express to come by. It's not a particularly pleasant experience to be photographed when you've just had a baby and you're not feeling very glamorous, but the picture was on the front page the next day, which was good publicity.

I stayed in hospital for a few more days to recover, which worked out well because it gave Trevor a little more time to get the house ready. It also gave my mum and dad the chance to come down from Manchester to see the baby. The strange thing was I couldn't believe how protective I was of Jay because when my dad tried to rock the little cradle the hospital had supplied, I got all edgy and had to stop him doing it.

Dad, being the good Jew he was, couldn't stop himself from asking the million dollar question when he saw his grandson for the first time.

I remember him looking at me and saying, 'So is he going to have the *brit malah*?' which is the Jewish religious circumcision ceremony.

I snapped back angrily, 'Like father, like son,' and that was the end of that, so to speak.

CHAPTER 15

BABY JAY

With Jay being born so close to Christmas it wasn't long before we were welcoming in a new decade. I have great memories of spending New Year's Eve at our lovely new home, which Trevor had done a fantastic job on, with all the champagne that friends had bought to celebrate Jay's arrival. But being a new mum I didn't have so much as a sip. Instead, I saw the New Year in with a nice glass of milk! Not only were we starting a new decade with a beautiful new son, I had also finally parted company with Alan Seifert, but not without quite a battle.

Even prior to the £48,000 tour debt, I'd known things with Alan weren't quite right. In fact it was Trevor who first realised that my arrangement with Alan was unacceptable. He believed Alan had a conflict of interests because he was not only signed to be my manager for five years, getting 25 per cent gross of everything I did, he was also acting as my lawyer and negotiating contracts on my behalf with the record companies. Clearly we would have been better advised to employ a separate lawyer.

It was while working in this dual capacity that he signed me to A&M Records 'in perpetuity', a couple of words which, at the time, I didn't understand the significance of. The contract was written in such a way that all advances for my albums and all my royalties were payable to Alan's company Music Lore; a contractual detail that definitely wasn't in my best interests.

When Trevor realised this he tried desperately to get

me out of the contract, but it was difficult to talk to Alan about this in a reasonable way. We asked him up to the Hammersmith flat where we confronted him over the way we felt I was being treated. But even the directness of that encounter didn't solve the problem as Alan somehow managed to see things out until the end of the five-year contract, which pretty much coincided with Jay's birth in December 1979. I remember him phoning me and asking what I was going to do.

I told him again I didn't want to continue and after a bit more argy-bargy that required the intervention of my solicitor, he finally decided to let go. I think he realised he didn't have a leg to stand on. The problem finally went away. It was a real shame because he helped to establish me as a solo artist and put me on the road to a successful recording career.

With Alan out of the picture, I was able to concentrate on being a mum. I wasn't scheduled to do a tour for six months and the only gig on the horizon was Knebworth on 21 June 1980. As I'm sure any mum would say, the worst thing about having a new baby is the lack of sleep, and our Jay, bless him, was a bit of a pain at night. He was so bad that sometimes we'd have to put him in the car and take him for a drive to try to get him to go to sleep. This, of course, worked a treat until you stopped and tried to get him back into his cot. I found the first couple of months hard going. As a result, I always say that it's easy to have kids, but it's hard bringing them up.

While I was at Queen Charlotte's Hospital having Jay, I met a great nurse called Diane, who came to do some part-time nanny work for me as I started to put the new show together for Knebworth. Diane proved to be a great help and I asked her if she would consider going on the road with us if we were to make the job full-time. Thankfully she agreed.

The preparations for Knebworth and the forthcoming tour went well, partly because the new house had a studio in the basement (built by its former owner Cat Stevens) and I was able to rehearse at home. Working hard on the show, I quickly got back into shape, both vocally and physically. My figure came back remarkably easily and I was able to wear a skin-tight dress for the show.

I've always thought the reason I returned to my pre-pregnancy size so quickly was the fact that I was in really good shape before I became pregnant. In fact my advice to anyone thinking of trying for a baby is to get yourself four or five pounds under your normal weight beforehand and then it's not so bad when you pile on the pounds.

The Knebworth gig went off amazingly well. The line-up was very strong with Lindisfarne, Mike Oldfield, The Beach Boys, The Blues Band and Santana, but what didn't go so well was the after-show party. Derek Green was upset that I couldn't stay to speak to all the record company people from America. I was still breastfeeding and wanted to get home as fast as possible.

I tried to be polite, saying, 'I'm terribly sorry, I've made plans with my nanny to be back at a certain time so I can feed my baby, and my plans can't be broken. If they're so desperate to see me, they can come back to the house because we're having drinks and nibbles.' I thought it was a very sensible and practical offer, but Derek didn't see it that way and was, once again, seriously frustrated with me.

After Knebworth I got stuck into rehearsing for the tour, and Trevor and I also took the decision to let Alec Leslie take over the management as he'd done such a great job turning my last tour into a financial success.

But before the tour, we started to get itchy feet. The Fulham house was lovely but the trouble with it was its location; it was in the same road as the band's favourite pub, which meant they were always at our house. It was very rare that Trevor and I sat down to dinner on our own, which was bad enough, but I'd also end up having to cook extra food for whoever else was around. With a little baby to look after, I didn't exactly have loads of time to cater for everyone.

I used to say, 'If you want some food, you're going to have to look after the baby.'

The best person at helping with baby Jay was our drummer Stretch. He was brilliant with him. He spent so much time at our house it almost felt as if he'd moved in. Stretch was a protective sort of guy because one night after a gig, a piano tuner we'd hired started moaning that he wasn't being paid enough, and before Trevor or I could do anything about it, Stretch had picked him up and thrown him out of the front door, which probably wouldn't have been too bad if it wasn't for the fact that we were five stone steps up from the pavement.

For a few months this mayhem was fun, but it quickly started to wear a bit thin. I think we'd both reached the point where we needed to be on our own. Strangely, it got to Trevor more than it did me. Trying to get away from the rest of them for a quiet drink he'd go to different pubs in the area but no matter where he went, they'd find him.

In the end he said, 'Elk, if we stay in London any longer I think I'm going to end up going to jail for hitting someone.'

As Trevor had always wanted to live in the West Country we came to the dramatic decision to look for a place there. His passion for hang-gliding was a deciding factor. He was going down every other week to his favourite spot at Woolacombe on the Devon coast so it seemed a logical place to look for a property. I'd been with him on quite a few trips there and had liked the area too.

So after only nine months in the Walham Grove house we decided to sell up, put our stuff into storage and move back into our flat in Hammersmith, and that way we would be ready to go if we found the right place in Devon. We moved back to Hammersmith towards the end of 1980 in time to celebrate Jay's first birthday. Within a week of putting the house on the market we'd sold it to TV presenter Peter Duncan of *Blue Peter* fame. As we had somewhere to live we weren't in a desperate hurry to find a place in Devon, we were more concerned about finding the right house. As a result, we were making trips down to the West Country every weekend looking at houses and indulging in Devonshire cream teas every time we were there; I suppose it would be rude not to, they're so good.

Eventually, we found and fell in love with a house in the middle of nowhere in the Quantock Hills in Somerset. It was absolutely gorgeous and had its own orchards. We decided to put an offer on the property, but we then had to go to America for a couple of weeks. While we were away Trevor rang to ask a question about the property at which point the owner told him he'd sold it. We were totally devastated. But, as is often the case in these situations, while we were angry at being gazumped, it actually did us a favour because very soon after we found another place, which we loved even more. We had just got back to the flat from yet another trip to Devon and were wading through the pile of property details we'd brought back with us when we spotted a house at Woody Bay, near Lynton and Lynmouth. We instantly loved the look of it so Trevor got straight on the phone and made an appointment to see it the next day. After a cup of tea we got back in the car and headed for Devon again. We had booked into The Woody Bay Hotel and the drive there was stunning. After turning off the A39 Lynton road at the old Woody Bay station we drove across a hill looking straight across the Bristol Channel to Wales; an awesome view. We then went down a steep hill to the hotel, which was literally at the top of this tiny road leading down to the house. The whole drive to the house seemed incredible.

Trevor said excitedly, 'This is it, Elk. I don't care what the house is like we've got to have it. This is amazing.'

The next day Trevor was glad he'd traded in his beloved Jensen for a Range Rover because we had to go down a bumpy unmade road and around a hairpin bend to get to the house. When we saw the property we were both surprised at its condition. The house was in desperate need of attention and the grounds were very overgrown too. Trevor, though, was still convinced it was the place for us, but I wasn't quite so sure because I couldn't see the sea, even though I knew it was only a few hundred yards away. Trevor saw its potential straightaway. I liked the location, despite not being able to see the sea, because it was away from everything. As soon as I walked down the road and saw the beach I thought it was perfect.

I can remember thinking, 'Wow, this is great. I can see myself walking down here with Jay.'

'Trees', our home from 1981 to 2002

After the briefest of discussions we both decided we should put in an offer. It was without doubt going to be a big change for us but I thought I could adapt. Bearing in mind what had happened the last time we were both worried but finally we got a call around Christmas time to say the owners had accepted our offer. We were thrilled.

All the legal stuff went through without any issues – surprisingly for us – and our new life in the country finally became a reality. We took possession of 'Trees', as it was called, in the summer of 1981, and the true condition of the house became very apparent. It was in desperate need of a complete makeover. The previous owners had been there for about twelve years and hadn't done anything to the place, but I knew my Trev and his sledgehammer could sort it out.

We had some time off, having toured from March to May, so I went back to London leaving Trevor at the house on his own to do his thing. He worked like a mad man, and in just a month knocked the place into shape for us. Many years later he told me a funny story about that time which involved going for a drink at the Woody Bay Hotel after a hard day working on the house. On this particular night, he accidentally left his favourite multi-coloured coat hanging up in the bar, which normally wouldn't have been too much of a problem, except on this occasion he had £5,000 cash in one of the pockets from tour merchandising money which we were going to use on renovations. He didn't realise what he'd done until the next day at which point he drove straight back up to find it. Despite the coat being ridiculously ostentatious, he found it hanging where he'd left it, with all the money still inside. I guess that's the difference between Devon and London.

When Trevor got the house into a liveable state in the autumn of 1981, I came down with Jay. I can remember wondering why I'd left a lovely warm flat in London to live in the middle of nowhere in a freezing cold house with radiators that were forever breaking down. But as long as I was with Trevor and Jay, nothing else mattered.

Not long after moving in I had to go to London to record some new songs for my album *Pearls,* leaving Trevor and

Jay at the house on their own at a time when North Devon was hit by one of the worst storms ever. More than 500 trees were blown down, like matchsticks. Trevor couldn't get out of the house because the road was covered with fallen trees. I suppose living at a place called Woody Bay in a house called 'Trees', there's always going to be a risk of that kind of thing happening, but it was definitely a shock to a city girl like me. Trevor wasn't too fazed. He's a practical bloke and he simply put his chainsaw to work, eventually managing to clear enough of the road to get supplies.

This was not only a landmark time for the little Jordan family, but an amazing time for me musically because A&M wanted me to make a record featuring some of my one-off singles like 'Lilac Wine' and 'Don't Cry Out Loud' that I'd made in between my albums, together with my hits from *Two Days Away* – 'Pearl's A Singer' and 'Sunshine After The Rain' – and some new songs. Derek knew the album would be a hit if he got Gus Dudgeon – a very successful producer who'd worked a lot with Elton John – to create some new material. Among the new songs we recorded were 'Superstar', 'Warm And Tender Love' and Chris Rea's song 'Fool If You Think It's Over'.

Derek and A&M knew they were on to a winner because they would only have to pay me half royalties under my new contract, which they'd drawn up in order to recoup the £48,000 I now owed them after the financial fiasco of the Andrew Miller tour.

Derek had originally put the idea to Alec who then suggested it to me. Initially, I didn't like it, assuming it was nothing more than a marketing ploy. I was very much into making a new, original album, not one that was made up of old material. However, I quickly recognised its commercial potential. Lots of artists at the time said it was too mainstream and it wasn't a good idea to do an album like that, but of course, most of them went on to do similar things later.

As had been predicted, *Pearls* proved to be my most successful album, selling more than 1.2 million copies and going platinum. It got to number 2 in November 1981 and went on to spend seventy-nine weeks in the charts. At the time it was also the biggest selling album by a British female singer in the history of the UK charts. I think it's probably the only one of my albums that A&M still sell on CD now, which I guess says something too.

In mid-December, not long after the album had reached its high point, we were given a taste of what life in the country can be like when the whole of the UK experienced terrible snowstorms. The effects of the snow were, of course, even more dramatic for us in our isolated North Devon home. Amazingly, Trevor's mum and dad and his younger brother Rob managed somehow to get down to celebrate Jay's second birthday and Christmas with us. Trevor put lights up round the house and the place looked spectacular. After only a few months in the house we discovered that the power was prone to going off in the winter, but that Christmas we were lucky and had a magical time.

Mother Nature had more in store for us in Devon and in the second week of January 1982 we were hit by the worst snowstorms for years. The snow was so heavy we got cut off from the outside world for two weeks. It was so cold we had ice on the inside of the windows. We had no electricity, no heating and no running water, but we did have an open fire with plenty of logs and we brought our mattress downstairs to keep warm at night.

We were well stocked up with food and cooking wasn't a problem because we had a marvellous little Calor gas stove, which we'd bought when we'd been camping with Trevor's mum and dad the previous year. For the first week it was all really rather romantic and we had a lot of fun. By the second week we just got on with it and coped. Having been cut off so severely we made a plan to get ourselves equipped with generators to make sure we would never be in that situation again.

In the midst of this terrible weather, which went on for weeks and weeks, I had 'Fool If You Think It's Over' in the charts. I was very proud of the song because it had been my idea to do a cover of it for the album. Most of the material had been chosen either by Derek Green or Gus Dudgeon. I had insisted that we did 'Fool'. Chris Rea has always been one of my favourite musicians and writers and I thought the song was pure class. Chris also happens to be a great bloke, which I was soon to find out.

Much to my delight the record did well when it was released and got to number 17 in the charts of February 1982, which led to an invitation to appear on *Top Of The Pops*. But, being cut off by the snow, the only way my manager Alec Leslie could get me to London was by helicopter. It was all rather exciting because the helicopter landed on the green at Martinhoe Manor, the house just below ours, with Alec having to show the pilot where to land because it wasn't easy to find.

Just a few hours later I was doing my bit in the studio in front of the dancing audience. When we'd finished recording I went backstage where this polite guy came up to me and asked me for my autograph. It took me a couple of seconds, but then I realised who it was.

I said cheekily, 'You've got to be Chris, you bugger.'

I'd not met him before so I suppose I was an easy target for a wind-up. We got on really well and we always laugh about that every time we see each other. But I never like to be caught out like that, so I was determined to get my own back. The perfect opportunity arose when we were both performing at a tribute gig to Leiber and Stoller at the Hammersmith Apollo in June 2001. I instructed Trevor to tell Chris that I was furious with him because he snubbed me at a showbiz bash a while ago.

Chris took the bait perfectly and came to apologise to me after the gig. I kept the tease going for a while until he started to look a bit worried at which point I gave him one of my big hugs and told him it was all a joke. We all had a big laugh.

CHAPTER 16

WOODY BAY

The journey home from *Top of the Pops* in the snow was equally eventful. The excitement of the helicopter had been swapped for a limo, which would have been fine had it not been for the treacherous conditions. My driver Dave Cole, who became a good friend, did an incredible job just to get me to the Woody Bay Hotel, but that was as far as his limo was ever going to go. The last mile down the hill to our house was definitely out of the question.

I'd phoned ahead and Trevor had made arrangements with our new friends Janet Corlet and her partner Brian Windsor, who lived a few hundred yards down the road from us at Martinhoe Manor. Janet kindly looked after Jay while Brian got out his classic grey Massey Ferguson tractor, which conveniently had a bucket on the back, and chugged up the hill through the snow with Trevor to collect me. Of course, they arrived early so they managed to squeeze in a couple of drinks at the hotel while they were waiting. When I turned up I was swiftly transferred from the limo to the tractor's bucket and taken back down the hill. It must have been a funny sight because there I was, supposedly a big star, stood on the back of a tractor with Trevor and all my cases. It didn't bother me at all: in fact I thought it was great fun.

Something that did bother me, however, was not seeing so much as a penny in royalties from my *Pearls* album because my cut of the profits was going straight to A&M to pay off my £48,000 debt. But while I wasn't benefiting financially from my record sales, the album did a great job in raising my profile and getting bums on seats on my tours, which with Alec in charge, became very profitable.

A&M realised they had struck on a fantastic formula and were keen for me to do another similar album. In early 1982 I was back in the studio with Gus Dudgeon recording *Pearls II*. This time we had to find new material that would suit me. I found 'Gasoline Alley', 'Going Back' and 'Nights In White Satin', songs that have become very much associated with me.

Funnily enough, 'Gasoline Alley' was released as a single after the album came out, which was quite the opposite of *Pearls* where they mixed my hits with some one-off singles and a few new songs. If I'm honest though, I'm not that keen on any of the tracks on *Pearls II*, apart from the three big songs of course, but I was wearing my business hat and knew they were all good for me commercially. It wasn't Elkie Brooks at her best, but the combination of me, good songs and with Gus Dudgeon producing meant A&M were on to another winner. All in all it was a good business decision.

Pearls II made it into the charts in mid-November 1982 and stayed there for twenty-five weeks, reaching number 5. None of the songs did that well when they were released as singles, not even 'Nights In White Satin' which was the best of the bunch, getting to number 33. Then again why would anyone buy it, because it was released as a single some time after the album came out?

To celebrate the albums having sold more than a million copies A&M threw a bash for me and invited Michael Parkinson to be the guest of honour. That was a nice touch because I'd known Michael since the Whisky A Go-Go days in Manchester and I'd sung on his chat show twice. On this occasion, however, I barely saw him to speak to, he just said a brief hello and then disappeared so I thought maybe I'd done something to offend him. The next time I saw him was during a promotional tour in Australia when Jay was a little boy and we were staying at the same hotel. He was very friendly so obviously I hadn't offended him. Bumping into Michael was the best thing about Australia because they were really nasty to me on the radio and in the press, treating me like a bimbo. I thought the men were very chauvinistic and I swore I would never do another tour there unless I was offered a serious amount of money.

Away from the excitement of having another hit album, we were getting used to living in our countryside hideaway in Devon. I was very slowly coming to terms with life away from London as well as being a mum, which was certainly not without its trials. There was one night in particular that scared me half to death. Trevor was down at the Hunter's Inn having a drink when Jay, who was about four at the time, started hallucinating. He had a terribly high temperature and an awful sore throat. I managed to get his temperature down overnight and took him to see Dr John Frankish in Lynton the next day. He diagnosed tonsillitis and said that it was quite normal for children to hallucinate when they get high temperatures. Poor Jay suffered so badly that he had to have his tonsils out when he was about eight. Trevor went down to Exeter with him and slept in his hospital room for two days. He suffered lots of bouts of hallucinations right up until he was about fourteen when he had an awful attack of mumps. His heart was thumping so fast that we thought he was going to have a heart attack. We succeeded in calming him down but at one point Trevor and I thought we'd lost him.

Our friendship with our neighbours Janet and Brian was one of the main reasons we started to feel more at home in Woody Bay. We met them regularly and this would often involve a drink up at the hotel, which was always fun, particularly because of our chosen mode of transport. While it wasn't Brian's old tractor, it was an equally precarious classic vehicle; one which had made something of a sudden appearance on the scene. One day, after working in London, Trevor bought a black Bentley, a T-series, which meant nothing to me. I tended to think of it as more of an old dog than a classic but it caught his eye and he had to have it. He bought it there and then. He said he thought it would be nice for us to go out and about in it, occasionally. Well, this 'occasionally' turned out just to be our trips up to the Woody Bay Hotel with Janet and Brian.

We'd drive 500 yards down to the manor to collect Janet and Brian then back up past our house to the hotel, and that was as far as the Bentley would ever go. It was such a short distance that the temperature gauge never moved. After lovingly caring for it for about two years, a process that involved Trevor polishing it whenever he could, we sold it to an undertaker in Braunton who promptly drove it into a wall. When he heard the news, poor Trevor was devastated.

Janet and Brian were responsible for another major event in our lives when they put Martinhoe Manor up for sale. A year or so after moving into 'Trees' we sold the Hammersmith flat for a reasonable price as the cost of keeping two places was getting too much. That feeling didn't last too long because before long we'd agreed to buy the manor. As a result Trevor and I became Lord and Lady Martinhoe. Never mind the hit records, now I thought I'd really made it!

The place, which was very run down and needed a fortune spending on it, consisted of twelve self-catering flats in 28 acres of land with its own beach. The manor also had the only real open space in the whole of Woody Bay that made it feel very special. This was our first experience of a self-catering business and, I might add, our last. All we had to do was run it, but because we were always busy on tour it was difficult to do two things at once. To make things easier we employed a manager and his wife to look after the manor itself and Trevor took charge of the financial side, doing all the books.

The business did well but we had to take out a second mortgage to buy it, which meant every penny we were earning on the road went towards paying it back. After two years, it became too much of a strain on our already busy lives so when a couple who came down every year – a merchant banker and his wife – expressed an interest in buying it we took them up on the offer.

I can't remember what we bought it for but we put another half on it again when we sold so we came out of the experience with a decent profit. Saying that, we also spent a lot of money on it including putting in a lake, which Trevor did in one weekend, much to the surprise of our neighbours, Dave Waller and his wife. They'd gone away for the weekend and come home to find they were looking down on a lake. Trevor doesn't do anything by halves!

One of my fondest memories of the manor was celebrating Christmas there with both the Bookbinders and the Jordans. As we had so much accommodation we were able to get all the families together. We had both sets of parents, my brothers, Auntie Sylvia, Trevor's aunt and uncle and his brother Robbie to name just a few. In total there were seventeen of us – it was a great buzz. Inevitably it was going to be a challenge cooking for so many at Christmas, but I never would've been able to imagine what actually happened.

Trying to be the perfect hostess I wanted to make sure there was plenty of food for everyone so I bought and cooked three turkeys. Everything went according to plan until we took the turkeys out of the oven to rest before carving. I then popped out to socialise with the family for a moment only to return to find Bumper, our young Alsatian, happily feasting on one of the turkeys. I was horrified. After calling Trevor into the kitchen we both saw the funny side and quickly forgave him, and went about carving the other two birds. Nobody went hungry and Bumper and the other dogs had a pretty good time eating turkey leftovers.

The manor had a marvellous bar area that we decided to turn into a rehearsal space for my *Minutes* album. I wanted it to be a contemporary record, my first since *Live and Learn,* which was recorded in 1979. Having had such success with the *Pearls* formula A&M weren't very keen, but let us go ahead anyway.

We got 10cc keyboardist Duncan Mackay to come down and write some songs with me. Duncan and I spent hours together singing and playing. After a long day writing we all used to have a drink at the bar in the manor. One evening I'd gone back home to bed leaving Trevor and Duncan still drinking and chatting. An hour or two later at about 2 a.m, Trevor decided to call it a night and said to Duncan that he was welcome to stay on and have a few more if he wanted. Before he went home, however, he left him with a very important piece of advice about getting back to the house which poor Duncan didn't take on board.

Trevor told him to make sure he followed the track up and not be tempted to go straight towards the lights of the house. I don't think he explained the consequences of going towards the lights, which might have been a good idea, seeing what happened to poor Duncan. Thinking nothing more of it, Trevor walked back up to the house and came up to bed. About an hour or so later we were both woken up by this horrendous noise outside. Trevor got up, put on his dressing gown and went downstairs to investigate, where he found Duncan standing on the other side of our fence freaking out, dripping in what Trevor very quickly realised was poo. Duncan had ignored Trevor's advice and headed straight up from the manor towards the lights and had fallen into our cesspit. If that wasn't bad enough, he was also wearing a brand new leather jacket. He looked at Trevor and asked him to help him over the fence.

Understandably Trevor said, 'No way. You'll have to get over the fence on your own.'

After somehow negotiating the fence, Duncan stood there covered in stinking slime, generally looking very sorry for himself. Trevor told him to calm down, go up to his room, take off his clothes, have a shower and go to bed. Duncan did what he was told, or at least we thought he had until Trevor went to see if he was all right in the morning with a cup of tea. He opened the door to see, to his horror and astonishment, Duncan lying on the bed, fully clothed.

After that mess, Duncan and I and Zal Cleminson the brilliant guitar player who was a founder member of The Sensational Alex Harvey Band in the 1970s, did manage to write some songs which we all thought were pretty damn good. But when Gus Dudgeon came down and listened to them he thought they weren't up to scratch.

Cartoon of Duncan Mackay

Gus said to me, 'If you want to do another album with me you'll have to go with my choice of songs because I don't want to go with these.'

On hearing this, Derek, who wasn't keen on the contemporary route, lost heart altogether and decided that this was going to be a low-budget album. As a result they hired a young producer, Jimmy Douglass, who is now a very big rap producer but was not a good choice for my type of music and the album we were hoping to produce. He came down on the last two days of rehearsal and we all very quickly got the feeling that he wasn't quite as good as he was cracked up to be.

Duncan Mackay's spoof music for Jimmy Douglass

Luckily, we were surrounded by quality musicians. As well as Duncan and Zal, we had John Giblin, the session bassist who had worked with Peter Gabriel and Kate Bush before going on to join Simple Minds, and Cliff Richard's drummer Graham Jarvis, who is sadly no longer with us. Graham was a fantastic drummer but he had a terrible drink problem and would have a pint of vodka for breakfast.

With musicians of this calibre working alongside a

producer like Jimmy, I suppose it was inevitable that we were going to have some fun and games. Duncan Mackay didn't let us down. He decided to catch Jimmy out by playing a trick on him which involved writing out a nonsensical, spoof piece of music and leaving it on the piano. Jimmy, of course, fell for it hook, line and sinker.

He came over to Duncan and studied the music for a moment and said to everyone, 'You know when you get to this bar here you've really got to lift it.'

With that Duncan fell off his stool in hysterics, while the rest of the band, who were in on the joke, burst out laughing. Nobody was taking this guy seriously.

Despite all this I thought the album turned out rather well. In the end the music did the talking, together with a little help from John Etchells, our excellent sound engineer.

My fears about *Minutes* being viewed as a minor album were confirmed when a little birdie in the art department at A&M told me they'd overheard the art director Mike Ross say that we weren't going to have any great photographers because it was a low-budget album. I hit the roof – not that it made any difference – because we'd put so much effort in writing and rehearsal. Looking at the album cover you can tell they didn't spend much money on it. I think the best you could say was that we ended up with an atmospheric cover shot: a picture of me standing on top of a rock at Heddon's Mouth, which is a beautiful spot near Hunter's Inn, not far from our house in Woody Bay.

Although the album was destined not to do that well it appealed to my Vinegar Joe fans and hung around in the charts for seven weeks in the summer of 1984, and made it to number 35. A&M put two singles out – 'Minutes' and 'Driftin'' – but without any real promotion neither charted.

Just before I headed out to promote the album on a fifty-show tour from September through to the middle of November, Derek Green gave me the bad news that he was leaving A&M to set up his own company called China Records. His final throw of the dice was to get me to make a safe and more commercial, live orchestra album with executive producer Bill Martin.

While it was, yet again, a low-budget record, it had a great feel to it. A super guy called Andrew Pryce Jackman, who sadly passed away in 2003, was the arranger and our friends from the Hammersmith flat Nigel and Chris Warren-Green were in the orchestra. I had a right laugh with them as we did our live recordings of an assortment of classic popular songs, most of which had been used in old films. I think Andrew was quite surprised and impressed that I was able to cope with the live situation and be so on it. There were very few overdubs, which I was very chuffed about. The whole thing suited me down to the ground because that's what I'd grown up doing singing with Eric Delaney and Humph.

By the end of the *Minutes* tour *Screen Gems* was ready to come out. This also coincided with Derek leaving A&M. Before he left he did a deal with EMI to release *Screen Gems* together and it became the first album to be produced on CD in the UK. Strangely, it also went to number 35 but was in the charts for a few weeks more than *Minutes*. Apparently, the original CD version is now a bit of a collector's item on eBay selling for up to £50 a time.

Without Derek Green, Trevor and I were very concerned that my career would suffer, particularly because of an incident that had occurred a little while earlier. Trevor had spoken to Derek privately about the possibility of getting my version of 'Don't Cry Out Loud' released in America, as it had already been a hit there for Melissa Manchester in 1978. He thought it was a good idea and said he would arrange a meeting for Trevor with Jerry Moss, the 'M' in A&M Records. Trevor went to see him in his hotel in London and talked to him while he was packing his suitcase to fly home.

When Trevor asked why A&M weren't promoting me in America, Jerry promptly replied, 'Trevor, there's no point because we've got thousands of Elkie Brookses in America.'

That just floored Trevor, which I have to say, is pretty hard to do.

With that Jerry curtly added, 'Are we done?'

Trevor answered, 'Yeah, I think we are.'

When Trevor told me what had happened, I wasn't all that surprised. After all, how can you have a record company called A&M and you've never met the 'A', and only barely spoken to the 'M'. Afterwards Trevor went to see Derek Green to tell him what had gone on and he said he'd had the same problems with the Americans for years, which made me realise that it wasn't as if Derek hadn't been trying to promote me in the US, he just couldn't get them motivated to do it.

With Derek off the scene we arranged for his successor – Brian Shepherd – and a colleague to come down to Devon in the spring of 1985 to talk about my next project. They were very vague and didn't seem to have the same enthusiasm for me that Derek Green had had. We had a fairly civil meeting but when we didn't hear from them for months after, it became clear that they didn't have any real interest in me as an artist and that my future as a recording artist didn't lie with A&M. Fortunately for me, Trevor was a step ahead of the game, and something truly amazing was just around the corner.

CHAPTER 17

JOEY

A year or so before this crossroads in my A&M recording career, we had been looking to hire an accountant and a friend had introduced us to Richard Cohen, who worked for an accountancy firm with a good reputation in the West End of London. When we met Richard we thought he was a fun, genuine sort of bloke so we decided to employ him. And it was through him that we were introduced to Mike Heap of Legend Records who put an offer on the table that we just had to go for.

We both got a great vibe from Mike and felt that he was being totally honest and transparent with us, a refreshing change from the murky business we had been experiencing. I would go as far as to say he has been the straightest person – outside of my family – I've ever worked with in the business.

Trevor and I both felt at ease with Mike and knew that he would do what he promised and that he was more than capable of getting the job done. Unfortunately for us, and Mike, the two guys who owned Legend Records were nowhere near as straightforward.

But this aside, Mike assured us that he was in charge of the music so we decided to go with the flow. Once we were committed to the project with Legend we had the smaller matter of my A&M contract to sort out. Knowing that I hadn't quite fulfilled the eight-album deal that had been agreed when they bailed me out of the £48,000 loss from the Andrew Miller tour, I wasn't sure how they would take it, despite the apparent lack of interest from MD Brian Shepherd.

When the time was right and everything was lined up with Legend, I went to the A&M offices in London to see Brian and he simply released me from my contract. I'm guessing the debt from the bail out couldn't have been big enough to warrant keeping me in the fold, but I'm pretty convinced I must have still owed them something at this point, I just didn't know how much. More importantly, it was obvious that Brian wanted to get rid of me because he didn't think I was capable of bringing in the money anymore. I think at the time he released a lot of other artists that he considered were dead wood. The downside of this was that I had to sign a release form which drastically limited the amount of royalties I would get from A&M in the future: something that still hurts today as they own all my early albums.

Having escaped the clutches of A&M we became fully focused on making a great new contemporary album. As part of this process Mike told us to go away and write and record the songs we wanted for the album with one stipulation – he wanted me to meet a song-writing contact of his.

He said, 'Elkie, you need to go and see Russ Ballard. He's a very successful songwriter and musician. I think you'll get on well together and be good for each other.'

We went with Mike to meet Russ, who of course wrote 'Since You've Been Gone' for Rainbow and Hot Chocolate's 'So You Win Again'. After all the initial chitchat was out of the way he told us he had three songs that he wanted to put forward for the album. He sang them to us at the piano. Trevor and I didn't say a word to one another while Russ was playing, but we both instinctively knew that the other wasn't very keen on any of the songs, they just weren't anything special.

Trying to fill the awkward gap after hearing the songs and

not having anything great to say Trevor said, 'What else are you working on, Russ?'

With that Russ said, 'I've been writing this song for Kim Wilde,' which he proceeded to play to us.

As soon as he had finished singing Trevor changed his tune completely, saying excitedly, 'That's it!'

Mike Heap, just as enthusiastic, agreed.

But Russ wasn't quite so sure as he protested, 'But I've written this for Kim Wilde.'

Trevor replied quickly, 'No you haven't. You've written it for Elkie Brooks.'

And that's how 'No More The Fool' came to be my song.

I wasn't anywhere near as blown away by the song as Trevor and Mike were. Yes, I thought it was a good song but for some reason I didn't feel as strongly as they did. Trevor always says that I never jump up and down about a new song, but I guess that's just me. I think the acid test of a song is always if you can sit and sing it yourself with only piano accompaniment, and it sounds great. Then you know that with everything else added in the mixing, it will sound amazing. 'No More The Fool' passed that test on both counts.

I hadn't experienced that level of enthusiasm from a record company since the early Derek Green days. I felt that Mike was going to put his heart and soul into this project and, having been the victim of many a lacklustre record boss, I was thrilled to bits.

I knew we had a big new song on our hands and so we got stuck into choosing the rest of the tracks for the album. We quickly picked two other strong songs – Alice Cooper's 'Only Women Bleed' and Bob Seger's 'We've Got Tonight', both of which I still perform regularly in my set. Russ Ballard provided 'All Or Nothing' and 'Don't Want To Cry No More'. I wrote two new songs for the album – one with Trevor called 'Blue Jay' which was about our son Jay and another called 'Hiding Inside Yourself'. The other two tracks were 'Hold The Dream' – the theme tune to the TV mini-series of the same name starring Deborah Kerr and Jenny Seagrove, which I believe was based on a Barbara Taylor-Bradford book – and another song called 'No Secrets (Call Of The Wild)' which we had to include for political reasons.

The making of the album also proved to be a major change from what I'd known in the past because, instead of a big studio in London, New York or LA, we downsized and recorded at our country house hideaway in North Devon. In fact, the whole of the *No More The Fool* album was recorded in our front room at 'Trees', except for the title track, which we recorded at Russ Ballard's house. And I have to mention that all the tracks were recorded on Trevor's famous Mavis quad board, which he'd built for Pink Floyd.

On this album we created a great level of enthusiasm and commitment from everyone involved, as we had when we were recording *Two Days Away* and 'Pearl's A Singer' in 1977. Mike Heap generated a huge excitement for the project and we had once again put together a strong line-up of musicians.

Trevor managed to persuade Duncan Mackay to come back down to play keyboards despite his terrible cesspit experience. I suppose he felt a lot safer knowing we'd sold the manor and he wouldn't have to do that treacherous walk again. We also had Zal Cleminson on guitar again alongside a new guy called Gary Hutchins and Mike Richardson, a fantastic new drummer who has been working with me ever since.

This was my first album that Trevor partly engineered and produced. He did four of the tracks; Russ produced another four, and Gary Bell and Julia Downes one each. The funniest thing about making this album in May and June 1986 was that I was pregnant and I hadn't told Legend. After all the problems I'd had the first time around with Derek Green and Alan Seifert, I decided not to tell Mike Heap for fear that he would react in the same way.

I'd always wanted to have another child but leading such a hectic life, and having Jay on the road with us, we'd never found the right time. After Jay I needed the chance to get back on my feet again. I'd also heard that children could get pretty jealous if the gap between them was too close. I used that as something of an excuse not to have another one. We finally decided to take the plunge when Jay, who was about six, said he'd like a little brother or sister.

Trying for a baby at forty, I thought I should go to see my gynaecologist in London, who promptly told me that I'd be very lucky to get pregnant at my age. I came home thinking I would never be able to get pregnant again but with a bit of determined effort, I was able to phone the gynaecologist a month or so later and tell him that he had been wrong. Trevor and I like a challenge!

My pregnancy was fine, just as it had been with Jay, and I didn't start to show for ages, which meant Mike Heap didn't have the slightest suspicion that I was expecting. I was due in December, yet again, which meant that there was going to be a clash with my big promotion tour, which was scheduled for the end of the year. This left me with no choice but to ask Mike if we could start earlier, perhaps in October. When I plucked up the courage to do so, he naturally asked me why and I declared, 'It would be a bit too difficult because I'm going to have a baby in December.' Despite the surprise and the logistical problems it no doubt caused, he was very understanding.

The pre-release promotion went extremely well. Mike definitely lived up to his promise to promote the album. They really went to town and even put ads in tube stations and on buses. The single of 'No More The Fool' was released in November and it sold so well over Christmas and into

January that it climbed to number 5 and stayed there for a fortnight.

With the birth of Joseph Jacob Jordan on 31 December 1986, weighing 7lb 7oz, I was almost too busy to fully appreciate that I was having the biggest hit of my career. 'Pearl's A Singer' – my best up until that point – had only got as high as number 8 in 1977.

My damaged pelvis from the fall at the Marquee and the Roundhouse in Camden all those years ago resulted in having another breech birth. From the X-rays from my last pregnancy, my gynaecologist at North Devon District Hospital – Mr McGarry – advised me that it was fine to have a natural birth. I was due on 1 January but he asked me to go in on 30 December and be induced on the following morning – he didn't want to work on New Year's Day. Everything went pretty much according to plan except the anaesthetist put the epidural in the wrong place. I was like a beached whale and just couldn't help myself. My legs were like jelly and I had real trouble pushing. They eventually found someone else to put it in the right place and I managed to get the job done. The labour was probably far shorter than I'd had with Jay but boy, did it feel longer.

Despite that little hiccup I came through the birth very well and so did Joey, apart from his bottom that is, which Trevor said looked like a dartboard from all the monitors they'd attached to it. It was just as well I felt okay because a week later I was doing *Top Of The Pops* and presenter Mike Smith introduced me announcing that the song could be number 1 next week. I was so busy that I didn't have the time to enjoy either the chart success or Joey's birth. It was much the same with Jay: I've always been doing two or three things at the same time which makes it very hard to balance your career and your family life.

A week or so after *Top Of The Pops* I was booked to do a promotion tour in Germany as the *No More The Fool* album had also been released in December and Legend were keen to push it far and wide. I wasn't complaining, but taking a very young baby on the road definitely wasn't straightforward. A conversation I had with a lady I knew at the dairy in Lynton, however, led me to a young trained nanny called Vicki Irlam. Vicki was great and was brave enough – or should I say crazy enough – to come on the road with Eddie Mcgillvray, my hairdresser, and me. I'd met Eddie in 1977 during my time with Alan Seifert. Alan had insisted I get somebody in to do my clothes, hair and make-up and Eddie was the person I'd hired. He was so good I worked with him for a long time.

On this tour, Eddie had to be far more than my hair and make-up specialist, he had to be tour manager too, which he did very well indeed. This was also the first tour I'd done for many years which hadn't been overseen by Alec Leslie. Alec had kindly stepped aside as Mike Heap didn't see him as being part of the new picture. He had done a very good job for me but latterly we weren't making the money we had done before, so I felt we'd probably gone as far as we could with each other. The split was amicable and many years later I did another tour with him.

The funniest thing about this tour was the look on Mike Heap's face at the airport when he saw Vicki, Eddie and me standing there with a crying baby, it was a real picture. After a brief 'hello' and 'how are you' he quickly got as far away as possible from us on the plane. Can't say I blamed him!

The tour went smoothly considering the inevitable stress of having a tiny baby on the road, and all the promotion paid off because the album made it to number 5 and hung around in the charts for nearly six months. I wasn't surprised it had done so well because sometimes you just know that a project is going to succeed, no matter what happens. I had the same sort of feeling I'd had with *Two Days Away*.

And better still, there was a lovely little irony too. On the back of the record's success A&M decided to put out two 'best of' albums in the same year to capitalise on my popularity. I can't imagine Brian Shepherd doing that, realising how he felt about me, but I guess he was a businessman and it was a chance to make money.

These compilation albums obviously sold very well because not long after I received my first ever royalties cheque from A&M for £16,000. The £48,000 debt must have finally been paid off and after all this time I was due some money. Sadly, this was at a much-reduced level because of the agreement I'd signed to be released from A&M to join Legend, but I wasn't exactly complaining.

For once in my life I thought things were at last moving in my favour. I should have realised that the music industry is never that straightforward.

CHAPTER 18

WOODY BAY STUDIOS

With a number 5 single and album to my name, as well as a beautiful new baby boy, everything was fantastic until we started working on the next Legend album. The contract we'd drawn up with Mike Heap gave me the option for another album, which we were naturally keen to do with so much recent success. Mike wanted us to do the same sort of thing but it quickly became apparent that, despite the verbal enthusiasm, there wasn't going to be the same level of financial backing for this project. This troubled us, knowing how much money *No More The Fool* must have been making for them, some of which we thought ought to have been ploughed back into my next album.

This time we didn't have the support of Russ Ballard and the other great writers, which, of course, had been such an important factor in my success. Deep down Trevor and I knew there was something wrong with this picture but we just went with it as you sometimes do when you're so close to a project. As time went by though it became apparent to us that they were just throwing mud at the wall to see if it stuck, and there really wasn't the same attention to detail that we'd had the first time round. Although we never felt Legend were ever fully behind this album – *Bookbinder's Kid*, a little reminder of Elaine Bookbinder who went on to become Elkie Brooks – we put our hearts and souls into making the best record we possibly could.

We chose some good songs to cover including Led Zeppelin's 'Stairway to Heaven' and a favourite of mine 'What's The

Matter Baby', which was a hit for the American soul singer Timi Yuro in the 1960s. I'd always been a fan of Timi's so it was a real treat when she phoned me from America to say that someone had given her a copy of *Bookbinder's Kid* and that she thought it was the best version of 'What's The Matter Baby' she'd heard anyone else do.

'Elkie, that's great, so good,' she said in a husky voice affected by the throat cancer she was suffering from.

I felt truly honoured because I absolutely adored the woman. Just like me she had been very influenced by black music but she didn't try to copy the black sound, which I always thought was an awful thing to do. It's fine to be inspired by something but I think you should keep your natural sound, and that's what Timi did, and I've always tried to do that myself. I hated that vogue, which was pretty common among a lot of back-up singers, of trying to sound like black singers. In fact, Timi, Sophie Tucker (one of the big red-hot mamas with a fabulous singing voice) and Anne Shelton, a dance band singer of the 1950s, were some of the few white singers that I admired.

Trevor and I also wrote a couple of songs together on *Bookbinder's Kid*, which we enjoyed. There was 'Sail On', which I always liked, and 'Keep It A Secret' which is the first song that we actually sat down and made a point of writing together; 'Blue Jay' on *No More The Fool* was probably the first one we wrote together, but that happened much more by accident than 'Keep It A Secret'.

Trevor had been in the studio one day and picked up on this rhythm and thought there could be a song there and asked me to put some words to it. He always says that I don't take him seriously when he has an idea for a song because he's a sound engineer and not a musician. I have to say, for the record, that that's not the case at all, Trev. Anyway I started writing some lyrics to this rhythm he'd found and we ended up with 'Keep It A Secret'.

Having recorded *No More The Fool* in our front room, Trevor decided to create a more professional set-up and built a studio in what used to be a logging shed at the end of our drive. It was only small but it did the job really nicely. This made it easy for us to record when it best suited us, which was particularly important with two young children to think about. It also led to us giving three North Devon musicians a chance to record with me. All three were really quite talented but sadly we had a falling out over a private function that we were booked to play in San Francisco. It was a great shame because none of them went on to do anything with music and they were all pretty good musicians.

When *Bookbinder's Kid* was released in 1988 we were pleased with it but we also knew that it wasn't up to the same standard as *No More The Fool*. I put this down to the lack of support from Legend. We eventually talked to Mike Heap about it and he confessed that Legend weren't really interested in the project and therefore the album wasn't going to be promoted. Not the kind of news that any artist ever wants to hear and sadly, I've heard it all too often.

If this wasn't bad enough, I didn't get any of the profits from the success of *No More The Fool*. We were told that all the money they'd made, which was a considerable amount, had been used to sign other artists instead of some of it being put back into my second album.

It turned out that Legend had been very clever. When orders for the album came in, they arranged to have them shipped from Germany rather than from the UK, which meant they wouldn't show up as a return against the £132,000 cost of making the album. They also had a bank in Panama, something we only found out about when we were visited by a team from Customs & Excise who were investigating them on another matter.

The result of all this clever manoeuvring was the debt of £132,000 never went away because the sales of the album didn't ever come into England: the profits were always sent to Germany and then out to Panama. In fact, I think there are still unanswered questions about this today, especially when you look at how many albums were sold in comparison to the £132,000 production cost. This must have been paid back umpteen times over but because there are no records, it still looks like it hasn't been settled. And this, of course, is why the debt remained the same no matter how many albums were sold.

To cap it all, Mike Heap also happened to mention one day that Legend had sold *No More The Fool* to Polydor for £500,000, giving them the rights to distribute it in Europe. And, because of the so-called debt, I wasn't entitled to any of the profits that came in.

We made our own investigations through Steve 'Jumbo' Richards, who was my driver at the time. He went through all the books and found that they'd been charging me twice, or sometimes more, for all my hotel stays during the promotion of the album. This was just another way of ensuring that I would never get out of debt with them; they just kept adding extras on to the cost of the album. I'm sure this isn't that unusual in the music business – even today – but as far as I'm concerned it should be stopped because it's totally wrong.

We thought about trying to sort out the mess with different lawyers but eventually came to the conclusion that we'd be wasting our money – money that we couldn't afford to lose – only to reach the same outcome.

The contract with Legend had an option for a third album but we obviously didn't want to take them up on it so we let the deal fizzle out. Until this very day I'm extremely sad that it ended the way it did, particularly our relationship with Mike Heap, but I can't say that any of it was of my doing, or his for that matter, we were just innocent parties. It's called the music industry and that was the business end of it, which I've always hated and I still do to this day.

With the highs, and now the lows, of working with Legend Records behind us we tried to move on with our lives. I'd finally adjusted to living in Devon. Trevor was convinced I wasn't happy living there from day one, which I can now say, having lived here for more than thirty years, was true. I think it took me a good five years to settle in and accept that I wasn't in London but in the middle of nowhere. After Trevor had done a few things to the house I suppose I started to come round to thinking that Devon wasn't too bad after all.

By 'doing a few things to the house' I really mean extending everything. Having been living in the Lynton area for six years, we'd made quite a few good friends, many of whom we got in to help with the building work. There was Kelvyn Dyer, Mickey Bell and Mark 'Billings' Cook, who are all probably best described here as 'characters'. They used to have a right laugh with Trevor, always winding each other up and trying to catch one another out.

Despite all the messing around the house got bigger and better. The kitchen, which Trevor had tackled first when we moved in, was improved yet again and the bedrooms were enlarged. When he wasn't working on the house with his friends, Trevor would be over at Woolacombe flying, and it was through a hang-gliding friend of his, Mick Stainer, that he got introduced to yet another leisure pursuit – jet skiing – and it wasn't long before I was doing it too.

Trevor and I, and his younger brother Robbie, all got into it. Kitted out with wetsuits, we spent many a happy hour at Lynmouth zipping around, jumping over waves. It was great fun. It took me a little longer than Trevor and Robbie to get the hang of riding the stand-up skis but I got pretty good in the end. I'm not one to give up. After a good few years of enjoyment, we started to feel a bit uncomfortable because it was gaining popularity and with it grew the noise and our fabulous, quiet beauty spot was turning into a fun park. We backed off and called it a day.

The next thing that we all tried ended up changing my life forever. When we were vegetarians, Trevor and I went to a restaurant called Wheel Farm, not far from us at Combe Martin, because we heard they had a good chef who excelled in vegetarian dishes. When we turned up we were the only ones in the restaurant, which meant we got talking to the chef and owner, an interesting man called Eddie Stratton. We instantly took to Eddie and thought he was great; in fact, I felt as if I'd known him all my life. Not long into our conversation we discovered that Eddie was an 8th Dan in the Japanese martial art of aikido. We thought the art sounded amazing because it involved using your opponent's force against himself. I told Eddie that our son Jay wanted to study karate but we hadn't been able to find a class for him locally. We discovered that Eddie ran a children's class at the school and he suggested that we bring Jay along to try it out. Jay, who was probably only five or six at the time, decided that he didn't like it.

After that we didn't see Eddie for a year or so until we bumped into him in the street in Barnstaple. We got talking about aikido again and said we'd like to try it as a family. With that he offered to give us a self-defence course at the house. A week later he came over to Woody Bay with three or four mats. We moved the table out of the kitchen and he gave us a lesson. We carried on like this for about three months until we had completed the course, at which point he persuaded us to go to one of his main classes at Ilfracombe School.

That was a major eye-opener for me. Wow! There I was, a 44-year-old surrounded by young people throwing them-selves around like nobody's business. I'm not ashamed to admit that I was absolutely terrible at the beginning; in fact, it took me years to get to grips with it. The worst thing by a long way was the falling. In order to practise you had to learn how to do a forward roll from a standing position. I can remember going home feeling battered and bruised, and thoroughly frustrated that I couldn't crack it.

Despite feeling totally and utterly useless as well as daunted by the whole experience, we kept on going as a family every Sunday morning at the unsociable time of 10 a.m., which meant leaving the house at 9.30 a.m. I would try my hardest but it often felt as though I didn't know my left from my right. I was so bad that other students avoided working with me because I couldn't get the hang of what I was supposed to be doing. I remember one of Eddie's senior students walking away from me in pure frustration. I don't think he meant to be unkind, I just don't think he knew what to do with me.

I suppose it was the challenge of aikido that kept me going, that and the pure fascination of it as I could never quite see how Eddie could throw and control the people that attacked him quite so effortlessly. Aikido was a complete brain tease for me from day one. I struggled just to get my co-ordination, something I never thought I had a problem with, especially having danced as a child and performed on stage since my teens.

To supplement our Sunday aikido sessions we decided to buy some mats and make our own little dojo – a martial arts training hall – in an old garage we had. It was pretty long and thin but it did the job and we had some very good training sessions there. Eddie, his daughter Emma 2nd Dan and one of his students, Simon Williams 3rd Dan, used to come round once a week to train. We also managed to recruit some locals from Lynton to join us, but they soon fell by the wayside.

After Eddie closed his class in Lynton, Trevor, who had achieved his brown belt, and Jay, who had got to orange, lost interest and stopped training. It was a great shame because they were both naturals. I was particularly sad about Trevor because he was so good, but I do have a great memory of seeing him do an amazing forward roll over eight people kneeling on the mat. Later on, Joey also started to train and took his brown belt pretty easily before also losing interest.

I, however, was completely fascinated by aikido. I used to drive into Barnstaple where Eddie eventually opened a full-time dojo. Simon Williams also used to come over to the house on a regular basis and train with me one-to-one, as did Jenny Herniman 3rd Dan who later became my long-term teacher and a great source of inspiration to me. By this time I started to get the hang of aikido, a bit, and knew that it was always going to be a part of my life. My experience of this new art touched me deeply and I did my best to capture some of the feelings I had about it by writing a song called 'The Ki' which featured on my 1989 Telstar album *Inspiration*.

Ki is the Japanese equivalent of the Chinese *chi*, which means life force or spirit, and is a very important aspect of aikido. I wrote the song when I started practising aikido and amazingly, despite my inexperience, I made a pretty good job of expressing what it's all about. I dedicated the song to Eddie but unfortunately on the album artwork 'sensei', the word for teacher in Japanese, was spelled 'sensie', a detail I'm still upset about. He wasn't bothered, he was just thrilled that I had been moved to write a song about aikido only a year or so after beginning my training.

The *Inspiration* album came about as a result of Telstar selling loads of copies of *No More The Fool*. Don Reedman at Telstar wanted me to do a compilation album with some big cover songs and some new material from Russ Ballard as well as a few of my own songs. We ended up doing sixteen tracks, some of which were very good songs. We also managed to do a version of an old track which I loved from my Vinegar Joe days; a song that I wrote with my first husband Pete Gage called 'Black Smoke From The Calumet'.

The covers included the Chicago songs 'You're The Inspiration' – which we named the album after – and 'Hard

Habit To Break', the Mr Mister hit 'Broken Wings', the John Farnham track 'Touch of Paradise' and a song that Toto recorded called 'A Thousand Years' which I still like singing today.

'Hard Habit To Break' and 'Touch of Paradise' were fantastic because we got Francis Rossi from Status Quo to do backing vocals with a friend of his called Bernie Frost. Francis is a great musician and was a pleasure to work with. He and Bernie had such a great rapport and sang brilliantly together. You don't have to be the greatest singer in the world to do great vocal backing, but there is an art to it. It's about finding someone that you can sing with and with whom you make a great sound, and this is what Francis had with Bernie. Some of the vocal harmonies were just amazing, particularly on 'Hard Habit To Break' which were pretty damn difficult.

Once again we made the album at home in Woody Bay Studios, this time with a lot of help from guitarist Gary Hutchins. Gary, who was a fairly intense character, was doing some hard drugs at the time and was a neurotic mess throughout his stay with us. At one point, Trevor felt Gary was in such a state that he needed to get him out of the studio to do something different so he arranged for him to go fishing with Lynmouth fisherman John Martin Jnr. He had a great day and felt much better, so much so that he wanted to go again the next day. This time things didn't go quite so well as he somehow managed to upset John, who dealt with the situation by throwing him overboard. I suppose that would have been fair enough if Gary had been able to swim! They ended up having to fish him out with some great big shark hooks. Poor Gary, and poor Trevor. He got so stressed out at working with Gary that he took up smoking again after not having had a cigarette for about four years. He's still smoking today. I can't stop him. He says, in his defence, he still hasn't got over making that album with Gary.

Trevor's return to smoking might also have had something to do with the power cut we had when he was mastering the album. The power went off at a crucial stage, which left a blemish on every single track prior to the vocals coming in. Trevor stayed up most of the night getting rid of every single one because the album was due to be sent off the next day to be duplicated.

When *Inspiration* was released in 1989, Telstar unsurprisingly didn't get behind it and it failed to make much of an impression on the charts. It got to number 58, one place lower than *Bookbinder's Kid*. We were disappointed because we both felt it was a very good album.

What was far harder to come to terms with, though, was the apparent end of my touring career, something that came about as a result of working with promoter Barry Marshall of Marshall Arts in 1989. I don't quite know how it happened but Barry managed to persuade me to do a farewell tour. I feel I should make it very clear here that I never actually had any intention of stopping and that I just ended up giving in to Barry and his insistence that it was the right thing to do to guarantee a sell-out tour. I should have stood my ground because I didn't feel it was right to mislead everyone like that, but I didn't. We went out on the road in the January of 1989 for three months, doing more than forty gigs across the country. Every night I had to do a little spiel about the fact that this was my final tour, which I always felt uncomfortable about.

There was one farewell, however, that I never wanted to say and that was to my wonderful mother. She passed away on 3 September 1989 at the age of seventy-six after going into hospital to have a minor operation. Sadly, Mum, who had suffered from lupus for years, was too weak to withstand the surgery. Mum's health had never been very good so I suppose it was inevitable something like this was going to happen eventually.

I caught the train up to Manchester for the funeral and was picked up from the station by my cousin Hilary. The funeral was strange because Mum, of course, wasn't Jewish at all, she had grown up as a Catholic and had married into the faith, but there we were giving her the full Jewish send-off. I'm sure that's what she would have wanted, having been married to my father for fifty years.

After the funeral, as the daughter, it was my responsibility to deal with Mum's clothes. I found it very odd but I was determined to do it because I didn't want my father's sister Betty, who Mum never liked (and neither did I for that matter), snooping through everything when she came round. I always felt my mother wouldn't have liked that so I made sure everything was bagged up and taken away before she had the chance to have a nose about.

As I was anxious to get back to Joey, we headed home two days after the funeral, leaving everyone sitting shiva in the house in line with the proper Jewish grieving process. It was a very short and sad visit back to Manchester, and one that I had always dreaded.

CHAPTER 19

THINGS GO WRONG

Not long after Mum died, Trevor and I found ourselves dealing with a different kind of grief involving our accountant. A close friend from the East End, who was also a client of our accountant's, told us he had a lot of money of ours stashed away that we didn't know about.

Naturally we were concerned and Trevor confronted him. He explained that he was holding a considerable amount of our money to pay a tax bill of mine. But as he gave the money back immediately and he'd always done such a great job for us and been a good friend since setting up his own business, we gave him the benefit of the doubt and let him carry on working for us. In hindsight this probably wasn't our wisest decision but you live and learn.

While Trevor was forgiving on this occasion there have been other instances in our time together when he hasn't been so generous. A promoter called Ray Nedas comes to mind. We were introduced to him by our accountant to do a tour and, looking back, we both wish we'd trusted our instincts about him. The bone of contention with Ray had been a sponsorship deal he negotiated with a brewery to hang a banner at every one of my gigs. He told us it was a £20,000 deal when in fact he'd been paid £34,000. Not bad work if you can get it! We, of course, weren't best pleased when we found out: I guess we would have understood if it had been a few grand more, but £14,000 seemed to us to be taking advantage.

Trevor took him to task after a gig at Wembley and he

was very callous about the whole thing. It turned out he thought it was perfectly acceptable for him as the promoter to make that kind of excessive mark-up. Needless to say that working relationship didn't last long. Trevor really isn't someone to upset; something a huntsman who encountered him on our property in Woody Bay was left in no doubt about.

On the day in question we were happily sitting in the garden with Jay and the dogs when all of sudden we were surrounded by thirty or more foxhounds. Luckily, our dogs weren't too bothered so we were able to tuck them safely into the house. Trevor, however, didn't react quite so well. He went inside and got his gun, and went about clearing the dogs off our property.

The lead huntsman appeared and asked, 'Have you seen the hounds?'

Trevor answered disgustedly, 'Seen the hounds, I've just got rid of them. They've been all over our garden.'

I guess if he'd stopped there everything would have been fine, but that's just not my Trevor's way. The next thing I knew he'd put the barrels of the gun under the huntsman's neck.

He said very coolly, 'I don't ever want to see you down here again, take your dogs and don't come back.'

The huntsman replied, 'Who are you?'

Trevor said, 'I live here and I don't want to see this, especially when my wife and I are enjoying a quiet afternoon in the garden.'

He seemed to get the point and quickly got in his Land Rover and drove off, but unfortunately for him he went straight down to the manor, which, of course, we owned at the time, so Trevor went after him, shouting that he was still on our property.

The next morning we had a visit from our local bobbies, Sgt Crocker and PC Parsons, who told us the lead huntsman was in hospital suffering from shock. Trevor wasn't too concerned to hear that and proceeded to tell the police that hunting in Woody Bay was forbidden in the Domesday Book, and the hunt was therefore in breach of that law. They asked if we wanted to press charges and we said we didn't. All we wanted was never to see the hunt on our property again.

My husband is a true animal lover and hates to see any form of cruelty towards animals, hence his strong reaction to the hunt. I first found out about his passion for animals when we were living in Hammersmith and he turned up to collect me from a rehearsal with Jean Roussel carrying a bag with this little head sticking out of it.

'What the hell's that?' I asked.

Trevor answered, 'It's the start of our family.'

I didn't have much of an answer for that. His defence was he'd been passing a pet shop and seen this little whippet standing there all alone, looking sorry for herself, and he didn't have the heart to walk on by.

Trevor was right; Winnie did become a fantastic part of our family. When she was young she was a complete tearaway, but she went on to be a fabulous dog. Trevor used to take her on his hang-gliding trips, as she just loved being with him. After years of accompanying him he had a feeling she might enjoy going up in the air, so he had a harness made for her. She didn't hesitate when he first put her in it, she genuinely seemed to love going up with him; it was an incredible sight. In fact, she was so at ease she used to get slightly out of the harness and lay on the small of Trevor's back, looking out at the view below with her ears blown back like sail planes. We took a picture of her and sent it to one of our local papers, which published it on the front page.

Winnie went on and on for years. One day when we were on tour in Newcastle we got a call from Dave West, who used to look after our house when we were away, to say that she was on her last legs. We had a day off the next day so Trevor drove hundreds of miles back to North Devon only to arrive fifteen minutes too late. He stayed up till 5 a.m. digging a grave and burying her.

Not long after acquiring Winnie, we extended the family with an Alsatian we named Betty. She was very much my dog and became super-protective of me; something which Alec Leslie found out one day in London when I was recording. Poor Alec was just talking to me about something or other and happened to gesture with his arm. Betty took it the wrong way. She flew at him, nearly taking his hand off in the process. Fortunately, I managed to stop her and no damage was done, apart from Alec's frazzled nerves.

When we moved to Devon we decided to get another Alsatian we called Bumper. He was another great dog with a lovely personality. Living in a fairly remote spot it was comforting to have two decent-sized dogs around, particularly at night. If Trevor was ever out at the pub I would go up to bed with all the dogs, and Trevor's shotgun for a little extra feeling of protection. One night, though, this nearly went horribly wrong when Trevor decided to surprise me by climbing up to the bedroom. On hearing this strange noise outside the window I grabbed the shotgun and was about to pull the trigger when I realised it was Trevor.

The next major additions to the Jordan menagerie were the birds. It all started not long after we first moved to Devon and it was a natural progression from Trevor's love of hang-gliding. As our friend Brian Windsor liked to shoot the wild pigeons, Trevor thought he'd make sure the local peregrine falcons at Woody Bay always had plenty to eat by buying thirty tumbler doves. They lived in a dovecote on our big wooden balcony overlooking the bay. The doves were very happy, and the peregrines were equally pleased with their arrival. When Brian died the wild pigeons came back and we had sixty doves. It all got a bit too much for me because there was bird poo everywhere.

With a dad obsessed with flying and birds, it was hardly surprising that Jay would be the same. One day he and Trevor went to the nearby Exmoor Bird Gardens and came back with a jackdaw that had been thrown out of its nest because of its deformed beak. We nursed him back to health and called him Jack. He became a great friend to the family and even I quite liked him despite the fact he drove me mad trying to keep the place clean; I was constantly putting bits of newspaper everywhere to stop him messing on my kitchen units. Rather than moan I went with the flow to keep the boys happy.

As well as Jack we had Silver, an African Grey parrot we trained to talk and sing. His party piece was singing the first two lines of 'Pearl's A Singer' and 'Sunshine After The Rain'. Poor Silver thought he was a pigeon. Every time they took off he would go with them. But while the pigeons were able to spin round in the air and land on the roof of the house, Silver could never quite manage it and would always end up crashing into the roof and sliding down. Other times he wouldn't make it back to the house at all and land in the oak tree opposite and sit there whistling for Trevor to go and get him.

Silver didn't like me at all. I always wanted him to, so I would try to get him to sit on my finger; he'd just bite me every time. I was covered in lots of little bites the whole time we had him. He lived in a cage in Jay's bedroom and every morning he'd hop off his perch, walk into our bedroom and climb up to Trevor where he would put his head on the pillow, waiting for him to wake up.

It all came to an end for Silver one day when he didn't return from one of his flights with the pigeons. We think he either got nabbed by one of the peregrines or stolen by someone because African Greys are worth quite a lot of money.

The most memorable of our so-called feathered friends, however, was Peggy, the Canadian cackling goose. Now if I thought Silver didn't like me, then Peggy absolutely detested me. Every day when I went down to get the post from the gates I would have to take my jo – a four-foot-long stick we use in aikido – for protection because she would be trying to peck me to pieces. She was a very good training partner! My martial arts awareness came on in leaps and bounds.

But the birds that really got on my nerves most were the peacocks. I was pretty annoyed the day Trevor bought them. Not only did they make a terrible noise in the mornings, they used to come into the kitchen and eat out of the dog bowls. One day I complained so much that Trevor threw a moccasin slipper at one to make it go away, but he accidentally hit it on the head and knocked it out cold.

Living with all these birds and animals was hard enough for me at times, but working among them must have been even harder for the nannies we employed over the years. Our first nanny in Devon was Vicki Irlam. She was brilliant and got me through the success of 'No More The Fool'. The one who probably had to put up with the most from the animal and bird antics was Sarah Harker. She had a fantastic relationship with Joey and he adored her. The most capable was Hyone Criscuolo and it wasn't until she came on the scene that Trevor and I ever went away on our own. Closer to my own age and with her own family, she was the only one we felt completely confident to leave the boys with.

Our last nanny, Alice Rollinson, who we hired for Joey was more of a teacher than a nanny. He started at the primary school in Parracombe as Jay had done but we moved him when someone suggested he might do better at Lynton Primary. He was there for a couple of years and hadn't learned to read or write so I thought something must be wrong. As a result we decided to take him out of school and advertised for a nanny who could also teach him at home. We eventually chose Alice, who was a qualified teacher, and she and Joey got on famously. She taught him to read and write which was brilliant. I found out later that he had been bullied at school and that's why he hadn't been learning anything. The other kids apparently used to put him in a dustbin and roll him round the playground. I made the right decision because today Joey's a computer whizz and very well spoken. In fact, you'd think he'd been to Eton the way he speaks. What's more, he's a real charmer with it.

Jay had more of a normal education, moving from Parracombe Primary to Ilfracombe Comprehensive when he was eleven. We always took the children on the road with us, which was fine when Jay was at primary school, but the teachers weren't so understanding at the secondary stage. When he was fourteen we pulled him out of school altogether. His teachers went mad with me, saying he'd miss out on the social scene and this, that and the other. I told them that he was already doing the job of a man on the road, sorting out all the drum kits and guitars. Everything worked out fine for Jay as he's gone on to manage me and produce my albums as well as working on the technical side of the recording industry.

I have some wonderful memories of the boys from my *Pearls III* tour in 1992. Not only did Jay help as a roadie and play guitar but he and Joey sang back-up vocals with me on stage. Trevor and I wrote a song called 'We Are All Your Children' and asked Jay to play for the record. We thought it would be a nice touch to get him to perform on stage too. He loved it and wasn't the least bit fazed.

Aside from that track *Pearls III* left a very bad taste in my mouth. Firstly, it should never have been called that. Freestyle Records came up with the idea, obviously thinking that making an Elkie Brooks album with 'Pearls' in the title would guarantee success. The album had nothing in common with *Pearls* and *Pearls II* whatsoever. A lot of the songs were home-grown where, of course, the 'Pearls' concept was a combination of hits, singles that hadn't previously appeared on albums, and some new covers. I was angry about this.

To compound this we made a big mistake with a guitarist we hired for the album and the subsequent tour. He got right up my nose early on because even though he had all the songs weeks and weeks before we started rehearsing he turned up not knowing any of them. Everyone else was bang up to speed, but this guy hadn't done his homework, which I always think is unforgivable since everyone ended up having to wait for him. What's more, his playing wasn't in the same league as Zal Cleminson, Al Hodge, Geoff Whitehorn, Tim Mills, Michael Caen, Melvyn Duffy, my son Jermaine Jordan and my current guitarist Rufus Ruffell.

The best thing that came out of *Pearls III* was finding my amazing keyboard player Andrew Murray. Meeting Andrew was proof that you should always listen to the tapes that people send you because that's how we found him. Being a North Devon lad he knew two of the local musicians we'd used on the *Bookbinder's Kid* album and he'd got my address from them and sent me a tape. Trevor and I listened to it and we couldn't believe how good he was. We were even more amazed when we realised he was only seventeen.

Over the years our opinions about Andrew have been proved right time and time again and I now always introduce him in my shows as one of the most talented keyboard players in the world today, which quite honestly he is. There are only two keyboard players who have ever truly played fabulously for me – Andrew Murray and Jean Roussel. While they are very different players, they share a great feeling for the music, and can move between classical, jazz and blues, which is quite a rarity in my experience.

Andrew's young talent started to come to the fore when we recorded *Round Midnight* in 1993. After the fiasco of

Pearls III, I wanted to do something more meaningful. It all came about when we got a message that John Beecher, managing director of Castle Records, was keen to produce an album that reflected my jazz roots.

We decided to keep the music as simple as possible so my voice would come through as the lead instrument. I got busy picking songs that I'd grown up listening to in Manchester, songs like 'What Kind Of Man Are You?' that I'd heard on an old Ray Charles album. I also chose the Mark Murphy song 'Spring Can Really Hang You Up The Most' and 'Cry Me A River', Peggy Lee's definitive version.

Recording at home in our tiny studio, we worked with Andrew, my long-time bassist Phil Mulford and a young trumpet player from nearby Braunton called Martin J. Lewison, who were all sympathetic to what we were trying to achieve. Consequently, the album turned out brilliantly. In total we did sixteen songs, which is a lot for one artist, but that was a stipulation from Castle Records. Even the album cover artwork, which had often been a disappointment in the past, looked superb. It had a fabulous sultry nightclub look and feel to it.

In the sleeve notes to the album, I wrote that I had always wanted to record these particular songs and I dedicated the album to those great singers that had influenced me over the years – Peggy Lee, Billie Holiday, Mary Ann Fisher, Ray Charles, Nancy Wilson, Dakota Staton, Dinah Washington, Mark Murphy, Nina Simone and Julie London.

Even without masses of promotion, the album was very successful, which led to an option of another album the following year. This time we went bluesy in tribute to other artists like Bessie Smith, Esther Phillips and Amos Milburn whom I'd loved listening to when I was a sixteen-year-old singing with the Eric Delaney Band on the American air bases in Germany.

The musician line-up was similar to *Round Midnight*,

with the addition of North Devon guitarist Tim Mills, who also did a great job of teaching Jay to play the guitar, saxophonist Duncan Lamont and trumpet player Derek Healey who Humph and his partner Susan had found for us. My long-term drummer Mike Richardson played superbly on both albums but one track caused him incredible grief. He and Trevor spent all day in the studio trying to get it right but for some reason poor Mike just couldn't crack it. Eventually, they took a break and came down to the house where Trevor and I proceeded to get Mike to unwind by giving him a jug of vodka, gin and orange juice. Once we'd got him a little more relaxed I sent him back up to the studio with Trevor where he managed to do a perfect take playing the drums, leaning up against the wall. He didn't even realise he'd got it right. We all listened back to it the next day and it was beautiful. Mike, being the modest man he is, couldn't quite believe how good it was.

Sadly, *Nothin' But The Blues* didn't do as well as *Round Midnight*. While the record wasn't selling like hot cakes, Trevor and I were pleased enough from a business perspective because we'd managed to do a deal with Castle that meant we owned both albums outright, ending the countless years of missed royalties. So even though we had another situation similar to *No More The Fool* and *Bookbinder's Kid* with the second album being more for the catalogue, we felt a lot better about it.

Elaine Bookbinder was finally getting somewhere with the business side of the music industry, something her dad would have been pleased to hear had he been there. Sadly he passed away on 16 June 1993 after suffering a massive heart attack at the time I was making *Round Midnight*. I remember getting a call from my brother Ray to say that he'd died. The next day we drove to Manchester.

Not comfortable with all the Jewish rituals, Trevor decided to stay in our van and let Joey and me go to the funeral on our own. The Orthodox ceremony was very tough on both of us since in Orthodox Jewish synagogues men and women are separated. It was hard for Joey, who was only seven at the time, because he was sitting with my brothers who he didn't know very well. To be honest, I was more upset worrying about Joey than I was grieving for my father as I'd never been that close to him. He had never paid me very much attention throughout my life, something that I deeply resented. And it wasn't just me that felt that way; my brothers Ray and Tony had the same response. At the funeral you could see they were nowhere near as emotional as they were at Mum's. They too felt as if they had been ignored. He was a very cold man, pessimistic and looked on the negative side of everything.

I last saw my dad a few months before he died on the way back from a gig in Carlisle. I was very tired but I just had this feeling that I had to go to see him. We had a strenuous journey which was made all the worse by getting lost on the way to Dad's flat from the motorway. I can remember him putting his arm around me and having this overwhelming feeling that he was full of regrets about all the things he should have said and done. Good times together with Dad were few and consequently memorable. I play a mean game of table tennis, thanks to Dad. He taught me, and although I didn't adopt his unique style, holding the bat like a pen between his thumb and middle finger, which he had adopted from the Japanese, I do have happy memories of my brothers dragging out the fold-up table from the garage and being invited to play.

He came to see me at the Albert Hall and at the Palladium when I started to become famous but prior to that he hadn't ever taken very much notice of me, or my career. I always felt very bitter about that. My mother, on the other hand, always came along on trips with me and was there for me whenever I needed support. It was very sad that he missed out on so much. The one thing I am grateful for was his financial generosity – he gave me the means to follow my dream.

In contrast, Trevor and I have involved ourselves in everything our children have done. I can't understand why people have children if they're not going to look after and care for them spiritually. Materially, of course, my father did look after me and I didn't want for anything, but emotionally I got very little from him. He had a habit of giving me something with one hand and then taking it away with the other. I think that pretty much summed up his whole attitude to everything he did in his life. Every time I give my children anything, I do it out of the goodness of my heart. They never asked to be born and all I ask of them is their affection.

I think my father's attitude towards me made me a harder person. I wrote a rather poignant song about my feelings towards him shortly after he died, which I couldn't face recording at the time, but could possibly do now. Maybe his harsh, unloving way actually spurred me on and gave me greater determination than I might otherwise have had, but I don't honestly think that was ever his intention. Maybe it also played a part in my choosing to follow the path of aikido, which has been an important part of my life, and which has contributed to my general health and well being, since 1988.

My persistence and determination with the art was rewarded on my fiftieth birthday on 25 February 1995 when I passed my first Dan grading with the Shudokan Institute of Aikido International. Some younger people achieve their black belt level in two or three years, but for me it was a seven-year journey. Touring and recording have prevented me from the regular training you need to progress. I have a lot of people to thank for helping me get to first Dan, especially of course Soke Eddie Stratton 9th Dan, but also his students: Simon Williams 3rd Dan, Jenny Herniman 3rd Dan and Robert Teague 2nd Dan.

After the grading we enjoyed a quick get-together in the pub and then I went home for a quiet bath. Just as I was getting out I heard Trevor shouting, 'Elk, you'd better get up to the bar, we've got a few surprises for you.'

When I walked in, the entire aikido club greeted me and Eddie's wife Marguerite had prepared a fantastic buffet. It was the perfect way to celebrate what I saw as the start of my aikido career. In my estimation, when you achieve first Dan you have only just climbed on to the first rung of the ladder. Anybody who says differently, I think is misguided. From time to time, I hear about people who have got to first Dan in a martial art and then give up, thinking they have reached the top. For me that's not what aikido and the martial arts are about. They are about learning humility, and that's something I learned from Soke Stratton's teacher, Master Thamby Rajah, when he came over from Malaysia to teach. He was a great exponent of aikido and a wonderful teacher; such a humble, beautiful person.

CHAPTER 20

'TREES'

While aikido has been good for me both mentally and physically, my dedication to it nearly cost me dear one snowy winter's night. Living in a remote place like Woody Bay, down a steep, rough private road, we always made sure we had four-wheel-drive vehicles. On that evening the journey home proved to be very difficult and my car almost ended up rolling hundreds of feet down the side of the hill on to our house.

I was doing fine until the last hairpin leading down to the house when I managed to get my car well and truly stuck in the snow. Joey and I clambered out and walked home. Trevor got the Range Rover and we all drove up to my stranded Suzuki. He hooked it up to the Range Rover and got Jay, who was probably only fifteen at the time, to sit behind the wheel. The plan was to pull it off the bank, but the trouble was it was lodged at a 45-degree angle, which meant you could see the lights of our house about 500 yards below, making the consequences of getting the operation wrong blatantly apparent. When Trevor yanked the car the front wheels started spinning and wobbling like mad, and it went further over the edge. Jay got out like lightning and he and Trevor stopped and reviewed the situation. After a couple of minutes they decided to re-attach the rope and give it another go, this time giving it loads of welly so that if my car went over the edge it would at least be secure. Trevor also got Jay to leave the door of the Suzuki open just in case he needed to jump out quickly.

When they went for it, my car lurched slightly out over the edge before eventually sliding free. That immediately caused a new problem. Jay, though, was one step ahead because he managed to bring my car safely to rest before it crashed into the back of the Range Rover by putting it into first gear and gently applying the brakes. It was a close thing though as the two cars were only an inch apart.

Jay is such a natural driver, quite the opposite of me. He started driving, as Joey did, in the hang-gliding field at Woolacombe when he was twelve or thirteen. Trevor always took the boys with him when he went flying so it was the perfect opportunity to teach them how to drive in complete safety. Jay picked it up incredibly quickly, and on one occasion he ended up driving us home one night while we were on holiday on the Portuguese island of Porto Santo. We'd had a little too much to drink and weren't in any fit state to drive so Jay took us home in the left-hand-drive Mini Moke we'd hired. He could only have been about fourteen, but the roads on the island were extremely quiet and we trusted him implicitly. The police on the island were a bit lax, which I suppose influenced our decision.

With a dad obsessed with flying it was almost inevitable that both sons would follow in their father's footsteps, or should that be in his slipstream? This hasn't always been easy for me, being a protective mother. The first trauma it caused me was when Jay was about twelve and was busy making a model aeroplane, complete with engine and propeller. In fairness to Trevor, he had told Jay not to mess about with the propeller, but Jay unfortunately didn't take any notice and decided to spin it round anyway. The propeller promptly took a slice out of his arm and there was blood everywhere. I had no choice but to rush him to the little hospital in Lynton, the trouble was the only vehicle I had at home was Trevor's Toyota pick-up, which I'd never driven. I managed to keep a cool head, or as my aikido teacher Sensei

Stratton would have said I 'held fast the centre' and got Jay to hospital without any further incident. I remember that year very clearly because Jay had been given an ostrich egg by a friend at the Exmoor Bird Gardens which he left on his bedroom window sill where it eventually exploded in the sunlight and stank the place out for ages.

Worse still for my nerves, Jay soon progressed from making model aeroplanes to learning to fly hang-gliders. Although I'd be lying if I said it didn't worry me, I knew that he was not only in incredibly safe hands with all Trevor's knowledge and experience, he was also very mature and more than capable. You can't stop a mother worrying about her son, especially when she's Jewish. By fourteen, Jay had not only learned to drive a car, he'd also learned to fly a hang-glider. In fact, he might even hold the record for being the youngest person ever to pilot a hang-glider single-handedly.

It was really no surprise that Jay had the maturity and ability to learn to fly because he had been working alongside adults on the road for years. We wanted to have the kids with us wherever we went, which meant that they were constantly exposed to things that would freak most parents out. But rather than having a negative impact on their upbringing, the experience of all the bad language and questionable tour bus behaviours actually had the opposite effect because both Jay and Joey have grown up to be very responsible people.

Thinking back to some of the crazy things that happened on the road over the years it's amazing the boys turned out to be such well-rounded human beings. For instance, when Jay was about twelve we had a caterer called Val, who we nicknamed 'Vodka Val' for obvious reasons. At the start of the tour John Cooper, one of the crew, got a new dustbin and filled it with every type of alcohol you could imagine. Val, unsurprisingly, was very keen on the punch and on this particular occasion in the early hours of the morning on the ferry from Liverpool to Belfast, she was in the back of the bus drunk, having had a good go at it.

On arrival in Belfast, Trevor discovered Val dragging two armed policemen on to the coach who she'd persuaded to direct the driver to the gig. By the time the coach got to the theatre Val was dressed in a police uniform, waving a 9mm machine gun around while the two policemen were sitting in the back, drunk on the punch. I should, of course, make it clear that before doing this the policeman had removed the gun's magazine. I was shocked, but not exactly surprised, to learn what had happened, especially as my boy had been asleep upstairs on the coach.

Although I know pretty much anything can happen on the road, and Trevor is more often than not at the centre of it, I also know that he's got a great head on his shoulders for the occasions when the shit really does hit the fan. A good example of his cool-headedness was around the time of my fortieth birthday in 1985 when we were in the Middle East doing a series of gigs in Oman and Dubai and one of our lighting guys chopped about six inches off a tree at the back of the stage, not realising that trees are as good as sacrosanct in Arab countries. The next moment the poor guy thought he was going to be thrown in prison for the rest of his life for his outrageous behaviour. At this point Trevor stepped in and successfully managed to defuse the situation.

Another time, however, Trevor was unquestionably the protagonist when he decided to teach the guy who was promoting my show a lesson about leaving a briefcase with £40,000 to £50,000 of cash lying around. Trevor probably wouldn't have minded had it not been our show fees he was being so careless with. As it was, he took the briefcase and hid it in a flight case. When the guy realised it was missing, he went mad. Of course, we were all very sympathetic and kept him going for a good couple of hours.

In the end Trevor pulled the case out and asked, 'Is this what you're looking for?'

The other funny story that came from playing in the Middle East involved one of my favourite guitarists, Zal Cleminson, formerly of The Sensational Alex Harvey Band. We were doing a show for the King of Oman but had been left waiting because the king hadn't arrived home from a trip to Europe. Things were made even worse when we heard his plane fly right over the top of the gig but he still didn't appear at the head table in front of the stage. Everyone, including me, was getting mightily aggravated at being kept waiting for so long. Zal, however, was obviously the most annoyed because when he came to do his guitar solo in 'Nights In White Satin' he walked straight down the centre of the king's table, kicking all the glasses over as he went. It was hilarious; in fact I've no idea how I managed to keep on singing it was that funny.

The African continent provided the backdrop for another eventful trip. I went to Sun City in 1984 as the support act for Shakin' Stevens on a three-night show. Things got a bit awkward when I received a better reception than the headline artist. I think he was pretty put out by it and, as a result, was quite unpleasant when we went to speak to him by the pool the day after the first show. It wasn't as if I'd done anything to hurt him; I was just doing what I do ... sing.

Soon after returning home, I did a gig at the Colston Hall in Bristol where I was greeted with an anti-apartheid protest. There were protests going on everywhere at the time so it wasn't a surprise. I think Shirley Bassey and Stevie Wonder, who had also been out to Sun City around the same time, had come in for far greater criticism.

Controversy, in some shape or form, never seems to be too far away from us; I really don't know what we do to deserve it. Then again my darling Trev does sometimes tend to attract trouble. The work we did to our house in the late 1980s and early 1990s, however, was definitely something we knew would one day cause an issue, having decided to just get on with it rather than seeking planning permission first.

From the moment we bought the house in 1981 we'd always wanted to make it bigger. The first thing we did was to extend the kitchen and the bedrooms above, which we did get permission for, but Trevor always felt we would struggle to get planning to add a studio, so everything else we did, we just took a chance on. By the time we'd finished we'd built a studio, three separate bungalows, a big balcony and an indoor swimming pool. Our first studio was in the living room, which after a couple of years we decided to move to the old logging shed. We then started building a bungalow next to it, with two bedrooms and an aikido dojo. This eventually became the studio and then a bar. We also built another bungalow for Jay so that he could have his own bachelor pad. They built it together, which was a great project for both of them. The other bungalow was for Dave West, our caretaker, and that was on the edge of our land, near the road.

Despite living in a very remote spot surrounded by trees, it was inevitable that the authorities would catch up with us so it wasn't entirely a surprise when a letter arrived informing us the local authorities wanted to come for a site inspection. This, however, was no ordinary planning visit. In total we had seventeen people looking round, made up of representatives from North Devon District Council, Exmoor National Park, the National Trust and the Highways Agency. Despite all the fuss, Trevor soon picked up from the head guy from the National Trust that we had done everything properly and the visit ended with a retrospective planning permission for everything we had done.

When we came to submit our application, we discovered

something annoying, but quite amusing. Our neighbour, who had bought the manor from us, had complained that we'd painted the house pink. He obviously didn't realise that we would see the letter, in which he described our house as looking like a birthday cake. Pink may be an odd choice of colour but when the sun shone on the house it actually looked more white than pink. It seemed like a silly complaint because for most of the year when the trees had foliage he couldn't see it.

In response, Trevor had a word with his firemen friends from Lynton and they turned up at the manor unannounced for a fire inspection and found so many things wrong, which led to the place being closed down. Shortly after, we received a letter from him, asking whether we would be prepared to patch things up. We tossed the letter in the fire and never spoke to him again.

Away from the retrospective planning problems we were busy in 1995 making *Circles*, a new album. We decided we wanted to make an organic, live album so we ironically picked a set of retrospective songs. We combined a couple of my standards – 'Pearl's A Singer' and 'Lilac Wine' – with some classic tracks like 'Mercedes Benz', the Janis Joplin song; Jimi Hendrix's 'Angel' and two Vinegar Joe tracks, 'Live A Little, Get Somewhere', which was a song my ex-husband Pete Gage wrote; and an interesting version of the Robert Palmer song 'Circles' which became the title of the album.

We recorded it over a period of two weeks, and being a live album, about a month later it was finished. The backing for the album came via John Lennard of Permanent Records who, just for a change, proved to have financial problems, which meant the album didn't get plugged at all and was pretty much wasted. I always felt we had some very good tracks, but perhaps we didn't have the standard of musicians we needed to create the right atmosphere for a live album like that, with the exception of Andrew Murray and my long-term drummer Mike Richardson. In fairness, I don't think it was one of the best albums I've ever done.

However, the live album *Amazing* that followed a year later in 1996 was, in my opinion, fabulous. John Howard, managing director of Carlton Premiere Records, instigated the project. Trevor got on so well with him that we insisted the contract was drawn up with a 'key man' clause, which meant if John left, either by choice or was moved by the company, the album would become ours. Lo and behold something happened after we'd finished making the album and he left the company so the record became our property.

The actual recording sessions proved to be an incredible experience. The idea was to re-record all of my hits – with the exception of 'Pearl's A Singer' – with the Royal Philharmonic Orchestra. For good measure we decided to include some other good material that I'd written with various musicians over the years.

The conductor, Tony Britten, had the toughest job of all as he was commissioned to write and arrange all the music. It must have taken him about eight weeks, or maybe even more, to do. He was an absolute joy to work with. He put his heart and soul into it, and the project was fantastic because of it. We got on fabulously and I did every song in one take over the course of three days at Lyndhurst Studios in London. I can honestly say the version I did of 'Lilac Wine' is the best I've ever done. But there were also some great live recordings of songs like 'No More The Fool', 'Paint Your Pretty Picture' and 'Nights In White Satin'.

My keyboard player Andrew Murray was outstanding on this project. He would be there with me at 8 a.m, practising for the recording session later in the day. I remember vividly halfway through recording one of the scores Andrew putting his hands up and waving, trying to get Tony's attention. The next thing I saw was Andrew –

wearing a baseball cap backwards, jeans and T-shirt, I might add – coming out of his booth and going up to the renowned conductor in front of the fifty-piece orchestra recording live, saying there's something wrong with the score.

Andrew said, pointing at the score, 'When we get to this bit here, it goes all wrong.'

Tony took a look at the section and said, 'Yes, you're absolutely right, Andrew.'

Only someone like Andrew with his superb musical ability and confidence could do that. He's a bit like the Nigel Kennedy of the piano. It was a very memorable thing for me to see that he had the bottle to do that in front of such a prestigious orchestra and conductor.

After *Amazing* was released and had done okay in the charts, I was asked to do a show singing the same songs at the Birmingham Botanical Gardens. Everybody was concerned about the high ticket prices for the gig, so I was thoroughly touched to hear that we not only sold all 8,500 tickets, but there were 2,500 people queued up outside trying to get in. Apologies if you were one of the unlucky ones.

The night before the show we stayed in a hotel nearby and had a bit of a drink with Tony. It would be wrong to think that only rock and roll and jazz musicians enjoy a drink because he and Trevor very quickly turned one or two quiet drinks into a full-on session. And it didn't seem to affect Tony as much as it did Trevor, because the next day he was bright-eyed and bushy-tailed as if nothing had happened. I just don't know how he did it. He must have had the hangover from hell but he managed two hours' rehearsals with the orchestra and then another hour with me, and then he went on to conduct the show in the evening. He is, without doubt, one of the most brilliant musicians I've ever had the privilege of working with.

The wonderful experience of making *Amazing* was followed by an equally amazing achievement in 1997 when

I was listed in the *Guinness Book of World Records* as being the most charted female album seller of the last twenty-five years. The funny thing was the album *The Very Best of Elkie Brooks* that gave me the world record was another 'very best of' which I didn't even know was being released. I'd had a year off and was in the charts again without having had to do anything. It was great.

Sadly though, the enjoyment of this was relatively short-lived because not even a year later our lives were turned upside down by some shocking financial news. Out of the blue, our accountant asked to come to see us. At the time, we thought nothing of it. How wrong we were.

Very quickly after arriving he sat down with us and sheepishly said, 'We've got a problem.'

Trevor asked, 'What sort of problem?'

He replied, 'A £250,000 tax problem.'

Dumbfounded, I said, 'What the hell's been going on?'

'I've got to put my hand up, it's all my fault, I've not been doing your tax returns properly for quite some time.'

With that we told him we never wanted to see him again.

CHAPTER 21

FINANCIAL PROBLEMS

We soon discovered the full extent of our financial problems when we were summoned to Barnstaple Magistrates' Court and questioned about non-payment of tax, which we, of course, knew very little about as we thought our accountant was taking care of everything. In fact that couldn't have been further from the truth because all he had been doing was paying the non-payment fines rather than the actual amounts owed. This could only have gone on for so long before the taxman caught up with us.

The tax people froze all our bank accounts. This, in turn, created a new problem. For every tour we would take out a loan to pay the musicians but now, with our assets frozen, we weren't able to repay the loan we'd arranged for my long 1998 tour. So instead of being in a good financial position after a hard tour, we found ourselves in a truly desperate state. We had a massive tax bill and a loan, which was rapidly spiralling out of control because the bank slapped the highest interest rate on it they could. I think it accumulated to something absolutely horrendous. Worse still, of course, we had no way of making the money we needed to settle our debts because we couldn't afford to pay the band to do another tour. And then there was the mortgage! After a few months the building society threatened us with repossession if we didn't meet our repayments.

To safeguard the house we came up with the idea of borrowing money from a finance company to do it up and rent it out. The company agreed to give us £250,000 but the deal went wrong at the eleventh hour because some paperwork from the tax office was needed, which they wouldn't provide as they couldn't put a final figure on what we actually owed. The wrangling with the tax office went on for several months, and the settlement figure changed constantly because we weren't paying our mortgage. As time went on, the building society got heavier and heavier, eventually giving us two months to get out.

Fortunately, a close friend Alan Henderson had mentioned our situation to his partner Claire and they very kindly agreed to lend us £25,000. This meant we could pay the mortgage and buy ourselves some time. They did this entirely on trust, without a single piece of paperwork, which was amazing. While this got us out of a hole, it was only a temporary fix; the hole just kept getting bigger and bigger because the tax people were taking so long to sort everything out.

By mid-1999, however, repossession was once again imminent which meant we had no choice but to put our house on the market. It broke my heart to think things had come to this, especially when we'd done nothing to deserve it, except employ the services of an accountant who had failed us spectacularly.

The house let us down because we couldn't get anywhere near what we needed to get us out of the financial mess. We had to carry on living the waking nightmare. The situation had become so dire that we were struggling to feed ourselves. The whole family was suffering. Jay and Joey were both badly affected. We didn't hide the seriousness of our predicament from them. We did, however, try to protect them a little by not telling them the full extent of the problem. Somehow I managed to stay strong through it all, but Trevor was devastated emotionally. I was really worried about him. I thought he was close to having some kind of breakdown, or even a heart attack.

The one thing that kept him sane was his hang-gliding,

and I even managed to spoil that for him on one occasion. Prior to the tax problem he'd bought a special hang-glider from America for two people so I could go up with him rather than just sitting around on the hill while he was flying around above. The first time he took me up nearly ended in divorce. It was a beautiful sunny day not long after we'd had the initial bad news of our tax problem and it was seriously playing on my mind. The flight began smoothly enough but I made the mistake of talking about our debts.

Trevor looked at me and said, 'Please, Elk, I do this to get away from all life's problems. For God's sake shut up.'

Apparently, I was talking so much that Trevor's hang-gliding friend John Meredith heard us on the ground. After that, things took a turn for the worse, quite literally, because Trevor stalled one wing of the glider, which he assures me now wasn't a problem, and all of a sudden we were heading towards the hill at a rate of knots which I found terrifying. And the way he rescued the situation was even more frightening! He dropped and accelerated even more to pull out of the stall, which sent my head smashing into one of the glider's uprights. I think this painful experience might have prompted one or two expletives. Suffice to say, I've not been hang-gliding much since.

Also around the time of this bad flying experience, a record label approached us about cutting a new studio album. In our current precarious situation we felt we had nothing to lose by exploring things further and Trevor went to London for a meeting with a producer. He wanted me to record an album and not very long after the meeting a contract was presented to us. We eventually agreed that I'd record a few songs to get the project moving.

The track we wanted to progress was 'Too Much To Lose' which was a great song written by the fantastic singer, songwriter and guitarist Al Hodge, my keyboardist Andrew Murray, Dave Quinn and me. We'd laid down most of the track quite easily but wanted to make it extra special by getting Courtney Pine to play sax and other instruments on it. He was keen to do the track and invited Trevor to his studio with the tapes. The recording session itself proved to be something of a challenge as there were not only several kids running round, but also a dog barked every time Courtney played certain instruments. Courtney did about ten takes and Trevor came home hoping he could find one track that didn't have the dog on it. Despite the difficult circumstances Trevor managed to mix and produce a fantastic song that I was really pleased with.

As it turned out, in what proved to be a very frustrating and unhappy experience, all the songs we recorded never saw the light of day as an album; a real disappointment because we'd made some amazing tracks. The only song that emerged was 'Too Much To Lose' which was released as a single. So many things have to fall into place to make an album work, and when the money isn't there or the production doesn't click or one of a hundred things goes wrong it can all fall apart.

However, a few good things did come from the association. As Andrew was busy writing songs with Russ Ballard's son Chris and doing other things, I asked my great friend Jean Roussel to get involved. As well as playing keyboards on all the tracks we recorded, he agreed to do the tour the record company was promoting for me. He also recommended a French rhythm guitarist, Michael Caen, who we hired for the tour, to play alongside Al Hodge on lead guitar, Roger Inniss on bass guitar and Arnaud Frank on percussion.

The other positive was collecting a Gold Badge from BASCA – the British Academy of Songwriters, Composers and Authors – in October 1999 at The Savoy. What was great was taking Joey, who was twelve at the time, with me to the ceremony. He wore a hand-tailored suit, which made him look so smart and grown-up. I didn't look too bad either in my off-white Max Mara suit.

Awards haven't featured very heavily in my career. In fact, only two come to mind. When I was in Vinegar Joe we got a Golden Ear award and I was named best female singer on a Noel Edmonds' Saturday morning TV show, receiving a lighter that didn't work to mark the occasion; a strange award, especially for a non-smoker.

The tour (ironically called the *Unfinished Business* tour) also led to an invaluable introduction to Haydn Dawkins who ran the coach company used by the road crew. After telling Haydn about our financial problems he put us in touch with a brilliant accountant called Paul Carvell. Paul, with the help of an insolvency expert called Peter Levy, eventually managed to get our debts reduced to £150,000. The two of them were fantastic. I really can't imagine how we would have coped without them.

The *Unfinished Business* tour began quite smoothly. It was one of the most memorable tours I've done because Jay's new girlfriend Joanna came on the road with us. The two met at the wedding of Trevor's brother Robbie in September 1999. Joanna was the bride's sister. They hit it off pretty much straightaway and she almost immediately moved in with Jay. Joanna quickly got into the spirit of being on the road, helping out with the merchandising. The touring experience must have been a culture shock for her, mostly because of the way we were organising my tours at that time. To save on expensive hotels we used motor homes. One of the big lows of the *Unfinished Business* tour was the standard of motor homes hired for us. They were uncomfortable, cramped and cold. At a gig in Scotland in sub-zero temperatures, I can remember thinking, 'What the hell are we doing here, freezing to death?'

I'm not sure what Joanna must have made of it all, but I guess she and Jay were just happy to be together, albeit sharing their motor home with Joey. This was a source of much amusement and we jokingly called it the 'school bus'.

The musical side of the tour was great from the very first rehearsal right through to hitting the road, but at the end of the tough tour in December 1999, we discovered that after two months on the road, we'd only made a small profit. It was a bad case of déjà vu.

Desperate to get away, we decided we had just enough money to take the motor homes through France to visit Trevor Morais – the drummer on my hit *Two Days Away* album – in Malaga. Jean Roussel, who I first met on that album in 1977, still worked with Trevor and had told me he wanted me to do some vocals for something he was working on.

Driving through France took our minds off our money worries and when we reached Luchon, one of Trevor's favourite hang-gliding spots, we had the first sign that things might just turn out okay in the end. It was 21 December – Jay's birthday – and we all went sledging – with our golden retriever Shadow, who we'd got just before our beloved Alsatian Bumper passed away. We were the only ones up the mountain, which made it incredibly special. In the midst of all this fun Trevor's mobile rang. He was on the phone for a while, chatting away quite seriously. It was Andy Williams's manager, Tennyson Flowers, asking if he would do a three-week tour of Europe with Andy in 2000.

This was just the type of news we needed and it was with new hope that we carried on our journey. Our next overnight stop was just beyond the Spanish border. It was a horrible, rainy evening and we parked the motor homes side by side, and got ourselves set for the night. Sitting chatting, Trevor looked at me and said, 'I don't think we're quite flat here, Elk, I'm going to move us to the other side of Jay and Joanna.'

Seconds after he'd moved us, there was an almighty bang

as a bolt of lightning lit up the sky. With that Jay opened the door of his motor home to see a burnt patch on the ground where he'd last seen our mobile home. He was standing there in a state of shock, trying to come to terms with his parents being killed by a freak lightning strike, when Trevor casually strolled round the corner, beer in hand, wondering what Jay was looking at.

Trevor said dryly, 'Mum and I moved round there, bit of luck wasn't it? Things can't be that bad, we're still here after all?'

The next morning we drove on down to Malaga, pleased just to be alive. Being at Trevor Morais's was great because he was so laid back. Well, what would you expect at a place called 'El Cortijo' – 'The Farmhouse'. In fact, it's a place where lots of famous artists like Madonna and Bjork have recorded. As well as a great studio, it's a bit of a haven.

We didn't tell Morais what was going on, but he may well have noticed something was wrong because it was pretty obvious at times that I was finding it difficult to get into anything creative. We spent a couple of weeks at 'The Farmhouse', and it proved a good escape for the whole family. We had a scooter on the back of the motor home so my Trevor was able to go off with the boys and Joanna and do their own thing while I was in the studio. I think it gave them some headspace and something else to think about for a change. It also proved to be the start of a new era for my touring career.

One evening while we were talking as a family over dinner Jay and Joanna suggested out of the blue that they wouldn't mind having a go at organising my next tour. And the very next day they started running with the idea, booking gigs from their mobile home, parked outside Trevor Morais's gorgeous house. Before long they had secured dates for me from mid-January through to early March. Trevor and I thought this was fantastic and felt it was another important step in the right direction in the Jordan family's quest to forge its own way forwards in the music business without having to suffer the pains of working with promoters.

This development made an already brilliant trip even better. The fact Jay and Joanna ran up a £1,000 mobile bill along the way was insignificant, especially considering how much we owed the taxman.

By the time we came to celebrate the millennium with Trevor Morais at a Chinese restaurant in Malaga, I was becoming cautiously optimistic that the year 2000 might be a little kinder to the Jordan family than the last two years had been.

A few days later we began the slow drive back to England, totally unaware that our nightmare was about to get even worse.

CHAPTER 22

RECORDING WITH HUMPH

Back at home in North Devon we turned our attention to preparing for Jay and Joanna's 2000 tour which was booked to run from mid-January to early March so Trevor could join Andy Williams for his UK dates as had been arranged on top of the mountain in Luchon.

Rehearsals went well, but I knew we were missing not having Jean Roussel or Andrew Murray on keyboards. Having worked with Jean again on the fraught *Unfinished Business* tour and the album that never materialised, circumstances conspired against us so that he wasn't able to tour with me in 2000. Similarly, Andrew had moved to London and was doing his own thing. This led to us working with a succession of different keyboard players including Jonny Dyke and Simon Carter. Although they were very proficient, great people who fitted into the team well, they didn't have the same kind of feel for my music as Jean and Andrew. But with no new album projects on the horizon and the financial crisis never far from our minds, we were very much focused on touring to make money and survive.

The tour kicked off in Norwich on 17 January and was running like clockwork thanks to Jay and Joanna's hard work until one awful night on the way from Skegness to Glasgow for a show at the Royal Concert Hall on 20 February 2000. Trevor and I were travelling in our motor home with Jay and Joanna following behind in theirs. I had gone to bed, leaving Trevor driving. The plan was to get us as far into Scotland as they could before parking up for the

221

night. In hindsight, Trevor now feels, that it was way too much to expect of Jay who was only twenty, especially after working hard during the day to set up the equipment for the show and then dismantling it afterwards.

What happened next nearly became any parent's worst nightmare. As Trevor was driving he casually glanced in the wing mirror and saw Jay's motor home drift out across all three lanes of the motorway and hit the central reservation barrier. Jay had fallen asleep at the wheel.

The whole vehicle almost went over but just as it did Jay woke up and managed to recover the situation, and pull over on to the hard shoulder. He got out of the motor home, and Trevor and I stood there cuddling him, in a terrible state of shock. The impact on the barrier was so great that Joanna was thrown out of bed into the front half of the motor home. It must have been horrific for Trevor to see our son and his girlfriend almost get killed. As we were on the motorway we had no option but to carry on so we kept an open line on the phone and I just kept talking to Jay to make sure he stayed awake until we got to some services. The only thing that saved Jay was the fact it was the dead of the night and there were no other vehicles around. Trevor still has nightmares about the accident now. He feels terrible about it and thinks he was pushing Jay too hard.

Having narrowly escaped being struck by lightning in Spain just a few weeks before and now Jay and Joanna nearly crashing on the motorway we were starting to realise just how lucky we were despite the money situation.

Another thing that was playing on my mind was my aikido teacher, Sensei Eddie Stratton, who had been suffering from cancer of the oesophagus for a year or two. Having seen him at one of my gigs at the Queen's Theatre in Barnstaple in February, it was becoming apparent that he wasn't going to win his battle. If anyone could have beaten the illness, it would have been him, and I'm sure his incredible spirit gave him quite a lot of extra time with his wife Marguerite and daughter Emma. Eddie had a rare form of cancer called malignant mesothelioma, which was caused by exposure to asbestos during his time as a chef in the merchant navy where he had to cook in terrible conditions.

He was in a wheelchair when he came to see me in Barnstaple and I remember him saying after the show that it was the best gig he'd ever seen me do, a remark which I have long since treasured. It was very sad to see him so weak and withered because he had always been such a big, strong man who was so full of life. The cancer had just eaten away at him.

When we got back to Woody Bay after finishing the tour, Marguerite told us that Eddie had got a lot worse and had been admitted to North Devon District Hospital. We went to see him several times and one occasion he asked Trevor to lift him up in bed. When Trevor went to take hold of him under his arms he screamed in agony, which was awful to see, knowing his unbelievable tolerance for pain.

Not only was he suffering terribly, he was annoyed at the poor level of care in the hospital.

On one of our visits he said, 'They're bloody useless in here. You can't even get a glass of water. I've had enough, I'm going home. I'd rather die at home.'

Shortly after, on 9 March 2000, we got a call from Marguerite to say he'd passed away on the settee in his sleep at home in Bideford. Trevor and I and the family were devastated.

He was only sixty-three, which is not old by today's standards, yet he had lived a hell of a life and he lived it to the full. As a youngster he had been a professional boxer, once fighting on the same bill as Henry Cooper. A few years later he volunteered to go to Malaysia for his National Service, where he studied aikido with Master Thamby Rajah in Seremban. Master Thamby, who is considered to be the father of Malaysian aikido, was also a pioneer of judo. I remember Eddie telling me how he had tried to attack Master Thamby but couldn't get near him; as soon as he did he found himself lying on the mat. From that moment on he was hooked on aikido and Master Thamby's teaching. He become an army judo champion and later went to Japan to study aikido with a very famous teacher called Gozo Shioda. Shioda created the Yoshinkan style after learning from the founder of aikido, Morihei Ueshiba. When Eddie came back from Malaysia in 1961 he introduced this type of aikido to Britain. Later he got involved with professional wrestling under the name of 'Doctor Kamikaze'.

Eddie was such a loveable man and a real character. I can honestly say that I don't think I would have stuck at aikido for all these years if it hadn't been for him. He had a major influence on aikido in Britain, introducing and nurturing so many people, several of whom I still practise with today. We still have aikido memorials to him every year in early March.

One particular story about him comes to mind that demonstrates his toughness. When Trevor and I were into jet skiing he said to us he'd always wanted to have a go at it so we arranged for him to have a try. We turned up on a very cold day in the spring at Instow, not far from Bideford where he lived.

We were all standing around waiting for him, wearing our wetsuits and gloves, when he appeared in nothing more than a pair of swimming trunks.

Trevor said, 'Have you got a wetsuit, Ed?'

'I don't need one of those,' he answered.

Trevor looked at me and whispered, 'I know he's tough, but we'll soon find out how hard he really is when he goes into that water.'

And with that Eddie walked into the sea to the jet ski without registering the slightest hint that he felt the cold. He wasn't pretending, he just didn't feel it. He got on and it was just like that episode of *Only Fools and Horses* when Del Boy rides the jet ski in Florida and can't turn it. All we could see from the beach was white water where he was hanging on to the jet ski. While he didn't manage to stand up, he was never ever going to let go.

He came back to the beach, got out of the water, dried himself off and went home as if nothing had happened. The sea that day was at its coldest after the winter. We all stood there amazed. He could not only talk the talk, he could walk the walk as well.

After the sad affair of Eddie's funeral, we focused on Jay and Joanna's forthcoming wedding in the summer. Jay and Joanna had hit it off from the very moment they met, so it was no real surprise Jay had asked Joanna to marry him. What did concern us was how in our current financial situation we were going to give them a good wedding and honeymoon.

Together with Joanna's parents we booked Armathwaite Hall, a superb wedding venue in the Lake District, for 9 July and we managed to take care of the honeymoon by agreeing to do some shows for Steve Wolski who had an old-fashioned, cabaret-style club up in Wakefield. For quite a bit of money, on a fairly regular basis, he used to ask me to sing there for a week. When he mentioned doing a stint in 2000 I wasn't too keen but, knowing Jay and Joanna were getting married, he suggested I did three gigs in exchange for two weeks on board one of his luxury yachts in the Caribbean. It wasn't a difficult decision.

The wedding was a fabulous occasion. Joanna looked absolutely gorgeous and Jay was as handsome as ever. Together they made a great couple. Mums are often said to be sad when their sons get married but with me, it was the exact opposite because Joanna is such a wonderful woman. I was so pleased for them both because they were totally in love with each other, and I'm pleased to say they still are today.

We'd made arrangements for Jean Roussel to come over to play the 'Wedding March' on the piano, which was a lovely touch. After the ceremony we all went outside for the photographs, as it was a beautiful summer's day, so beautiful that it inspired our friend Mickey Bell to strip off behind a hedge and streak across the croquet lawn. I'd never been that keen on croquet, but the memory of Mickey's performance and having the chance to play at the wedding has given me a new perspective. Nowadays, Trevor and I play whenever we stay at a posh country hotel; always, it has to be said, with a wry smile on our faces.

In the evening Jean was at the piano and I decided to get up and sing. My brother Tony who was the drummer for Billy J. Kramer and the Dakotas, played drums. But, being a rock 'n' roll drummer, he didn't know the meaning of trying to accompany a singer, which is why I found it impossible to sing with him making such a bloody racket. I turned round to him at one point and jokingly said, shaking my finger, 'You're so bloody loud I can't hear myself sing. That's the reason why you've never played drums for me and you never will again!'

Joanna's mother Mary had a few to drink and made the mistake of trying to get Trevor up to dance, something he never does, not even with me. She had a bit of a go at him for being boring and went to pull him up, and promptly fell over backwards on her arse, which caused quite a laugh.

After a great wedding day Trevor and I hoped the honeymoon would live up to its billing. Fortunately, it surpassed it. Jay and Joanna had a fabulous time. They were treated like royalty on board the yacht as they were sailed all round the Virgin Islands. They didn't have to lift a finger. They had cooks and waiters, all they had to do was eat, drink and swim. They loved it.

When they came back they were so grateful for the time they'd had. Trevor and I were just so happy we'd been able to give them such a fantastic honeymoon despite not having any money. Evidently, Jay and Joanna had also spent some time talking about getting more involved in managing my career as a natural progression from booking my last tour, and had decided they were going to take on the management full-time.

I was thrilled that they wanted to come on board, especially knowing how bad the situation was. I also knew they would be totally committed and as such would probably be the best people to try to turn things around. They immediately asked whether we had any recordings we could sell to make some quick money. Trevor mentioned he had recorded my week at the Palladium in 1978 on 16-track, which apparently was quite something at the time. He dug it out of the archives, mixed it, and Jay and Joanna arranged the packaging and marketing. It did the job by bringing in some much-needed money. Now I think it's actually become something of a collector's piece.

They got busy booking dates from September through to early December. And Jay had the idea of making a contemporary album with me and was planning how we could make it happen. He felt we were lacking a really talented keyboard player so we came up with the idea of getting in touch with Duncan Mackay of 10cc fame. Despite the unforgettable memory of falling into our cesspit and living in South Africa, Duncan agreed to come back. We were pleased when he agreed because he is a seriously accomplished musician, who is not only a great keyboard player but also a pretty reasonable violinist and an exceptionally good writer.

Our enthusiasm very quickly disappeared when he arrived at our house and we saw one of his fingers was heavily bandaged. He said he'd hit his hand with a hammer while mending a fence. To be honest, this wasn't the only problem. We later realised he was taking some pretty heavy drugs and drinking a lot, which wasn't good knowing his alcoholic past.

He told us not to worry about the finger but after three or four days of him not performing to his usual standard and then not turning up one morning for rehearsal, we knew something was seriously wrong. Trevor went down to The Hunter's Inn where he was staying and couldn't get any response from knocking on his bedroom door. He got a pass key and found Duncan lying in a pool of sick, looking like death. We got him to hospital where we found out his immune system had been weakened by the booze and drugs he'd been doing, and that he was suffering from septicaemia.

He came back a few days later after having had a course of the right sort of drugs and we finished rehearsals. As Duncan's such a natural musician he was able to catch up. It didn't last. Our first gig was a warm-up at a club in Bradford called Pennington's. It was just after the July 2001 riots, which meant it was pretty scary as we were parked up at night in the motor home at the back of the venue.

Midway through the show we realised Duncan must have taken some pills and had a drink because he kept wobbling about on his stool, looking as if he might fall off at any time. Friend and tour manager Alan Henderson got a grip of the situation quickly and came up on stage and held Duncan in place by the hips. Somehow we managed to get through the gig by the skin of our teeth. Luckily, it was a bar-type set-up, which meant it wasn't as intense as being in a theatre. After the show Trevor went to speak to Duncan about what had happened; one minute he was standing having a drink and the next he had fallen on the floor in a heap. Trevor had seen enough and told him to go. As we had a week before the start of the tour proper we managed to get Jonny Dyke to replace him. After the trauma of that night, the rest of the tour went very smoothly.

The start of 2001 saw Trevor doing the sound for the second of Andy Williams' three UK shows. At the end of January Jay, Joanna, Joey and I went to see one of the concerts at the Colston Hall in Bristol. Andy put on a great show and the sound wasn't bad either. It was brilliant to see Trev doing what he does best for someone other than myself. After the show we all went back stage to see Andy; I hadn't seen him since our honeymoon in Las Vegas in 1978. Having chatted for a while Andy asked, 'Elkie, how would you feel about Trevor coming over to America to do the sound at my theatre in Branson for three months?'

Without as much as a pause, I replied, 'Yes please, how soon can he go?'

Another good earning opportunity wasn't to be missed, even if it meant losing my 'Jord' for a few months. Everything was agreed and we planned my next tour to coincide with Trevor flying out to Missouri, on 11 September 2001.

In the meantime, Jay and I were hard at work writing and putting songs together for what became our first album together, *Shangri-La*. It was an amazing experience making an album with Jay. He is so creative and so talented. *Shangri-La* was a very experimental album. And, unusually, I had a hand in writing most of the songs on the album.

The title track came from a composition by North Devon music student Tim Petherick who we got to know through Alan Welch who played keyboards and did a lot of the arrangements on the album. I loved the melody he'd created and I decided to write some lyrics to it. Jay and I were very pleased with the result, but I will never forget Tim's reactions when he came to see me in concert with his parents. He was just so overwhelmed that I'd recorded the song and made it the title track of my album.

As the album wasn't due to be completed and released until the following year we decided to promote it heavily on the road. 'The Strange Fruit Tour' – named after the protest song Billie Holiday made famous which I'd covered – began on 22 June at the Gaiety Theatre in Ayr.

In an effort to make some money we wanted to record a show for a live CD but we hit a major problem when the band refused to play on it unless they were paid a ridiculous amount of money. Consequently, we weren't able to afford to record anything. It was a real chicken and egg situation. Our desperate financial position, coupled with the fact gigs always paid us so late, meant we were falling behind on paying the band, and we of course needed the band's support to get a record out to try to make some money.

Early into the tour, we had to go to London so that I could sing 'Pearl's A Singer' at a tribute concert for song-writers Leiber and Stoller on 4 July at the HMV Apollo. As we were already travelling in the motor home we took it to London and parked in the alleyway next to the theatre. Joey, who is super-confident, got talking to Tom Jones while I was rehearsing and somehow mentioned that we were touring in a motor home. The next minute he was showing Tom around the motor home. Joey said he really liked it. I have to say I was far more concerned about how tidy it was.

Jerry Leiber was very kind to me at the concert. I always liked Jerry and admired him as a lyricist, but I was never quite as keen on Mike for some reason. The gig also gave me the chance to catch up with some other people I hadn't seen for years, most notably soul singer Ruby Turner and Ben E. King who I thought was as brilliant as ever, even though he must have a good few years on me.

When I came to go on stage, Jimmy Tarbuck gave me a lovely introduction. I've always got on extremely well with Jimmy over the years and I think he's actually a genuine fan of mine as he very often comes to my shows at Cadogan Hall in London. I was upset not to get the chance to talk to boxer Barry McGuigan, who was introducing one of the acts, as we discovered we were both big fans of each other.

Bumping into each other several years before in a corridor in a TV studio, it was a case of who could find a pen first to get the other's autograph.

After our diversion to London we got back to the hard work of touring, gigging pretty much every night until we finished on 9 September in Limerick. We had to rush back to North Devon to say our goodbyes to Trevor who was due to fly to America for his three-month stint with Andy Williams. But the tragic events that took place on 11 September 2001 meant he had to wait a couple of days before he could get another flight to Missouri.

Having always been together throughout our marriage it was strange not having Trevor around. Fortunately, I had Joey, Jay and Joanna to keep me company. I had also planned for us to visit Trevor a couple of months into his stay. We went over for two weeks and after we left, Jay and Joanna flew over. Joey and I found Branson a bit boring so we went to LA to see my cousin Michael Gochin and his beautiful wife Carolyn. It was great to see Michael again because, despite being close when we were growing up, we hadn't seen much of each other in our adult lives. Even after living in LA for more than thirty years he still speaks with a Manchester accent, which always impresses me. Joey, who is into fashion, loved the shops and the glitz and glamour of Beverly Hills.

In Branson Andy took us out for Sunday lunch. I remember him remarking about how much I ate. People are always amazed at how much such a small-framed person can pack away. Andy clicked with Joey: I think he could see that he has something of a star quality about him. I'm just so proud of how people seem to love my boys.

During our trip I met some fantastic people. I got on like a house on fire with Andy's drummer Rosa Avila. In fact, we got on so well she and Andy's percussionist Thomas Dostal did a tour with me, which meant that I had two drummers. She is without doubt one of my favourite drummers of all time. Not since the days when the lovely Trevor Morais was in the band have I enjoyed it so much. She was brilliant.

Andy's show in Branson featured the legendary Glen Campbell. What a musician! What particularly impressed me was how he changed his set around depending on how he was feeling. He didn't do the same show two nights in a row. He's quite a hard-drinking, tobacco-chewing individual, but I couldn't help but like him. After one show, I was invited into Andy's dressing room with Joey and Trevor; Andy's very classy wife Debbie was serving drinks. His dressing room was like nothing I'd seen before: it was grander than some of the posh houses I've been in. Glen and Andy were in a great mood and with Andy's older brothers, who helped start his singing career, they launched into all these great songs. I couldn't help joining in here and there although I didn't know the lyrics; it was just such an honour to be around all this talent.

Trevor came home just in time for Christmas, the day after Jay's birthday – 22 December – with his mum and dad, and Robbie and his wife Yvette. Even though we'd been on the road and Trevor had earned well with Andy in Branson, Christmas 2001 was a frugal affair. I had to do something I'd never done before – ask Trevor's family to help us out with money for the food. In all our time at 'Trees', Trevor and I had always laid on Christmas so while I didn't feel embarrassed to ask, I was definitely disappointed that things had come to this.

The tax problem was hurting at every level, and we couldn't afford to make the payments on Jay and Joanna's motor home. Not long after, the company came and repossessed it. It was heartbreaking to see them emptying it and taking it away. Later we found out the company had sold it on for far more than it was actually worth anyway.

Trying to stay positive while the financial problems got worse and worse was hard but we did our best to make the most of 2002. *Shangri-La*, my first album with Jay, was released. It was also my first album since *The Pearls Concert* in 1997 so I apologised to all the 'Elkaholics' that it had taken me six years to make it. Little did they know what I'd been going through. Self-funded and without the big push of a major record company, it was never going to have an impact on the charts. However, it certainly did well, as all the money it made came directly to us.

One promotional interview, however, stands out – an interview with Michael Parkinson for his BBC Radio 2 show *Sunday Supplement*. At the time I was at a real low with all our financial worries.

Jay gave me a very strict brief, he said, 'Just keep to the album, Mum. Talk about the music, don't go on about the aikido.'

I know I have a tendency to talk about aikido given any opportunity, so I took Jay's advice on board. Despite having known Michael for years, I was – for some reason – incredibly nervous. I guess my confidence was shattered because of the worry over our financial troubles. Michael kept telling me to relax which only made it worse.

The conversation went well until he said, 'Tell me a bit about this aikido then?'

I said, 'Well, I've actually come here to talk about my music and the new album.'

He retorted, 'You stick to the singing and I'll do the interviewing.'

It felt very uncomfortable at the time, but all the family thought the interview was great. This still didn't stop me thinking I could have done better. After that I hoped Michael would one day interview me again and we could put the record straight.

Also that year, I recorded with my long-time mentor

Humphrey Lyttelton. Humph had come to see my show in Leicester in 2000 and afterwards we got talking about how we'd never done an album together. I had guested on one of his albums prior to going to America to do *Rich Man's Woman* in 1976 but that was as much as we'd done on record together. It took us a while to get everything organised, but by early 2002 we were ready to record what became the very aptly named *Trouble In Mind* album live in our studio with Humph's band.

While it was a real high to be working on a jazz album with Humph, I was also struggling emotionally as the taxman was looming large. Humph was in a great mood and his band were brilliant to work with. Trevor made a little vocal booth for me, which is probably best described as a telephone box, so that I could be in the studio with the band.

One of the beautiful songs we did on the album was 'Some Other Spring' which is a favourite of mine written by Billie Holiday's arranger's wife Irene Kitchings. I love it so much I nearly always play and sing it in my practice sessions at home. I also recorded lyrics to Humph's hit 'Bad Penny Blues' which he'd sung into a dictaphone one day in his car after going to hospital to visit his wife Jill who was very ill. I have to say I'm very proud of the result, which we named 'Mister Bad Penny Blues'.

It was wonderful to be working with the incredible jazz saxophonist Kathy Stobart, who must have been about seventy-seven at the time. I remember one morning when she wasn't feeling too well she still managed to play an amazing sax solo. The funny thing was, she wasn't happy with it because there was a tiny blip on it. Consequently, she wanted to do it again even though everyone agreed that the quality of performance was there and we didn't need to do it again. But Kathy insisted on doing it again, so we did. Very often, however, when you go to correct one thing in a live recording you lose something elsewhere in terms of the overall performance, and this is what Trevor felt happened here so he ended up going with the first recording. Joey helped Kathy get over her disappointment by going to the decanter, which was full of Glenmorangie, which I'm quite partial to, and getting her a big drink to help her circulation problem.

I will always treasure the four days it took to record *Trouble In Mind*. Both Trevor and I thought it was a complete pleasure to work with Humph, Kathy, Ted Beament, Jimmy Hastings, Mick Hutton and Adrian Macintosh. We all got on so well and a lovely little joke developed about it being time for a glass of wine. We would start work at 10 a.m. and finish at 6 p.m. but at about 4.30 p.m. one of us would raise an imaginary glass to their mouth, which was a signal that it was 'wine o'clock'. Being old pros we didn't get carried away, we'd have a little drink and then finish it off having a laugh in the studio.

We still have some footage that Jay shot of Humph and the band performing. There is a lovely piece of him sitting in the control room on the sofa with Joey. Jay and Joanna also have a souvenir from the session, some bongos that he played for one of the tracks and on which he drew one of his fantastic cartoons.

Humph and I did a few gigs together in the summer of 2002 to show off some of the tracks we'd recorded. We did the Marlborough Jazz Festival, Oakengates at Telford and my local theatre, The Queen's Hall in Barnstaple, which was a very special occasion. Sadly, the incredible high of working with Humph again wasn't to last. Just a few months later our circumstances changed dramatically and we found ourselves moving out of our beautiful home in Woody Bay to live in a mobile home in the middle of a field.

CHAPTER 23

REBORN IN THE USA

We'd had the house on the market ever since we understood the seriousness of our tax problems in 1998 but we never had the slightest bit of interest, which was probably due to its location and the fact we'd transformed it into such a specialised property. While we didn't want to sell the home we loved, we were also under no illusions that it offered the best solution to escaping the financial predicament we were in. By the same token, we thought it was more likely to get repossessed by the building society than sold by us for what we felt was a very reasonable asking price.

After yet more letters from the building society, we had all but given up hope when twenty-four hours after taking it off the market in the summer of 2002 a young, scruffy-looking guy strolled up the drive, asking if we were selling. Trevor, giving him the benefit of the doubt, said we were, to which he asked how much we were looking for.

We later found out he had been referred to us by Dave and Brenda Waller who had just sold their cottage further up the road. They'd told him we were trying to sell and he'd come down on the off chance of talking to us. It then also became apparent that he was enquiring on behalf of his girlfriend's mum and dad who were looking to buy and, better still, they had the money to pay for it.

After that, things moved quickly and they made us a good offer. We accepted. It was so ironic because when we really needed an offer earlier on we couldn't get anything remotely decent at all. We agreed contracts and everything seemed fine, but as is very often the case, things slowed right down for about four months.

From our side, the situation got more complicated because the insolvency people said we couldn't sell the house until a certain part of our debts were paid off. At this point Trevor started to get ill with worry. Luckily, all the problems were eventually ironed out and the sale was agreed, and we moved out of 'Trees' on 5 December 2002. We drove up the lane for the last time without saying very much at all to each other.

Our new home was a field on a farm at Woolacombe, a few hundred yards away from Trevor's favourite hang-gliding spot. He had done a deal with Steve and Vanessa Malin, who own Little Roadway Farm, to park the motor home there. Steve found us a nice place to park and we hooked up the power and got settled in.

As soon as the money from the sale of the house came through we were able to pay off all our debts. We owed a fortune to the bank, and we had lots of other debts, which we had accrued along the way as we struggled to get by, like the £25,000 we had borrowed from Alan Henderson's partner Claire. We also paid the outstanding balance on the motor home and bought a decent second-hand car for touring because I didn't want us to take the motor home on the road if it was going to be our permanent residence. We ordered a trailer with a slide-out for Joey so he could live next to us and helped Jay and Joanna rent a one-bedroom flat in Woolacombe.

By the time everything was sorted out we were left with a sum of money, which was significant but not substantial enough to be able to buy another property. Besides which, of course, we were far too scared to take on any debt having just sorted the last fiasco out, not that anyone would have given us a mortgage anyway.

For the first time in four years we were free from debt and all the worry it brings. You can't explain the relief we all felt. While the previous Christmas had been a frugal affair this one was even stranger, living in a motor home as opposed to our beautiful house. There would be no more big meals round the table at 'Trees'. We spent Christmas with the kids and Trevor's parents at a bistro in Woolacombe. It was a bizarre experience; it was as if life was imitating art and I'd gone back to my Vinegar Joe days and we had actually become rock and roll gypsies, which was the title of our second album.

Although it was all very sad in one way, it was fantastic not to be burdened with all those debts. While we had to come to terms with what had happened, we were understandably a little concerned about what people thought so we spent quite some time pretending that things were great and that we were moving to a beautiful, remote island in the South Pacific, 1,000 miles north-east of Australia, called Vanuatu, which was an amazing place for hang-gliding. With our temporary story in place we got used to our new lives. After a while we even started to go out for the odd meal, which we hadn't done for ages. Trevor built a deck between the motor home and Joey's trailer and in the summer we would sit outside, have a barbecue and enjoy the Woolacombe sunsets from high on the hill.

We were relieved to find that we could actually sit down and enjoy ourselves without worrying. Saying that, I think it took the whole family at least two years to enjoy a decent night's sleep again. But what inspired me was the knowledge that the Jordan family could survive and that we had been given the chance to start again. And that's exactly what we did, despite the inevitable scars.

The whole 'moving-out of Trees' process had been a truly horrible experience, not least because we were moving from a beautiful, large house to a motor home. To say it was a shock to the system would be an understatement. Downsizing radically we had to be ruthless about what we took with us, what we sold and what we put into storage. What really hurt was when a friend of ours who deals in bric-a-brac came over and took it all away to sell for us, knowing we would get very little back for it. It also hurt when our buyer's brand new kitchen turned up before we left and we had to store it in the garage.

During the sale process we negotiated, in writing, to sell all the fixtures and fittings. We had a lot of decent stuff that we couldn't take with us and didn't want to put into storage; we had already filled two containers. A few months after leaving we received a letter from the new owners saying they had to hire two skips to get rid of all our fixtures and fittings. We were flabbergasted because they had bought them.

Then to cap it all, they called Trevor asking if he would go back and tell them how to look after the well and keep it clear of Japanese knotweed, which can be very hard to control unless you keep on top of it. After spending a good while with them, Trevor left with the feeling they hadn't taken his advice in properly.

Lo and behold, a few months later when we're out on the road he gets a call asking if he'd go back and help them because everything was clogged up again. He'd found it difficult going back once to the house he loved so much, he sure as hell wasn't going to do it a second time.

Prior to leaving 'Trees', Trevor took a phone call from the producers of the television show *Reborn in the USA*. It led to one of the oddest experiences of my career. When Trevor explained the show was to take ten music artists and acts from the UK that were unknown in America around the capital cities, singing songs appropriate to each, and let live theatre audiences decide who they liked most, I said I quite fancied it.

He then had to drive his parents down to France for a holiday, which meant Jay, Joanna and I carried on the talks with the production company. In total, I had three meetings with the producers before they asked me to take part. My decision to accept was always a bone of contention with Trevor. He always felt I shouldn't have done it, convinced it wouldn't turn out as they'd promised and that the very concept would make me seem like a has-been.

I, on the other hand, thought the show would give me a great opportunity to sing to a new audience, both in America and on TV at home. The fact the show involved being in another country on a tour bus also didn't bother me. I was, however, a lot more concerned about being away from Joey as we are very close. At one stage I talked to the producers about letting him come with me but they wouldn't have that. They said he could come over to visit, but I had to do the show on my own.

I flew out to New Orleans on Sunday 2 March, the day after our twenty-fifth wedding anniversary. I was on the same plane as former Imagination singer Leee John and Spandau Ballet front man Tony Hadley. Being together from the very beginning allowed the three of us to bond and as a result we all got on well throughout the filming. We used to go out to soul restaurants and have a good laugh together. Leee and I had a lot in common and I soon discovered that he is a great music historian; it was also obvious that Tony had a bit of intelligence about him and that he wasn't half bad in the old vocal department. Leee and I are still friends and he comes to see me perform whenever he can, which gives us the chance to keep up the *Reborn* tradition of going out for meals together.

I also enjoyed the company of David Van Day from the pop duo Dollar. His singing partner Thereza Bazar, who's a Jewish girl like me, was good fun as well. We all went to the Mardi Gras street parade a couple of days after arriving in New Orleans. The celebrations were amazing but after a while I'd had enough and decided I wanted to go back to the hotel.

David realised this and said, 'Elkie, I don't think you're going to be able to find the hotel on your own, let me come and give you a hand.' That was a very kind thing for him to do. Someone had obviously told him I'm completely useless at finding my way around.

A few days after the excitement of Mardi Gras, we did the first show. I chose songs that I felt would be reasonably compatible with my voice and, I have to say, I thought the guy who did the backing tracks did a very good job. I was the first to sing. I guess they thought they'd better let the old girl get things going. I sang 'Love Letters' which I was relieved to see went down quite well with the audience. Afterwards Davina McCall, who was hosting the series, asked if it was scary going first.

I said, 'Well somebody's got to do it.'

When everyone had sung, the New Orleans audience voted, which resulted in Sonia (of 'You'll Never Stop Me Loving You' fame) and Dollar being put up for eviction. This led to a big falling out between them all. In the end Dollar lost out on the UK phone vote and were sent home. I felt David was portrayed very badly on the show, especially with the whole Sonia argument thing, which came after the two of them were put up for eviction. They made him look awful when in fact he's a very nice guy, and a bit of an old pro like me.

Travelling on the tour bus and staying in cheap hotels was like water off a duck's back to me. It made me laugh because all the other contestants spent so much time moaning and throwing their toys out of the pram every five minutes, instead of just getting on with it. I found it a lot easier because I'd been on the road the rough way, and none of them had. What they considered to be terrible times –dodgy hotels and awful travelling – was just normal to me. It made me think of my friend, the comedian and folk singer Richard Digance, who was always able to see the funny side of any bad situation.

Richard did support for me for many years in the late 1970s and early 1980s when I was going through a stage of hardly saying anything on stage. Having comedians like Richard, or Ian Irving, meant I didn't have to worry. Over the years though, I've changed and now can't stop talking at my gigs!

Our second show was in Philadelphia where I sang 'The Rose' which didn't go down too well with the audience as I was put up for eviction with Gina G. I managed to survive the phone vote and moved on to Detroit where I did The Supremes' song 'You Keep Me Hanging On'. My version wasn't popular with the audience either and I was up against Tony Hadley for being thrown off.

I made my final appearance in Memphis where I sang 'Mess Of The Blues' and lost the vote, unsurprisingly, to Tony. This meant I didn't go to Nashville. Strangely, I think they were glad to get rid of me. I didn't play the show-biz razzamatazz; I was too down to earth. I should have listened to Trevor, he never thought it was a good idea.

In truth, the show had been a pile of rubbish. The venues they chose were dreadful; a lot of them were clubs seating only a couple of hundred people. We had been promised proper theatres. I felt we had been sold down the line. I remember Tony Hadley looking at me and saying, 'This isn't what we were told, was it Elkie?'

I said, 'No, it bloody well wasn't.' As far as I recall we were told we were going to be playing good venues and the show was going to be televised all over America, not just in the UK and some parts of Europe.

Several positives did, however, come out of the experience: my friendship with Leee John, I gained some new fans on both sides of the Atlantic and with time on my hands I managed to write a few new songs which later went on to my *Electric Lady* album. I wanted to make the most of my downtime in hotel rooms so I asked the production team to hire me a piano, which they did. This enabled me to do some practice and try a few things out. Actually, I'm pretty sure I was the only person on the show that could play and sing.

I came home slightly better off than I thought I would. Having been through the mill financially, I went to America without a credit card to my name. Jay and Joanna made sure I had lots of traveller's cheques and a fair amount of cash, but while that was fine most of the time, it was a bit embarrassing in the hotels when I came to check in and they wanted a credit card. I always had to put cash behind the desk: I expect some of the others were wondering what the hell I was up to. The production company gave us a daily allowance of $20. Most of the cast spent it. I, on the other hand, took a more prudent approach, spending only on essentials, which meant I still had nearly all my traveller's cheques when I came to fly home in late March.

Back in England, I put *Reborn* behind me and got back into doing my own thing with a handful of shows in the summer months of June, July and August, as well as preparing for a more intensive tour due to start in mid-October.

A few weeks before we were due to leave I received a phone call that left me reeling. I was vacuuming the motor home on 26 September 2003 when I answered the phone to be greeted by the voice of Anne Palmer, Robert Palmer's mother, who was calling to tell me Robert had died of a heart attack in a hotel room in Paris. Apparently, he'd been taking a two-day break after recording a TV show in the UK. I was devastated by the news, as it was such an out of the blue thing. He was only fifty-four, which is such a young age to die.

I felt terribly sorry for Anne, who I'd got to know very well over the years since meeting her in the Vinegar Joe days. She always comes to see my shows when I'm in or around Scarborough where she and her husband Les, who passed away in 2007, brought up Robert. Robert was born in Malta where Les was a British naval intelligence officer, but the family moved to Scarborough when he was about ten.

At fifteen, while still at school, Robert started his first band, the Mandrakes. He then went to art college and began his career as a graphic designer before getting his first singing break when he joined The Alan Bown! We came together as part of Dada, and then Vinegar Joe. As a musician Robert did very well for himself. I followed his career with close interest and I still have all his records in my collection. Robert was a great songwriter. He had a great sound, which people loved, and he used this to maximum effect and made a lot of money. As well as having big hits and number ones all over the world with songs like 'Addicted To Love' and 'Simply Irresistible', I think it was because he wrote most of his own material that he was so successful. Lots of his songs have been covered by very famous artists such as Tina Turner and Rod Stewart. Not having written any of my hit songs has meant I've never been fortunate to have that additional lucrative second income. This is why I've spent so many years on the road – I could never relax and just wait for the money to come in, I always had to keep working.

Robert was ultra cool, always following all the latest trends, and his fashion consciousness helps explain the designer-suit-wearing stage image he created. He loved the finer side of life, especially clothes, food and drink. When I first met him he hardly drank but by the time he left Vinegar Joe, however, it was a different story. Many years later I met up with some people who had worked with him doing hair and make-up and they said he could quite easily knock back a bottle of vodka as well as being partial to cocaine. If I had to guess what brought on the heart attack I would say it was probably a combination of things – good living, booze and drugs. Life often has a terrible way of catching up with you.

A little while after he died Anne sent me a video of his last interview at Ronnie Scott's where he had been making a DVD as a tribute to all his favourite singers. I think it was filmed a week or so before he died. When I watched it I was struck by how terrible he looked; I'd known him when he was young and devilishly handsome. He was just so good-looking that everybody wanted to be near him. There was even some talk in the papers that he'd had an affair with Princess Diana. Knowing Robert, I wouldn't put it past him. All I know is that wherever we went as Vinegar Joe, the girls used to go crazy for him, and they all hated me because they thought we were an item, which of course couldn't have been further from the truth. Deep down, I loved Robert and did until the day he died, but it was more of a brotherly love than a romantic one.

I'm still sad we never saw or spoke to each other again after our last meeting at Steve York's flat in North London shortly after Vinegar Joe split up. My fondest memories of Robert are the times we spent together away from the band. Sometimes, when the rest of them went for fish and chips, we would go off and find a restaurant and enjoy a good meal and nice bottle of wine. We wouldn't talk about anything in particular; we'd just enjoy each other's company and then make our way back to the gig feeling quite good about the world.

Trevor tried several times over the years to get us back in contact. His mum Anne told him to call me, but for some reason he never did. While I don't know his reasons for not picking up the phone, I was very pleased to hear from Anne that he had been voting for me on *Reborn* from his home in Switzerland.

CHAPTER 24

ELECTRIC LADY

A few weeks after learning of Robert's untimely death I was back on the road.

Some time earlier, we had made a family decision to stop touring and instead, do a series of one-off gigs throughout the year. This meant Trevor and I could drive up the day before a gig, stay in a nice out-of-town hotel, set up, do the gig and then drive home as soon as the show was finished. We felt this would give us sufficient income and, more importantly, an improved quality of life by cutting out the gruelling daily performances and nights in the motor home in theatre alleyways.

The formula has been so successful I've been doing it ever since. It also enabled us to bring Jean Roussel back into the band as he could quite easily fly in from Paris once a week. Having a truly talented keyboard player back on board meant we were able to achieve something we had been talking about for a while. Not long after Jay and Joanna had decided to get involved in my management we had all sat down in the conservatory at 'Trees' and had a conversation about my shows. I never wanted to do songs from my old albums, other than the songs everyone expects me to sing.

Jay said to me, 'Mum, why aren't you doing songs from the old albums?'

I replied, 'I'm not really sure. I didn't think anyone was that interested in my old stuff. Maybe I will then.' At which point Trevor looked up in amazement because I'd been telling him for ages that I didn't want to do that material. He was delighted because he felt he could finally put together a show that people would appreciate more.

Jean, of course, had played on all my early albums, which meant he was the perfect person to bring those songs to life on stage with me. This important change in personnel didn't come to fruition until I'd finished recording the *Electric Lady* album, a process that was spread over several years due to our changing living arrangements.

We began laying down tracks for the album at Woody Bay after finishing *Trouble in Mind* with Humph. Living in a motor home in the middle of a field was obviously a challenge from a recording point of view, but Jay and I used the experience to write 'Trailer Trash', a very personal song, which summed up our feelings about the whole tax episode. It has some very emotional lines, which people wouldn't have understood at the time because we kept our story a closely guarded family secret. Now, however, you can see the meaning in them, especially lyrics like:

'They took my home and all I owned in taxes, but they'll never take my soul or dignity' and 'The boys and I just want to make a living', and 'I don't feel that I did anything wrong, I certainly won't go down without a fight'. This was very much how I felt at the time and still do for that matter. In fact, I even recorded the vocal in a trailer. As we didn't have anywhere to record, we bought a new six-by-six trailer, which we soundproofed and got some power to. This gave us our own little studio, albeit not quite as sophisticated as our previous one.

We also recorded some of the album in the front room of Jay and Joanna's flat in Woolacombe and at the house they went on to rent in Braunton where they turned one of the bedrooms into a studio. We finished the album there and I also tried to record a new vocal to 'Trailer Trash' but I could never get it to be as good as the one I'd done in the little trailer, so Jay insisted we went with the first version.

Jay and I wrote six other songs for the album, some of which I had come up with while on the *Reborn in the USA* tour. Among them was the title track 'Electric Lady' which comes from a nickname I had before moving to Devon that went on to become a company – 'Electric Elk'. I'm also very proud of 'Try Harder', 'So Good Looking' and 'White Girl Lost In The Blues' which was my take on Sonny Terry and Brownie McGhee's version of Michael Franks's song 'White Boy Lost In The Blues'. Even though I liked theirs, I re-wrote the lyric completely, making it personal to me.

The record as a whole was a very gritty mix of my own material, alongside great songs like Bob Dylan's 'The Groom's Still Waiting At The Altar', Tony Joe White's 'Out Of The Rain' and Paul Rodgers' 'Muddy Water Blues'. I've always admired Paul's singing ever since Vinegar Joe supported his band Free and I think this song is terrific. I haven't seen Paul for years, but I have a special memory of trying to sing 'In The Midnight Hour' with him at Boz Burrell's house to the accompaniment of Tim Hinkley on piano. I say trying to sing because I didn't really know the words.

I still play many of these *Electric Lady* tracks in the second half of my shows, which always tends to be a bit more rocky. It was a real pleasure making the album with Jay, and the difficult and changing recording circumstances only made it more fun. The whole family was delighted with how the album turned out when it came to be released in 2005 and I was thrilled that it was well received by both fans and critics, who said it was one of the best things I'd done for many years.

The promotion of the album went well. This was partly down to working with Laurie Jay who I had first got to know on the Don Arden show in 1960 when he was the drummer in the backing band, The Echoes. We met Laurie again by going to see our friend Mike Patto's son, Mike

Patto Jnr, sing at Ronnie Scott's. We had no idea at the time that Laurie was managing Mike Jnr so we were very surprised to see one another. Laurie was interested to hear about *Electric Lady* and asked for Trevor to send him some songs. When he heard them he got excited and arranged a meeting with Jay and Joanna to discuss how he might be able to help.

Having paid for the entire recording ourselves, Laurie offered to fund the photography and the promotion. This included doing a week-long showcase at Ronnie Scott's in mid-February, followed by dates throughout the rest of the year under the title of 'Elkie – The First 45 Years'.

I had last performed at Ronnie Scott's following the release of my first album *Rich Man's Woman* in 1975, again as part of a promotional campaign. The place hadn't changed very much. You still had to do two sets, and for me the second is always too late. I did my usual show, but just split it in half. The first show was at 9 p.m. and the second at about 11 p.m. I didn't enjoy it because I've never liked singing late at night.

During my week at Ronnie's, Trevor had a fun surprise visit from someone he used to work with in the early 1970s. He was down in the green room one evening with the band when he was told that someone wanted to see him upstairs about a lot of money he owed him. Having been through everything we had, he was getting ready for the worst when all of a sudden Jack Jones poked his head around the corner. Apparently, he always took great enjoyment in winding Trevor up and couldn't resist the opportunity when he saw I was performing at Ronnie's. It's always amusing to see someone get the better of Trevor in a wind-up, as he's usually the one causing all the trouble.

Jack came to see me after the show and said, 'You really sing the blues well.'

Not a bad remark coming from such a well-respected

singer. I remember thinking, 'Well, he must think I'm all right.'

After the dates at Ronnie's things just fell apart with Laurie because of a difference of opinion about which track we should go with for the single. As a result we went our separate ways. The album, however, did rather well for us. Trevor always maintains it would have been in the top 10 had it gone through a major record company. I think that's probably a slight exaggeration, but we were all very pleased with its performance.

The following year we decided to embark on another live album project featuring some of my favourite and most successful tracks, alongside a couple I hadn't sung before. To add a little extra magic we came up with the idea of inviting some special guests to play on it including the great steel player Sarah Jory; jazz guitar player Martin Taylor, who I got to know at the British Academy of Songwriters, Composers and Authors awards ceremony; and Humph. By now we also had a really strong band in place with Jean Roussel on keyboards, Geoff Whitehorn on guitar, Brian Badhams on bass, Stephen Jones on sax, Lee Noble on backing vocals, and not forgetting my long-time drummer Mike Richardson.

To give us a good merchandising opportunity at gigs Trevor and Jay came up with the idea of making a DVD and getting all the guests who had played on the album together at Shepperton Studios to make a film version of the album.

We were also lucky enough to get Rick Wakeman to play keyboards, as he was a friend of the studio owners. I hadn't met Rick since his days in Yes. What a terrific musician! He fitted in with the rest of the band straightaway as if he'd been playing with us for years. Trevor, being the sympathetic man he is, spent ages talking to Rick about his problems with alcohol over the years only to finish the conversation by standing up and saying, 'Right, I'm off for a pint.'

Prior to *Electric Lady* going on sale I managed to persuade Trevor to let us move out of the motor home into a rented flat in Woolacombe. After two years of living in such a confined space I wanted to be in a proper building again. If I'd left it to Trevor we'd still be there now. Being so close to his regular hang-gliding spot he had no real desire to be anywhere else. We took a three-bedroom apartment at Camelot Court, which was, conveniently for Trevor, across the road from The Golden Hind pub.

In fact, it was at the Hind two years later that we arranged to meet up with my former keyboard player Andrew Murray who I hadn't worked with since the *Amazing* album in 1996. One day, completely out of the blue, Andrew got in touch again to say he was coming down to see his dad and brother in nearby Bideford and would we like to get together for a drink. Knowing that Jean Roussel was finding it hard work flying over from Paris for my gigs which were now, of course, far more spread out than they used to be, Trevor asked Andrew whether he'd consider coming back on board. And, much to our surprise, he said he'd love to.

Having been living in the relative comfort of Camelot Court for a couple of years a friend happened to mention he was about to move out of a rented cottage in the neighbouring village of Mortehoe. We went to have a look and decided it would suit us, being in a quieter spot than the flat. We eventually moved in October, which was roughly the same time as Jay and Joanna moved from their house in Braunton to a village nearer us.

The decision to carry on renting was, by now, one of choice rather than necessity. Trevor and I talked about buying again and went to see a lot of houses in the Woolacombe area, but we couldn't seem to find one that was right.

Staying in the Woolacombe and Mortehoe area was a must as all three of my boys – Trevor, Jay and Joey – are flying mad. Trevor taught both Jay and Joey to fly hang-gliders in their early teens and subsequently paragliders. Both boys are excellent pilots and are active members of the North Devon Hang-gliding and Paragliding Club; in fact Joey was the club secretary and Jay is the site officer. Joey has incredible passion for paragliding and has excelled in the sport and at nineteen won his class in the 2006 British Open Paragliding Championship. Trevor and I were very proud parents. He and Jay have now turned their passion for flying into a business by setting up the North Devon Paraguiding and Paragliding School.

Joey's such a confident and trustworthy pilot he has taken me up several times. It was a great buzz, quite different from my hang-gliding experiences with Trevor. I prefer hang-gliding because it feels more like flying as you're lying down next to the pilot as opposed to sitting upright in a para-glider. Maybe, one day I'll go up solo to understand what excites Joey so much about the sport. Joey's enthusiasm for flying and paragliding is something he always used to talk to Humph about whenever he was down. Humph, whom Joey always referred to as 'the genius', was very keen to go up in the sky in a paraglider. He even sent his son Stephen an email in early 2007 saying that he planned to let Joey take him up in the spring.

The email read, 'He is a fully trained expert and takes his mum aloft regularly, so I have no qualms. What an experi-ence it will be, floating silently above North Devon among the seagulls.'

He and Susan da Costa – his manager and partner – came down one weekend with a view to him going up in the air with Joey but the weather wasn't suitable. Humph's busy schedule didn't allow him to get back down to Devon again, and sadly he passed away the following year without ever having the opportunity to experience flying in a paraglider.

I remember very clearly where I was when I was given the news that Humph had died. I was in Jersey on 25 April – a beautiful spring day, the day before a show at the Opera House. Susan rang and said very simply, 'He's gone.'

It was a horrible shock but I had no choice but to carry on working. And that is exactly what Humph would have expected. We had known Humph was going into Barnet General Hospital in North London to have an operation but we didn't dream it would turn out as it did. We later discovered he had gone in for an operation to repair a very large swelling in the abdominal area of the aorta artery, which, if left, would have burst and caused him to die in great pain. Despite the procedure being very risky he felt it was his only chance so he decided to go ahead.

The hospital did a week of extensive health checks and they found his heart and lungs were fine, which was pretty amazing at the age of eighty-six. The biggest danger of treating such a big aneurysm, however, is the chance of debris escaping and damaging organs, which is exactly what happened to Humph.

Before the operation he said to his son Stephen, 'This is a win-win situation for me. If the operation goes to plan I will wake up with my family all around me. If it doesn't then I will know no different but you will all be okay.'

It took me a long time to come to terms with his death as he had always been such a great friend and mentor to me. From the moment I got to know him on our train journey to an RAF base in the mid-1960s I found him to be a source of both wisdom and inspiration, and this became greater as the years went by. Humph had a massive influence on my singing career. He gave me confidence at a time when I had very little. Without his words of wisdom and support I'm not sure I would be the singer I am today.

Humph and I formed a connection almost instantaneously, and it grew into a bond that would last more than forty years. He became a close friend of the whole family, coming down to visit us lots of times over the years. He always remembered everyone's birthdays and would always send a card with one of his trademark cartoons. We have them all and we'll treasure them always.

Our friendship, at first sight, might have seemed quite unlikely as Humph came from a very distinguished, well-educated background whereas I come from a simple, yet affluent Manchester family. Even though he'd had a some-what privileged background Humph never looked down on anyone and he never talked up or down to anyone. This was something I felt came through on his Radio 4 show *I'm Sorry I Haven't A Clue*. I always thought he made the show accessible to a very wide audience because of the way he was. Now I feel it's aimed at a more upper-class section of society, which is a shame. In my opinion it's not the same without him.

I was honoured when Susan asked me to sing at his funeral, which was to be a non-religious affair near his home in North London. As he'd given me the confidence to be the professional I am today, I agreed without hesitation. I sang 'Trouble In Mind' – the title track of the album we made together – with the accompaniment of Humph's great keyboard player Ted Beament and saxophonist Jimmy Hastings. As Ted and Jimmy had both played on the album and we'd performed numerous gigs together, we only needed half an hour's rehearsal before the funeral to get used to the acoustics of the venue. And, despite it being the funeral of our dear friend, there was still time for an amusing moment. As I was singing without a PA system Jimmy very quickly realised Ted's piano playing was drowning me out, so turning to him he said, 'Turn down man for heaven's sake, Elkie can't hear herself think, let alone sing.' He was great, he was like my musical director and sound engineer rolled into one. It was all good-natured stuff, especially as they are a right pair of jokers.

Singing with Humph lying there beside me in his wicker

basket coffin, complete with trumpet on top, was a bizarre experience. I later learned, from a story Trevor told me about the reaction of a particular mourner, that I must have been singing from the heart. His funeral was absolutely chock-a-block and the only available seat in the whole place was a tiny space next to him, which would have been fine had someone small wanted to sit there. Trevor therefore knew it was going to be a tight fit when Stephen Fry arrived late and tried to squeeze in beside him. Evidently, Stephen was so moved by my singing that he started crying. I either sounded bloody awful or he found it very moving – I'd like to think it was the latter. I can well understand how he must have felt because it was a struggle for me too, but I wasn't going to let Humph down.

After the funeral we went back to Humph's house in Barnet. Everyone was there: Barry Cryer and all the *Clue* team. I found it very strange being in his house as none of his friends, including me, had ever been there. It felt a little impersonal and odd that we were all milling in and out of his study, which he must have regarded as his inner sanctum.

Humph was a very private, clever, interesting, humorous and genuine person, but he could also be very silly and schoolboyish, especially when he was tired. I remember one day during the recording of *Trouble In Mind* he just started throwing his hat around at everybody. Another time he found Joey's whoopee cushion and took great enjoyment getting Kathy Stobart to sit on it. He also liked a drink but, in all the years I knew him, I never saw him drunk. He was a very controlled man, which I think is why he liked his privacy.

A week or so after the funeral, Susan phoned me and said she and the family had been talking about what to do with Humph's ashes. Realising he had always wanted to go up flying with Trevor or the boys, they asked us to fulfil this wish by taking him up in a paraglider and releasing his ashes over Woolacombe.

Naturally we agreed, and made arrangements for Humph and his urn to come down to Devon one last time for his final send-off. As Humph had meant so much to me I was very keen to go up in the paraglider with Joey and scatter his ashes myself. Unfortunately, the flying conditions and my availability conspired against us, which meant Humph's urn was left on the shelf by our television for the whole summer, waiting for the right moment.

Having Humph in our living room was an odd but entirely pleasant experience. Trevor and Joey would both say hello to him whenever they walked past and I too found myself talking to him every morning and evening. I have to say it was lovely to have him there. He was great company. Eventually though, one beautiful day in September the weather was right and I was at home so we all headed up to the hill. Joey took me up and I let Humph go with a few fond words of farewell.

As Susan and Humph's family weren't able to share in the occasion, the boys filmed the whole thing. Jay took a camera in his paraglider and Trevor attached one to the wing of his hang-glider. Afterwards they set the footage they shot to Humph's 'Bad Penny Blues', together with still photographs of his band members and an audio clip of the last *Clue* show he did the night before he died. They finished the film with Humph saying his catch-phrase, 'That's it.'

Susan and the family were delighted with the film and Humph's son Stephen gave us a statuette of a goshawk that he found when he came to clear out his father's belongings. He thought it would be a fitting reminder of Humph and his flying desire. The goshawk now sits in the same spot on the living room shelf where we'd kept Humph's ashes. I find it comforting to know we still have something of Humph close by.

Since saying goodbye to Humph for the last time, for some reason, which I can't really explain, I haven't been up in the paraglider with Joey. However, every time I walk the few miles from our home in Mortehoe, down to Woolacombe village and up to the hang-gliding hill to see Trevor and the boys, I always do so happy in the knowledge that Humph is all around me.

And, while I'm not necessarily the most religious or spiritual person in the world, I was intrigued by a story Trevor told me recently after coming home from flying. One of his hang-gliding friends had apparently been on the sand dunes having a quiet barbecue with his family when they heard the bizarre sound of someone playing the trumpet. Whatever the explanation, I think it's safe to say that Humph's spirit is definitely still with us.

CHAPTER 25

MEETING WILF

Although working with Laurie Jay on the *Electric Lady* promotion hadn't worked out, in the longer term he did unwittingly play a crucial part in my forming a very important new friendship. My daughter-in-law Joanna had got bored at a meeting in his office one day, which is easy to do because he can go on a bit, and spotted a book called *One Of The Family: The Englishman and the Mafia* which she borrowed.

After reading it she passed it to me, certain that I would enjoy it. I read it in no time at all and was completely enthralled and intrigued by the true life story of Wilf Pine who, as I learned, had gone from being a bouncer in clubs on the Isle of Wight to being a successful music promoter before, ultimately, becoming the first Englishman to be accepted by the Mafia in America. I was fascinated by Wilf's life, not only because of what he'd done but also because he had worked with lots of people I'd known, not least Don Arden, the man who discovered me and always scared me half to death.

Although the book had made quite an impression on me, I didn't think too much about it again until the summer of 2007 when I did an interview with John Hannam, who does a talk show on a radio station on the Isle of Wight. We arranged to do the interview at the Cannizaro House Hotel in Wimbledon, as John always prefers to do face-to-face interviews. After recording our conversation in the garden I told him I'd read this amazing book about a guy called Wilf Pine who lived on the island.

I said, 'You don't happen to know him, do you?'

'Know him, I grew up with him,' he replied. After mentioning we knew quite a few of the same people John said he would get in touch with Wilf and set up a meeting between us.

Wilf agreed and we arranged to meet at a pub he regularly used for important business get-togethers. It was a bizarre experience, even for someone like me who has seen a few things in their time. The pub was in a strategically remote location and we were the only ones there, except for Wilf's bodyguards that is, who were discreetly placed so they could keep a close eye on everything around.

I sat down to talk to Wilf and Trevor got talking to one of his friends, Clive Jenkins, known as Jinxie. As soon as Wilf and I started chatting, we instantly clicked. It was one of those magical moments a bit like when Trevor and I met my aikido teacher Eddie Stratton. In fact, I've always felt Wilf and Eddie were a bit alike. They had both led tough lives, and while they had followed very different paths they undoubtedly shared several traits, in addition to being of similar build.

Wilf and I got on like the proverbial house on fire. It just felt like we'd known each other for ages. There are some people in life with whom you just seem to get on from the outset. We had so much in common. Naturally, we shared stories about Don Arden, who had left a mark on both our lives, and then there was my friend Steve Marriott of the Small Faces who Wilf had managed when he formed The Steve Marriott Allstars. He also managed Black Sabbath, The Groundhogs and Stray.

Wilf clearly felt a similar connection because we've gone on to become firm friends. In fact, Trevor and I have come to think of him as our 'godfather'. Not long after we got to know one another I remember him saying to me, 'Please don't take this in a disrespectful way, but I think you're kind of like a female version of me. You can be so hard and then you can watch a silly movie and burst into tears.'

I definitely didn't take it the wrong way, and it actually meant a lot to me because it showed he understood who I am. While I've obviously had a very different life from Wilf's, I've had to be hard to survive as long as I have in the music industry. My experiences in the business have made me who I am today: someone who is outwardly very tough, yet who, as my family will tell you, has a much softer side. And that's something my son Joey enjoys teasing me about when he sees me watching a sad film. He'll say, 'You're not crying again, are you, Mum?' And Wilf is, it appears, very similar as I remember giving him a fairly ordinary birthday present at which point he just melted into tears. He's a very hard man who really appreciates friendship because of the very hard life he's lived.

Although we've only known each other for a relatively short period of time, he's become an important influence on me. He and his wife Ros, who he calls his rock, have been wonderful to us and have made us feel so welcome every time we've been to see them. And without Wilf's encouragement I almost certainly wouldn't have got round to writing this book.

It was Wilf who was the inspiration behind my 2010 album *Powerless*. The journey to *Powerless* began when he suggested I take part in a concert at the London Palladium in August 2008 to celebrate the work of his good friend composer Don Black on his seventieth birthday.

Despite never having sung a Don Black song I was keen to sing in the show – entitled 'Lyrics by Don Black' – as I've always admired his great songwriting talent. I chose to sing the Olivia Newton-John song 'Sam'.

When I met Don at rehearsal we got along well and he was extremely complimentary about what I'd done to his song, saying, 'This is fantastic, Elkie, you've made it your own.'

As is often the case at these types of gigs, artists tend to keep themselves to themselves. However, the person who

I did get to speak to was Lulu, who I often run into. I admire what she's achieved. She's got a lot of savvy, which has helped make her very successful. She's one of the few female artists of a certain age who hasn't gone all mumsy. I also had a great time sharing a dressing room with Marti Webb. I remember being very envious of this incredible fold-up mirror she had. I thought, having experienced the many shortcomings of British theatre dressing rooms over the years, it would be invaluable. I eventually managed to get one and I've been using it ever since. The concert also gave me the chance to accidentally worsen my relationship with Michael Parkinson, who was the host for the evening. Having had that rather uncomfortable interview with him in the middle of our financial problems it would have been good to set the record straight. Instead, Trevor told me afterwards, I blanked him by mistake as he was complimenting me to the audience. I just didn't hear what he said. He must have thought I was still annoyed about the interview. That's two things I've got to put right with Michael.

The following month I was supposed to have been doing a gig with Humph at the Buxton Opera House. Rather than cancelling, I decided to go ahead by doing my normal show but with a special tribute for Humph at the end. I told the audience the story of how he'd made up the lyrics to 'Bad Penny Blues' after going to see his wife in hospital. I said I was going to play the tape and sing along to Humph playing, which they thoroughly enjoyed.

The tape, of course, finished with Humph saying his trademark, 'That's it'.

Prior to the Don Black concert I took part in a charity event organised by the newspaper publisher Richard Desmond at London's Old Billingsgate Market following a request from Nikki Lamborn and Catherine 'Been' Feeney of the band Never The Bride. Richard, who owns the *Daily Express* and *Daily Star* among other things, had put together a charity band called 'The RD Crusaders' with Roger Daltrey and a varying line-up of other musicians. The concert I took part in featured Richard on drums, Pete Townshend's younger brother Simon on guitar and Russ Ballard, who wrote my hit 'No More The Fool', also on guitar, and the excellent bass player Rick Wills of Foreigner and Bad Company. It was strange to see Russ playing guitar, as I'd only known him as a keyboard player and songwriter. It has to be said, he's also a pretty damn good guitar player. It was also a real privilege to play with Simon. Never having met him before, I found him to be a very sound person, and a hugely talented guitarist like his brother.

Through Nikki I'd arranged to sing 'Pearl's A Singer' and a duet with Roger of 'Baby, What You Want Me To Do'. As Roger and I didn't know one another I thought this would be a good song for us to sing together because it's a fabulous bluesy number. I'd appeared at a big rock 'n' roll event with Roger in his Who days, but I don't believe we'd ever met properly. Getting to know one another at rehearsals was fun, especially when I discovered he hadn't learned the words from the CD I'd sent him a few weeks earlier. As I've said before, I'm not too good with people who haven't made the effort to prepare. While Roger was understandably a little slow getting to grips with the lyrics, I very quickly found out he was a performing force to be reckoned with and that he was not only an accomplished guitarist, but an exceptional harmonica player to boot.

When we came to do the show he did a great job, although I have to confess I ended up taking one of his verses when he was slow to come in. We didn't have words about it after, but we did exchange a bit of a look.

It was also fun working with Richard Desmond. Not being one to be fazed by anyone's importance I made sure he knew what I expected from him as a drummer, which was not to get carried away and to play fairly quietly so I could hear myself singing. And, to be fair, he did a pretty reasonable job. With such great musicians around me I didn't have any worries about the quality of the performance. If I did, it wouldn't have mattered because I had my keyboardist Andrew with me, and we both knew that if all else failed we had got each other.

Despite fitting these two one-off gigs in my already busy work schedule which had me performing an average of five shows a month throughout the year, I was still keen to take on the challenge of making another studio album with Jay. The process began when Wilf asked Don Black if he had any songs that might suit me. Don kindly sent a whole selection of songs to Wilf and me, and unbeknown to one another we both picked 'Powerless' as our favourite. When we talked to Don about it he said another female singer, whose name I don't remember, had recorded it and it had failed miserably.

With one great song identified our conversations very quickly turned to making an album together, with Wilf as executive producer. As he's not a well man he wanted to do something that he felt would make a lasting difference. We both agreed to go away and come up with a selection of tracks to be considered for the album, which by now we thought should be called *Powerless*.

Wilf chose 'Someday We'll All Be Free' by Donny Hathaway, the Bonnie Raitt song 'I Can't Make You Love Me' and Leon Russell's 'A Song For You'. Jay and Joanna suggested the Prince track 'Purple Rain', which I have to admit I hadn't heard but instantly took to. Trevor, who never liked Prince or the song, now acknowledges that it was a good move as it is one of the most requested songs from the album.

Jay and Joanna put forward the Bob Dylan track 'Make You Feel My Love' which Adele covered on her album *19*. I preferred Dylan's version and used it as my inspiration. As soon as I heard it, I knew I could make it my own. We included a great song written by my vocal backing singer and second keyboard player Lee Noble called 'Why'; and my own songs – 'Dancing On The Tables' and 'Holding On To You' which was a tribute to everyone who has been there for me throughout the ups and downs.

I am particularly pleased with 'Dancing On The Tables'; it's my favourite track on the album. It started life as an instrumental track that Jay made for me, which, when I listened to, conjured up images of lap dancing. This led me to create Nona and the story of her lap-dancing career. I decided to name her after the beautiful American vocalist Nona Hendryx who sang as part of the Labelle trio. I think the lyrics are probably the best I've ever written, and Jay developed with my sax player Steve Jones a wonderfully sleazy sound that is absolutely perfect for the words. I think it's also a good example of how well Jay and I work together: it usually starts with him creating a piece of music, which he then gives to me to put words to. Over the years it's become a really enjoyable and highly effective way of working for both of us.

The photography for the cover of *Powerless* was done by Christophe Cohen who did my hair and make-up for several albums, including *Shangri-La* and *Electric Lady*. After suffering a motorbike accident which damaged his arms and hands and forced him to give up hair and make-up, Christophe has gone on to become a very accomplished photographer.

When *Powerless* came out in 2010, Wilf sent a copy to a friend in prison who played it to some of his fellow inmates. The next thing we knew Wilf asked for a box of CDs to be sent in as they all loved 'Dancing On The Tables'. Aside from being popular in prison the album has received some great reviews. It has sold well at gigs and on the web, which everyone involved in the project is very pleased about. When we finished recording the album in 2009 we did have a short debate about whether we should go to a major record company with it or not, but knowing the few independents still left were struggling to avoid being swallowed up by the bigger labels, we decided to keep doing our own thing.

I know I still have a good fan base, judging by the number of sell-out gigs we have week in, week out, so we've just had to come to terms with not getting the glory of public popularity in the charts and do what had to be done in order to survive the rough patch. And now that everything is back on track, there doesn't seem to be any point changing the formula. After all, if it ain't broke don't fix it.

I feel *Powerless* is probably the best album I've ever done. Just as well, really, because it came out five years after *Electric Lady*. The album was also timed to come out in the year of my fiftieth anniversary of being in the music business. A milestone that Universal Music took advantage of by putting out a compilation of my old material called *Sunshine After The Rain – The Collection*.

To support the album, I agreed to do a series of promotional interviews for them, one of which was with Simon Mayo on his *Drivetime* Radio 2 programme. This proved to be a strange interview because I went into it having been told about a conversation Simon had had with film critic Mark Kermode a few months earlier on Radio 5 Live. They'd somehow got talking about 'Lilac Wine'. Simon apparently made a remark about me, which led Mark to say that he thought I was a better contemporary act than U2. They argued about this for a while before Mark asked the listeners what they thought. Simon said there wasn't much point asking everyone for their opinion because the answer was bound to be U2. But the listeners kindly proved him wrong by coming back saying they preferred me.

I went into the Radio 2 interview with Simon all geared up to mention it. Simon, however, conveniently managed to avoid it, although Trevor, who was watching from the control room, said he looked a little cagey throughout. Perhaps, in the back of his mind, he was worried I was going to bring it up. As well as my new album, we also talked about Humph's celebration concert, which was arranged for Sunday 25 April at the HMV Apollo, Hammersmith, exactly two years after his passing. I'd been briefed by Humph's son Stephen Lyttelton to talk about the concert as a celebration rather than as a tribute, a point which I made sure Simon and his listeners completely understood.

The concert, which Stephen asked Trevor to put together, was also the launch pad for The Humphrey Lyttelton Royal Academy of Music Jazz Award and The Humph Trust. Stephen set up the award in memory of his father's contribution to the world of jazz and the trust to raise money to support young jazz musicians in building their careers.

When I arrived at the Apollo I spoke to the technical manager who I've known for years. He asked if I knew where I was going to get ready for the show and I asked in return if I could have the same dressing room I'd had for The Beatles Christmas Show in 1964, right at the top of the building. He very kindly sorted that out and then showed me a book that had the actual poster of me with The Beatles and all the other people on the show.

The Humph concert was a great celebration of his life. There was a superb line-up including Charlie Watts, Jools Holland, Acker Bilk, Kenny Ball and umpteen other jazz guests as well as those Humph worked with on *I'm Sorry I Haven't a Clue* like Barry Cryer, Jack Dee, Graeme Garden, Tim Brooke-Taylor and Rob Brydon. I also met up with trumpet player Tony Fisher who I used to work with in the Eric Delaney Band when I was starting out in 1960. I sang 'Till The End of Time' with Andrew, my keyboard player, and Steve Jones, my saxophonist, dedicating it to Susan da Costa, Humph's manager and partner. I also did 'Every Day I Have The Blues' with Humph's band.

After the show I was in my dressing room when I heard a knock at the door. Only a brave person decides to knock on my door after a concert, as it usually has a very large 'do not disturb' sign on it. I opened the door with a heavy heart only to be greeted by Jools Holland.

He said, 'Elkie, I just have to say that was fantastic.'

I was touched he'd made the effort to come all the way up to say that, especially after our last meeting. We had both been performing in Dublin and after our respective shows we found ourselves in the same hotel bar. Jools was smoking a cigar, which Trevor realised was playing havoc with my throat. Not the most diplomatic person in the world, he told Jools in straightforward terms to smoke his big cigar outside. Jools, I'm relieved to say, kindly obliged and nothing more was said.

I was very impressed with Jools at Humph's celebration gig. The way he communicates with the audience is marvellous. I've found that side of performing difficult and always admire anyone who does it well. And, it has to be said, it doesn't get much better than Jools Holland. He did a great job of finishing the Humph concert with Charlie Watts. In fact, everyone on the show combined beautifully, making for a totally brilliant two-hour gig. Sadly, the BBC only used forty-five minutes, most of which was around the *Clue* team.

This would have been fine if they hadn't made Trevor work so hard mixing it for the radio. He'd been told by Susan that they wanted to air the recording in mid-May. But a week after the show, having just got back from one of my gigs on a Friday, Susan rang in the early hours to say the BBC wanted the show mixed by Tuesday, which meant he had to pull an all-nighter to get it done. They even sent a bike to pick up the tapes. Despite this they didn't put it out on the Tuesday, in fact it took six months for them to play it and then we were all disappointed with how little they'd used.

In December, however, I had something far more emotional to contend with when Joey left to go to Banff in Canada to train to be a ski instructor. Being such a close family and with Joey still living at home, I dreaded him being away for three months, let alone in such a far off place. We'd already decided that I wasn't allowed to go to the airport to see him off because of how upset he'd been when I left to do the *Reborn in the USA* tour, so we said a heartfelt goodbye in Devon before Trevor took him to Gatwick.

Fortunately, with modern technology we were able to see and speak to him every few days via the Internet. This made his time away far easier for me to bear. He came home at the end of March 2011 having passed his instructor qualifications – being a Jordan man – with flying colours. And, the word 'flying' appears to have played a larger part in his trip than Trevor and I realised.

One evening at home in Devon, Joey had a little too much to drink and let slip that he'd very nearly killed himself on the slopes in Banff. Evidently, he had been skiing down a fairly advanced route with a few friends when he missed a crucial turn by a 20-foot drop. He went straight over the edge, down on to a small plateau and then over another larger drop. He waved to one of his friends who he spotted going up on a chair lift as he was flying through the air. Amazingly, he landed safely and in one piece, albeit in a heap.

His instructor, who had seen him go over the edge, said it was the biggest wipeout he'd seen. He couldn't understand how Joey had managed to survive unscathed as everyone else who'd fallen there in the past had either been killed or badly injured. The instructor believes he escaped because the rucksack he was wearing had absorbed some of the force of the fall. Thank goodness for the rucksack, otherwise it might have been a totally different story.

CHAPTER 26

TODAY

Today my home and work life couldn't be better. I have so many great people around me who make everything happen as smoothly and efficiently as anyone could wish for, letting me focus on being the best singer I can be. Jay and Joanna take care of the business side of things. Their input in the management of my career has made a massive difference. They work very closely with my backing vocalist and second keyboard player Lee Noble who has taken on the responsibility of booking my shows.

Lee had been coming regularly to my gigs since 1994 when he was fourteen. Over the years he became involved with the fan club and got to know Trevor and Jay, and through that he started helping with a bit of promotion here and there. Knowing that he was keen on singing, Jay invited him down to Devon to try doing some backing vocals for the *Electric Lady* album.

When I listened to what he'd done I was so pleased I had to phone to thank him. Since then he's become an integral part of the Elkie Brooks operation, additionally handling most of my promotion, arranging interview schedules and booking gigs. He wrote the song 'Why' on the *Powerless* album. When he first played it before a show at a festival in Taunton, I was moved by the lyrics. Lee was thrilled when I included it in my live sets and I recorded it for *Powerless*.

Lee introduced us to his music degree course friend big John Eden who now takes care of all the merchandise at shows. Between them they're great at spotting anyone famous who might happen to come along to one of my gigs. Apparently, I'm quite popular with a couple of senior Labour politicians; John Prescott and Harriet Harman have both been seen in audiences. Terry Venables, the football manager, has also been sighted.

I'm very fortunate to have a great group of musicians who I work with most weeks, several of whom have been with me for years. Mike Richardson, my drummer, has been around since *No More The Fool* in 1986 and I've known Andrew Murray, my amazing keyboard player, for nearly as long. Bass guitarist Brian Badhams, who's worked with Ruby Turner, Bernie Marsden and Sheila Ferguson of The Three Degrees, joined in 2001, and Steve Jones, on sax, I met in 2005 at Ronnie Scott's in the week's residency that Laurie Jay organised. As well as being a gifted saxophonist, Steve is also a songwriter, producer and pianist who has worked with Alice Cooper, Rick Wakeman, Kim Wilde and former Spice Girl Mel B. The newest member of the band is lead guitarist Melvin Duffy, who joined in 2008. An accomplished session musician, Melvin has worked with Sam Brown, Jools Holland, Solomon Burke, KT Tunstall, Joe Cocker, Leo Sayer and Robbie Williams.

Together we put on a good show for the thousands of loyal fans who come to see me perform every year all around the country. To keep up with this talented bunch I have to work hard to be on top form. When I'm not working I try to keep fit, stay healthy and look after my voice. Usually, I do some fitness work in the morning and sing in the afternoon or evening. I like to do about 100 skips and 300 hula hoops every day as well as some aikido. If I don't do some kind of aikido warm-up, some basic movements, or some exercises with the jo for at least an hour in the morning, I can't be well.

When we're away from home I still have to do my daily workout. Every morning in the hotel I will religiously go through my exercise routine. This often includes doing something we call backdrops, which involves sitting down on the floor from standing up and rolling backwards on your back towards your head. I used to make quite a lot of noise doing this until Trevor pointed out that I wasn't curving my back enough as I went down. Anyone who's stayed in a hotel room below me will be quite relieved to know that I've finally got the hang of it and I am so much quieter than I was.

Aikido, as you can probably tell, has become an intrinsic part of my life since I took it up in 1988. I'm a lot better at it now than I used to be. I suppose I just don't like to be beaten and that's why I've persevered with it for so long. In fact that's true of my life in the music business too. I just can't accept being beaten by anything. Even though it's been fifteen years since I took my 1st Dan black belt grading, I still feel like a white belt beginner. My teacher, or sensei, Jenny Herniman 3rd Dan, wants me to take my 2nd Dan but I don't think I'm ready for it yet. There are so many things I've been doing wrong for so long, I'm determined to get out of those bad habits before I do another grading. That's what keeps me going.

Jenny has been running the Shudokan Institute of Aikido club in Braunton with Sensei Morgan Mills 2nd Dan for about ten years and together they have worked hard to help me improve. Jenny trains with me privately whenever I'm at home. But the demands of my work have made my progress slow.

I feel extremely privileged to have two such brilliant teachers who are prepared to give me so much of their time. They are both very humble, and these days that can be something of a rare quality in people. I think humility is an essential when studying aikido. And that sadly is something a lot of singers today are lacking. I admire people who are talented in whatever they do, but if they're full of themselves, that's a big black mark for me.

Whether I'll ever get to the next level I don't know. All I know is that I enjoy practising aikido and that for me is enough. I employ the same approach with my singing. I'm very dedicated with my practice and I'm still as determined to improve as a singer as I was when I was starting out all those years ago in Manchester. Since learning how to accompany myself on the piano in my early twenties – something I'm grateful to my first husband, Pete Gage, for – I've always practised. Over the last fifteen years, however, I've become far more disciplined. When I'm at home I generally sing everyday for an hour or an hour and a half; if I'm working, I only practise every other day. And if I'm in a bad mood, I don't bother as there's just no point trying. I completely relate to what I read about Billie Holiday not singing when she was in prison for illegal drug possession because she was so unhappy.

When I practise I always start off with something in the mid-register and work up until I get to my high end, which is a top D. I can sometimes hit an E flat and bottom D on a really, really good day. I suppose my voice is a low contralto with a good two-octave range. That isn't bad, but it's not brilliant especially when you think singers like the wonderful Aretha Franklin had at least two and half octaves in her heyday. She would easily hit F and G. She's one of my favourite singers, but I'm also very fond of all the low voice singers like Gladys Knight, Mavis Staples and Etta James.

At school I also loved listening to the singing of Kathleen Ferrier, who had a fantastic contralto voice. I've always felt that it's not about how high you sing, it's more about the quality of what you sing. I believe people should sing within their limitations. That's why I hated it in the late 1960s and early 1970s when I did backing vocals on people's records and the other girl singers always seemed to be singing higher than was comfortable. Any backing vocalist who is guilty of this should listen to the Raelettes on some of the early

Ray Charles records. They sang within their vocal abilities and sounded beautiful as a result. They paid great attention to the low register, which, in my opinion, made the big difference.

This is why I make sure everything I do in practice is within my range. I can go up high, but only after I've warmed up my voice. I also tend to sing songs that aren't in my show set as I think it's important to explore songs that push me mentally and vocally. I'm particularly fond of a lot of the songs I did on the *Trouble In Mind* album with Humph. I often sing 'Some Other Spring' which was a challenge to learn, as was Duke Ellington's 'Sophisticated Lady'. That's not an easy song to sing because of the intonation that subtly shifts from one note to the next. I also enjoy doing a lot of Paul Rodgers's songs like 'Muddy Water Blues', 'Weep No More' and 'Holding Back The Storm'.

But whatever I sing, I always try hard to do what my singing teacher, Rabbi Berkowitz, told me in the lessons I had with him when I was seventeen. Rabbi Berkowitz, like his father before him, was the cantor – the person who leads the prayers and singing – at our synagogue. I think I was probably one of a chosen few that he used to teach because I was never aware of him having any other pupils. I used to go round to his house, which was conveniently only a few doors away, two or three mornings a week. The lessons were always early, as he wanted to hear me sing before I'd had chance to speak to anybody or even had a cup of tea. With my voice at its freshest, he felt he could hear my strengths and weaknesses and identify what I needed to improve.

Even though he made me sing all these old Hebrew songs I enjoyed my lessons with him very much. I also remember finding him very intriguing, because, not having a beard, he didn't look as Jewish as other rabbis I'd known in my life or, for that matter, as Jewish as some of his congregation. I saw him as a very modern-thinking man, as was his wife, but I never knew why he was like that. I finally discovered the answer only recently when someone who'd heard me speak about him sent some information to me via the fan club.

It turns out he had been captured by the SS while he was in Frankfurt during the war and put into a concentration camp from which incredibly he managed to escape. On the run from the SS, he pretended he wasn't Jewish. That must have been very hard to do when you were such an Orthodox Jew. This obviously had a profound effect on him and explained why he didn't have a beard like most rabbi and why he had a very different outlook on life compared to others I'd encountered.

The most important thing Rabbi Berkowitz taught me about being a vocalist was the correct way to project my voice, especially on certain notes. But singing so many pop songs on the way to establishing myself as a recording artist, I threw away his advice for many years.

Around the millennium, however, I realised the error of my ways and started projecting my voice in the way he'd taught me. It's made an unbelievable difference to my singing. I feel I have much better breath control and can hold notes longer and far more easily than I used to be able to. When I do interviews and they play an old track of mine like 'Sunshine After The Rain' or 'Don't Cry Out Loud', I think there are light years between how I sang those songs then to how I sing them today. It is so effortless now.

This improvement has given me more confidence, which is very strange because confidence was something Rabbi Berkowitz was helping me with originally. As a teenager I thought I was the best singer in the world, but Don Arden shattered my confidence when he told me I had a long way to go. As it turned out, of course, he was absolutely right. Rabbi Berkowitz, however, had quickly realised that my singing was suffering because I didn't have any belief in myself as a person.

Once I remember him saying to me very kindly, 'How can an intelligent person like you have no confidence in yourself?'

With plenty of encouragement like that he managed to bring out the best in me and helped me to think differently about myself: something for which I will be forever thankful. I'm just sorry I didn't get the chance to tell him before he died. I kept in touch with him for quite a while but we eventually lost contact when I became successful with 'Pearls' and, in my misguided wisdom, tried to distance myself from my Jewish roots. His teaching has, without doubt, left an indelible mark on my life, a fact borne out by the visions I often have of him, as I'm about to go on stage.

CHAPTER 27

LOOKING FORWARD

I don't tend to spend too much time thinking about the future. When I do, however, I am filled with happiness at the thought of what we have now compared with how things were after the horrendous tax bill news of 1998.

Prospects look very promising for the Jordan family, not least because in 2010 we purchased a plot of land, which we see as being the key to our future. It all began one day when Trevor was on the hill talking to one of his hang-gliding friends and overheard a conversation about a piece of land that was for sale in Mortehoe. When he heard the guy say he didn't know what to do with it, he said we'd buy it.

Before meeting me in 1977, Trevor had a strong desire to get out of the music industry and move to North Devon to start his own business. Strangely, his vision is now becoming a reality as we're using the land to set up a fruit farm. So while we lost our beloved bricks and mortar 'Trees' we seem to have gained some real ones. Despite 2011 having the driest March on record we've already had the thrill of seeing tiny apples appear on our trees.

As for work, I have to come to terms with the fact that I'm getting older and performing week in and week out is demanding, even in the controlled way we do it now. At the moment though we've got a fruit farm to get off the ground so there's a need for money to be coming in until it gets established.

There's still so much I'd like to do when I have the time. I love learning new things so I'd quite like to try golf, tennis, clay shooting, badminton and, dare I say it … paragliding. After all, if you can't beat them, join them. I've also now got a son who's a qualified ski instructor so I've got to give that a go. I definitely won't have a problem finding things to do when I eventually stop performing.

Of one thing, I am certain: I don't want to be one of those performers who continues on for too long. I recently saw a very well-known singer on television who not only couldn't hold a note but looked diabolical too. I'm definitely going to put my microphone away before that happens!

But for the time being, I've got my health and I'm still enjoying working, not least because I have an amazing team around me. I've always said that I sing my best when I'm part of a good team, and this couldn't be more true than it is today as I've got a great band who make every performance a pleasure.

I feel extraordinarily happy that I'm still here doing what I love best – sing:

I was young when I first got started
Things didn't always go my way
I will never lose the hunger
To make a stand, survive another day

I feel my spirit growing stronger
I must admit, it's taking its toll on me
They took my home and all I owned in taxes
But they'll never take my soul or dignity

I played the game right down the line, I was honest
I can't believe people can be so cruel
The boys and I just want to make a living
Oh, but what do you do when you're surrounded by a load of fools?

I held my own and I don't need no sympathy
Just ask my friends and they will put you right

I don't feel that I did anything wrong
I certainly won't go down without a fight

You bet I'll be coming back
You can depend on that
I look the other way when they call me trailer trash
You bet I'll be on the attack

Oh, they won't get away with that
I look the other way when they call me trailer trash
When I get to where I'm going I'll take some time out
Reflect upon the good times I've had

I'll keep on moving south in my trailer
There'll be no time to be bitter or sad
You bet I'll be coming back
Oh, you can depend on that

I look the other way when they call me trailer trash
You bet I'll be on the attack
No, they won't get away with that
I look the other way when they call me trailer trash

You bet I'll be coming back
You can depend on that
I look the other way when they call me trailer trash
You bet I'll be on the attack
No, they won't get away with that
I look the other way when they call me trailer trash
I look the other way when they call me trailer trash

('Trailer Trash', written at the height of our troubles, sums up the story of my life in the music business)

Elkie's a singer.

MUSICIANS I HAVE WORKED WITH

KEYBOARD PLAYERS
Jean Roussel
Andrew Murray
Duncan Mackay
Tim Hinkley
Don Shinn
Dave Thompson
John Hawken
Mike Deacon
Bruce Foster
John Mitchell
Chris Stainton
Gary Hutchins
Brandon Fownes
Johnny Dyke
Simon Carter
John Richards
Ian Parker
Pete Wingfield
Ted Beament
Mick Pyne
Dave Ellis
Russ Ballard
Alan Welch

Rick Wakeman
Dave Wilkie

DRUMS
Eric Delaney
Trevor Morais
Mike Richardson
Martyn Harryman
Gerry Conway
Stretch Scretching
Keef Hartley
Pete Gavin
John Woods
Conrad Isadore
Graham Jarvis
Andy Newmark
Paul Burgess
Matthew Letley
John Lingwood
Rosa Avila
Peter Baron
Adrian Macintosh
Tony Mann
Paul Bilham
Ronnie Pearson
Alan Powell

PERCUSSION
Gasper Lawal
Simon Morton
Frank Ince
John Chambers
Duncan Kinnell
Thomas Dostal
Arnaud Frank

BASS PLAYERS
Jermaine Jordan
Steve York
John Giblin
Brian Badhams
Paul Westwood
Jerome Rimson
Phil Mulford
Joe Hubbard
Roger Inniss
Brendon Taylor
Jerry Knight
Dave Green
Mick Hutton
John Rees-Jones

GUITAR PLAYERS
Pete Gage
Geoff Whitehorn
Zal Cleminson
Jermaine Jordan
Robert Ahwai
Mike Cahen
Russ Ballard
Bernie Marsden
Jimmy Page
Simon Townshend
Martin Jenner
Les Martin
Martin Taylor
Dave Leverton
Tim Mills
Jim Mullen
Isaac Guillory

Elliot Randall
Les Martin
Al Hodge
Paul Stacy
Paul Dunne
Melvin Duffy
Rufus Ruffell
Nigel Spennewyn
Bob Wilson
Keith Beauvais
John Edmed (steel guitar)
Sarah Jory (steel guitar)

HORN PLAYERS

Humphrey Lyttelton
Courtney Pine
Tony Coe
Kathy Stobart
Steve Jones
Jimmy Hastings
Bruce Turner
Pete Strange
Barry Duggan
John Lee
Jim Lawless
Tony Fisher
Roger Ball
Malcolm Duncan
Mike Rosen
Dave Brooks
Malcolm Capewell
Annie Whitehead
Nic Clark
Duncan Lamont
Martin J. Lewison

ELKIE BROOKS

Ray Wordsworth
Ernie Lauchlan
Karen Sharp
Derek Healey

VOCALISTS I HAVE SUNG WITH
Robert Palmer
Cat Stevens
Roger Daltrey
Chris Farlowe
Paul Korda
Jimmy Chambers
Herbie Goins
Gene Williams

BACKING VOCALISTS
Joseph Jordan
Lee Noble
Francis Rossi
Bernie Frost
Barry St John
Russ Ballard
George Chandler
Lee Vanderbilt
Tony Jackson
Ruby James
Simon Bell
Jerry Knight
Jimmy Chambers
Mike Patto Jnr
Darlene Love
Venetta Fields
Julia Tillman Waters
Maggie Henry
Jim Gilstrap

FINDING MY VOICE

Oren Waters
Clydie King
Carl Hall
Peggie Blue
Mary Ellen Johnson
Barbara Ingram
Evette Benton
Carla Benson
Edna Wright
Marcie Levy

CONDUCTORS
Andrew Pryce Jackman
Tony Britten

CREW
Sound engineer
Trevor Jordan
Assisted Trev in the early years: Huw Richards, Robbie Jordan

LIGHTING
Phil Freeman
James and Liz Loudon
Peter Canning
Mark Powell
Ian Bintliff

BACK LINE TECHNICIANS
Jermaine Jordan
Joseph Jordan
Steve Bootland
Justin Crew
John Cooper

ELKIE BROOKS

TOUR MANAGERS
Colin Hannah
Matt Clarke
Pat King

CATERING
Des Harkness
The Beez Neez
'Vodka' Val Jevons